Dr. Sprinkle's

Spectacular

Sex

Annie Sprinkle, Ph.D.

Jeremy P. Tarcher/Penguin

a member of Penguin Group (USA) Inc.

New York

Dr. Sprinkle's Spectacular Sex

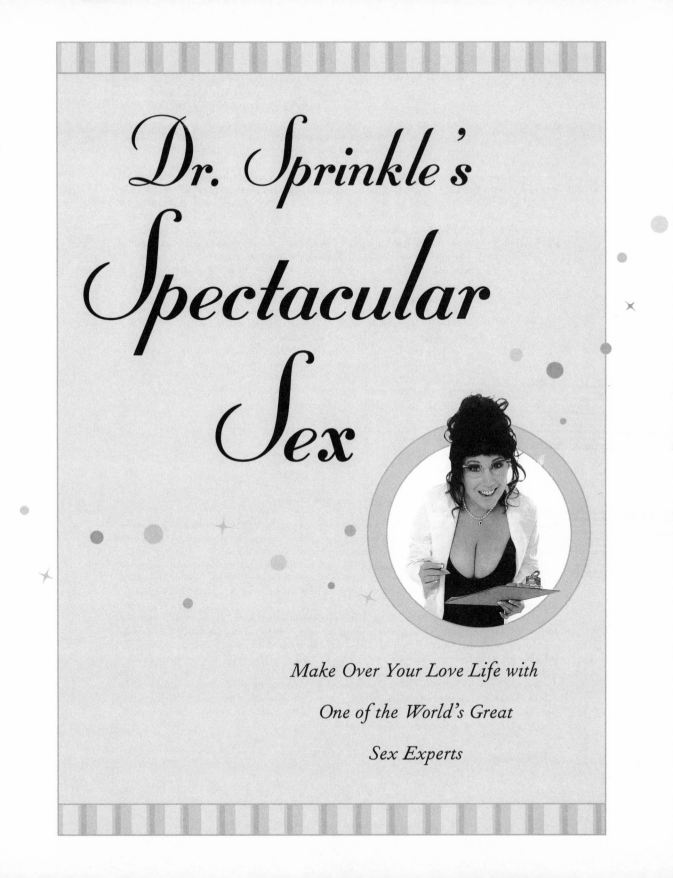

Make Over Your Love Life with

One of the World's Great

Sex Experts

JEREMY P. TARCHER/PENGUIN
Published by the Penguin Group
Penguin Group (USA) Inc., 375 Hudson Street, New York, New York 10014, USA • Penguin Group (Canada),
10 Alcorn Avenue, Toronto, Ontario M4V 3B2, Canada (a division of Pearson Penguin Canada Inc.) • Penguin Books Ltd,
80 Strand, London WC2R 0RL, England • Penguin Ireland, 25 St Stephen's Green, Dublin 2, Ireland (a division
of Penguin Books Ltd) • Penguin Group (Australia), 250 Camberwell Road, Camberwell, Victoria 3124,
Australia (a division of Pearson Australia Group Pty Ltd) • Penguin Books India Pvt Ltd, 11 Community Centre,
Panchsheel Park, New Delhi–110 017, India • Penguin Group (NZ), Cnr Airborne and Rosedale Roads, Albany,
Auckland 1310, New Zealand (a division of Pearson New Zealand Ltd) • Penguin Books (South Africa) (Pty) Ltd,
24 Sturdee Avenue, Rosebank, Johannesburg 2196, South Africa
Penguin Books Ltd, Registered Offices: 80 Strand, London WC2R 0RL, England

An application to register this book for cataloging has been submitted to the Library of Congress.
ISBN 1-58542-412-9

Printed in the United States of America
1   3   5   7   9   10   8   6   4   2

This book is printed on acid-free paper. ∞

Book design by Meighan Cavanaugh

Most Tarcher/Penguin books are available at special quantity discounts for bulk purchase for sales promotions, premiums, fund-raising, and educational needs. Special books or book excerpts also can be created to fit specific needs. For details, write Penguin Group (USA) Inc. Special Markets, 375 Hudson Street, New York, NY 10014.

Accordingly nothing in this book is intended as an express or implied warranty of the suitability or fitness of any product, service, or design. The reader wishing to use a product, service, or design discussed in this book should first consult a specialist or professional to ensure suitability and fitness for the reader's particular lifestyle and environmental needs.

Neither the publisher nor the author is engaged in rendering professional advice or services to the individual reader. The ideas, procedures, and suggestions contained in this book are not intended as a substitute for consulting with your physician. All matters regarding your health require medical supervision. Neither the author nor the publisher shall be liable or responsible for any loss or damage allegedly arising from any information or suggestion in this book.

While the author has made every effort to provide accurate telephone numbers and Internet addresses at the time of publication, neither the publisher nor the author assumes any responsibility for errors, or for changes that occur after publication. Further, the publisher does not have any control over and does not assume any responsibility for author or third-party websites or their content.

This book is dedicated to

E. Marshall Stephens

for being

my collaborator in love/art,

my *Spectacular Sex* test-subject,

and the love of my life.

Contents

Orientation

Every person is an erotic universe waiting to be explored.

Welcome to Dr. Sprinkle's Sex Life Makeover Center and Spa. I am Dr. Annie Sprinkle, center founder and your transformation facilitator. I invite you to enter into an experience that promises to transform your heart, mind, body, and soul as far as you will let it.

The purpose of any spa is to refresh and revitalize. The same goes for this spa with the additional goal being that you explore and enjoy the many benefits of spectacular sex. After all, what more rejuvenating, nourishing, invigorating force is there than sex? It can put a glow in your cheeks rosier than any cosmetic and a spring in your step higher than any amount of StairMastering will give you.

Let me start by telling you what I mean when I say spectacular sex. I mean an experience that goes way beyond the physical ins and outs. Sex is an awesome miracle: It can create whole new human beings, increase intimacy in relationships, not to mention that it can feel really good physically. These things are petty spectacular in and of themselves. But what I am inviting you to explore with me in this book are the multiple benefits of awakening to the full experience of your own special erotic power.

Spectacular sex can take many different forms and has countless uses and effects. Just to name a few, sex can be:

- A force for personal growth
- A source of physical and emotional healing
- The inspiration for self-realization and spiritual nourishment

- A fountain of joy that promotes relaxation, intellectual stimulation, emotional well-being, and physical health

Having spectacular sex means you are communicating perfectly what's deep inside you and are truly being heard. It means you're feeling life-force energy stream through every part of you and expressing your sexuality in your own unique way. Spectacular sex involves feeling deeply loved and adored, whether you are with yourself or with another person. It is when you are sexually satisfied and content to the core of your being. Spectacular sex is countless things, many of which will be revealed to you as you go through this program.

Go Forth

As we go through this makeover program together and you get to know me better, you'll come to understand why my credo is "Let there be pleasure on earth and let it begin with me." There's so much pain, suffering, and sadness in the world that we need to balance that out with as much pleasure, bliss, love, and happiness as we possibly can. I firmly believe that a sexually satisfied person is a happy person—and a happy person makes those around her/him happy, too.

As a person in today's world, you are free to live your dream. How fortunate we are that we have so many opportunities to be sexually free, to love whom we choose, to have access to information about sex and our bodies. Never forget your erotic heritage. Many women, men, and multigendered people have come before you and fought for the freedoms you have and enjoy today. Freedom isn't free. You are able to be fully who you are now because of them. Never take that freedom for granted.

Why do we all desire a spectacular sex life? Why is SEX the most downloaded subject on the Internet? True, we are biologically programmed to reproduce our species. But beyond that, I believe it is because when you get to its essence, sex is a great way to give and receive love—with ourselves, with others, and with the universe. It's because it is human nature to seek out ecstasy, to desire openness, and to want to share life, to connect and bond with others. We want to feel good in our bodies, to have peak experiences and adventures. We yearn for inner peace, and we can find that peace in the afterglow that permeates our lives when we are sexually content.

Dr. Sprinkle's Sex Life Makeover Center

During your visit to our center you will be offered a world of options just as at other "spas" and "retreats," but here there is solid emphasis on the treats: sensual rubs to bring your body to life, provocative lessons to tickle your awareness, lush recipes to whet your appetites, and healing therapies to keep you supple, hard, and moist.

Perhaps you really like your sex life as it is and feel you need just a mini makeover. If that's the case, then I will help you make small adjustments to enhance and take your sex life to a new level. Or maybe you want an X-treme makeover, to fix a sex life that is not just unsatisfying but possibly depressing and frustrating or has even been nonexistent for years. If that's the case, do not despair: Dr. Sprinkle is here to help.

Like most folks these days, you may have a very busy schedule, and I want to thank you for sharing some of your precious time with me. I promise it will be worth your while. Follow the steps in this guidebook, and you can turn even an icky, unsatisfying sex life into a spectacular, yummy one. The methods I present in the following chapters are tried and true, having proven themselves effective for the many people from all different backgrounds and situations with whom I have been privileged to work over the years.

In real life, my Makeover Center is located in my lovely three-story Victorian home in the middle of a city. But my dream is to have a sprawling, lush villa by the sea surrounded by an abundant garden filled with fragrant possibilities. So, let's have some fun, and put ourselves there. As we move through the grounds, note that there are signposts that direct you to specific areas: the cleansing pool, the healing hot tub, the feminine fountains, the massage room, my study, and, of course, the temple of lovemaking. The chapters in this book describe each area and its purpose. I recommend that you follow the path as I have laid it out for you chapter by chapter, but if you feel a strong desire to wander a bit, please feel free. In the end, I'm not going to tell you exactly which path to follow for your sex life makeover. I will happily lead you through a variety of possible paths and cheer you on as you walk—or float, as it were—down whichever path you choose. But ultimately you will find your own way. If there's one thing I know about sex absolutely it's that everyone has different needs and desires. There isn't one right way; there is only *your way*.

My Unusual Credentials

But first—why should you trust me to help you with your sex life?

When I was a teenager, like most girls of my generation, I felt intense peer pressure both to be, and not to be, sexually active. I felt like the ugly duckling who wanted to be a beautiful swan but hardly dared dream that it was possible. I was excruciatingly shy and insecure, and terrified by the mere idea of sex. No one could ever possibly desire me, I thought. Desperate, I used to browse through magazines for ads or articles about makeovers and study the before-and-after photos. I hung them on my bedroom walls—they gave me hope.

My fear and confusion about sex were holding me back in so many ways that I finally resolved to face my fears head-on and overcome them. I set out to learn everything I possibly could about sex, and then use the knowledge to slay my own sexual dragons. Thus began what has now been thirty-three years of intense sexual research and exploration. Sex became my favorite hobby—and the focus of my life's work. A year after I was relieved of my virginity, at eighteen I became a hippie, exploring "free love." Then I got a job in a "massage parlor." In my naïveté, I thought I was just an enthusiastic masseuse with horny clients; but in fact I'd stumbled into the world's oldest profession. From there it wasn't such a big leap for me to take work as a porn star, a stripper, professional dominatrix, and a nude model. Eventually I would go on to direct my own brand of sex films, work as an erotic photographer, and write hundreds of articles for sex magazines. In my mid-thirties, I crossed over into the art world and toured internationally, performing one-woman plays about my life in sex to sold-out audiences. Today my "groundbreaking" theater and performance work is studied in art-history and gender-study classes at many major universities.

In the process of learning about all facets of sexuality I have also traveled far and wide, seeking out the best sex teachers and studying the most modern and some very ancient sexual practices. Then I went on to learn the academic side of sex. Three years ago, I earned a Ph.D. in human sexuality and became a sexologist. For years I've taught innumerable sex workshops and assisted many people as a one-on-one sex-life coach.

I've tried out a wide variety of sexual relationships. I've been monogamous, promiscuous, polyamorous, and even celibate. I've been straight, gay, and bisexual, as well as totally uncategorizable. I've enjoyed and experimented with sexual intimacy and sex without any intimacy. I've done it every which way with people of every gender, color, shape, nationality, and personality, having sex with literally thousands of people! As a result, I've amassed an incredible collection of life experiences. As I'm sure you're aware, this wide an amount of sexual experience is not common for women in our culture, but I think it laid the perfect foundation for me as the creator of this sex-life makeover program.

There are too few positive sexual role models or mentors for us to turn to for inspiration. I wish I had had one when I was younger. I don't think it's too presumptuous to say that I now feel qualified to offer myself to you as just such a role model or mentor (whatever you prefer!)—not because I know every last thing there is to know about sexuality but because the chances are good that, whatever your challenges are in your efforts to have a satisfying, healthy, and spectacular sex life, I've probably had them and gotten past them, too. I am no longer afraid to make mistakes (and I have made plenty of them), because mistakes have often helped me to learn some of the principles that I will be sharing with you.

My sex life has had many ups and many downs, as well as ins and outs. It wasn't always fun, and it was certainly not always easy. There have been times when I was scared and felt jaded or confused. There were phases when I felt horrible about my body and times when sex became routine. I've been sexually mistreated. I've had my heart broken and had to pick up the pieces and move on. At times I've had almost no libido, and at other times I've had such a high libido that, no matter how much sex I had, I felt frustrated. I've been with sexual partners who, for a variety of reasons, weren't right for me. Once I was in a relatively long-term nonsexual lover relationship. I've been with partners who wanted more sex from me than I wanted to give. I've contended with jealousy, lies, danger, disappointment, and sexually transmitted diseases. In short, I've been through the entire array of sex-life challenges.

One thing this means is that I have surely had some magnificent ups! I've had great sexual adventures and have known what it feels like to be a real sex goddess. I've had incredible lovers, with whom I've experienced deeply satisfying, miraculous sex, and I am proud to be a part of a dedicated international, sexually knowledgeable, and experienced community, some of whom will be introduced to you here. Through the transformational power of sex I've lost my painful shyness and inhibitions. As I learned to appreciate myself and cherish my lovers more, I lost my old anxieties about being an ugly duckling. I've experienced sex as a healing and spiritual act. Through lovemaking I have generated, given, and received huge amounts of love. I have known great joy through sex and had mind-blowing orgasms of all kinds. ("Orgasms of all kinds?" If you're wondering just how many kinds of orgasms there can possibly be, just wait until you get to Step 13.)

Today I am fifty years old, I certainly don't look like a "porn star" anymore. I'm a bit chubby, I haven't had any plastic surgery, and my signature large breasts have definitely drooped. But I can honestly say that my sex life is more wonderful and satisfying than I would ever have dreamed possible. Far better than when I was a young porn star. Today I'm satisfied to the core of my being. I adore my partner, sex is easy and fun, and it feels like we never do the same thing twice—unless we want to. I am more orgasmic than I could have ever imagined I'd be. I appreciate sex as part of my spiritual life and know that it helps me stay healthy. For me, sex is a natural antidepressant and stress reliever. One day I might, and most likely will, run into difficulties yet again, but I have the knowledge and tools to make over my sex life again and overcome any hurdles. In spite of any sexual hardships I've been through, I've come out of all of them a total winner.

So can you!

Why Are You Here?

There could be many reasons why you've chosen to visit Dr. Sprinkle's Sex Life Makeover Center. Perhaps you are curious and want to know exactly what "spectacular sex" is and if you're having it or not. Maybe you have a great sex life but want to make it even better. Or perhaps your sex life is somehow not working. You want to change but don't know how. Maybe you're afraid, insecure, or having trouble getting turned on, or maybe you want to learn more about orgasm. It could be that you want to know how to create more love and intimacy in your relationship or life, or you're looking for uplifting ideas to take you out of a frustrating rut. Or maybe you have boring sex, or feel empty after sex. Whatever it is that brought you here is perfect. I'm just glad you came.

Annie Sprinkle Herself Before and After

Before: I thought I was the ugliest, least sexy girl in the world—excruciatingly shy, insecure, and with very low self-esteem. I was afraid of sexuality and didn't like my body much. I thought I was horribly fat. I wanted to be like the other girls so I wore this bikini, but I felt totally uncomfortable and self-conscious.

After: Finally, I made a commitment to myself to change. I faced my fears head-on and set out to learn all I could about sex, to build my self-esteem, and learn how to communicate my feelings and my needs. In time, I learned to love my body and myself and to receive all the gifts that sexuality holds. I'm so grateful that I took this journey. What a spectacular adventure!

Whom Is This Guide For?

I've tried to make this guide useful to all kinds of people from all walks of life. Whether you're married or remarried, single, divorced, living with someone, describe your lifestyle as traditional or alternative, whether you identify your orientation as heterosexual, bisexual, or homosexual, if you are rich or poor, vanilla, chocolate, or strawberry, I'm quite confident that there are many great techniques and tips here for you.

If I use colloquial or slang expressions or words that may not be part of your regular vocabulary, please don't be offended. For example, I often use the word *lover* to refer to sex partners. You might never use the word *lover* but *my husband* or *my wife* or *my partner* or *my girlfriend* or my *boyfriend*. Just substitute your own terms. You and I are just speaking different dialects of the same language, the language of love, pleasure, and intimate communication.

For many years, as an adult entertainer, my work catered mostly to men. While I still love and adore men, it is mostly women I work with now. It is mostly women who seek me out for advice and support, and who come to my center and workshops. In fact, most of the sex-life makeovers that I've facilitated have been for women, or for couples. So this guide is in many ways geared toward the gals. Besides, I'm a gal myself, and much of what I can share is from a female's experience.

If you are a man reading this, you may need to translate a few parts that are geared toward women, to fit. But you will likely learn more about female sexuality from the parts geared for women, and that's a very good thing for you, and your female partners. I'm very glad you are here.

If you're transsexual, "pansexual," and/or intersexed, this book is for you, too. Please be pro-active, and translate the parts for "male" or "female" or "penis" or "vagina" as you wish. Be creative. You are more than welcome at my Makeover Center.

You Are Not Alone

If you feel insecure, confused, or troubled about sex, you are not alone. Research studies show that huge numbers of women and men have significant sexual problems at various times in their lives. And I'll let you in on a little secret: Even the most experienced sex experts in the world occasionally feel inadequate or confused or end up in a rut. Sexual "problems" are absolutely normal. I prefer to call them "lessons." As long as you learn and grow from them, you win.

There is a reason I have located the Sprinkle Center near the ocean. The sea is a great metaphor for human sexuality. Sex, like the sea, can be calm and peaceful. Or sometimes it's rough, stormy, and dangerous. The tide comes in, and the tide goes out. Sexual energy comes and goes. The beach is healing and nurturing. Sex can be healing and nurturing. It can be polluted with trash or clear and sparkling. The sea is a great mystery. And so is sex, no matter how much you know about it.

Think of your sexuality as a huge treasure chest filled with magnificent gems, gifts, and secrets. Maybe you've never really looked into your sexuality treasure chest, or you've looked into it but haven't really tried things on for size. Perhaps you feel as if your sexuality treasure chest has sunk to the bottom of the ocean, is rusted closed, pirated away, or hopelessly lost. You've all but given up on having a spectacular sex life. Again, do not despair. I will help you mine your abundant treasures. Opening a sealed or lost treasure chest may sound like hard work, but I promise that your sex-life makeover won't be drudgery or difficult. It will be fun. And you will feel very sex-sea. As I always tell my clients, you are already at the right place at the right time in your own personal sexual evolution. I'll bet you've got a lot more going for you at this moment than you realize. If you're willing to learn and change, you've made a fantastic start.

Our sexuality can be an extremely wonderful, useful, joyous, positive, and miraculous part of our lives. It can also be painful, confusing, difficult, scary, and frustrating. Sometimes there are complex issues to deal with and obstacles to overcome on the way to having a spectacular sex life. The good news is that fortunately most of us have a lot of control over how we choose to lead our sex lives. We have the power to change ourselves. We have more freedom and greater access to information about sexuality today than at any other time in history.

I've seen people radically transform their sex lives in a single weekend workshop, or as the result of seeing the right movie or show, or of reading just one inspirational book at the right moment in their lives. Sometimes, just one key piece of wisdom can initiate a major breakthrough. Sometimes change takes longer and requires patience. Just as there isn't one right or best way to live one's life, there is not just one correct way to live one's sexual life. But there is only one way to approach how you make choices about your sex life—

by ensuring that your choices are true to your desires and are the best choices for you. Here at the center together we will create a sex-life makeover that's custom-made for you and your lifestyle.

Logistics

The center program consists of various exercises, experiments, and questions. For some of these you'll need something to write with and an empty journal or notebook. Or you can write directly in this book if you want to. Besides any required writing, please do also add any thoughts, feelings, realizations, dreams, ideas, and fantasies you might have along the way.

I will also be telling you some stories of other people, some of whom I have taught, some who have been my teachers, many who have been both. To be discreet I've changed names. Whenever I use just a first name, unless I state otherwise, you can assume it is a pseudonym. If I use a first and last name, it is that of a real person who prefers to be identified.

It's All About You

Now, I invite you to do a warm-up exercise. Close your eyes and imagine a person who would be your "absolute ideal lover." If you have a lover at present, just for a minute pretend that you don't, and let yourself see an imaginary perfect person you'd want to spend time with. Think about the qualities or traits this ideal lover would have. For example, does he or she have humor, sensitivity, creativity, and intelligence? Is it someone who is romantic, passionate, smart, honest, or peaceful? Just write whatever pops into your head first.

All done? Good. Now, look over the list and take note of to what extent the person you have described may, in fact, resemble you or the you you'd like to become! How many of the qualities you listed do you yourself possess? Could it be that you are the lover you've been looking for? Perhaps you might want to cultivate these qualities in yourself even more. Or if you listed any qualities you don't possess but would like to, think about how you can adopt these qualities.

The point of this exercise is to discover that rather than looking outside yourself for an ideal lover, you can actually give yourself many of the things you enjoy and need. And this will free you up to enjoy a lover or lovers who may have qualities different from yours or qualities that you might not have thought you'd appreciate. This will help you avoid the ever-present temptation to ask your partner to change.

You can transform what goes on externally in your sex life by first transforming yourself internally. The way you think and feel about yourself is of utmost importance to your sex-life makeover, so a good part of this guide's first half is devoted to getting to know,

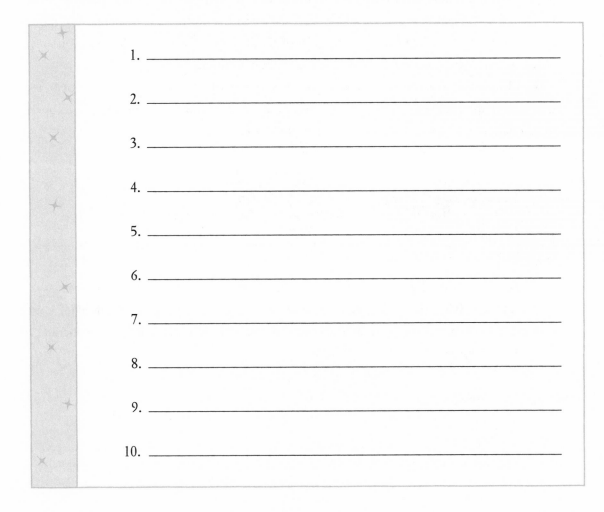

1. _____

2. _____

3. _____

4. _____

5. _____

6. _____

7. _____

8. _____

9. _____

10. _____

and falling in love with, yourself. Once you've explored your inner landscape, you can have lots of fun playing with your outer one and enjoying other people for who they are, rather than being needy.

Part of the purpose of my program is to inspire you. You may find that you already know some of the tips I offer, either consciously or subconsciously. But perhaps reading about them in the context of your sex-life makeover will help you put them into action and use them to your greater advantage.

So, are you ready to begin? Are you sure? It's only fair to warn you that there are some downsides to having a fabulous sex life. There are lifestyle issues to consider: You might miss some good television shows. There are also housekeeping issues to think about: You might have a lot more dirty laundry, and not always have time to wash it. There are even career-advancement issues to consider: You may find that you want to spend a lot more time having sex and less time working. And don't forget the inevitable beauty issues: Having lots of great sex can be absolutely brutal on your hair.

But I'm going to assume that you've decided to embark on your sex-life makeover regardless of the challenges and risks of success. If that's the case, you have only to open your imagination and turn the page to open the door.

Know Your Top-Ten Turn-ons in Life

Make a list of ten things that you enjoy doing more than anything else in the whole world, the activities that bring you the greatest pleasure. They don't necessarily need to be sexual. Put them in order—make number one your most favorite and go down from there.

For example:

1. Massage
2. Riding on a motorcycle
3. Making love
4. Reading in bed

5. Cooking
6. Going to the movies
7. Walking on the beach
8. Singing in church
9. Learning new things
10. Listening to music

MY TOP-TEN TURN-ONS IN LIFE ARE:

1. _____

2. _____

3. _____

4. _____

5. _____

6. _____

7. _____

8. _____

9. _____

10. _____

Take note! The more time you spend doing the things on your list, the more happy, excited, energized, and turned on you will be. If you can make a living doing something on your list, then so much the better. As you expand your concept of what sexuality is, you will come to understand that doing the things you love most is part of enjoying your sensuality and sexuality. Hang this list on your mirror and review it often. Your list will also keep you aware of how you balance your time. Do you feel you spend enough time doing the things you love to do most? Can you do them more? Did you have difficulty even coming up with a top ten? That, too, is important information.

It's good to redo this list at least once a year, because your top-ten turn-ons can change as you yourself grow and change. Have your lover make a list, too, and share your lists with each other. Then you will know what really turns each other on.

Step One

Make Over Your Mind

A sexy mind is a terrible thing to waste.

We'll begin your program in my private study, where two comfy armchairs await us. Notice the many books and artworks that line the walls. They represent some of the greatest thoughts on the subject of human sexuality. Through the windows you can see the beautiful grounds of the center. Here inside this study we will focus on your mind.

Your mind-set is *ultra* important when it comes to making over your sex life. You might be thinking, "Oh well, it's perfectly fine for *other* people to have a spectacular sex life, but *I'll* never have one because I'm too (fill-in-the-blank) . . . too old, too depressed, too wounded, too unattractive, too tired, too busy, too *whatever*." Almost anything at all can become an obstacle to a satisfying sex life if you're looking for obstacles, and if you're *looking* for obstacles then it's more likely your mind-set that's the problem, not whatever you put in the blank.

If you've had some bad luck or bad times with sex, I can understand coming to believe that sex is less than joyous. Maybe it's been a frustrating chore at times, or a source of insecurity, or you've been rejected, or hurt. If this has been your experience, I applaud your courage in trying to create change. The trick will be to use these difficulties as inspiration. I've seen so many people experience miraculous sexual awakenings and transformations, and all of them begin with one simple action: They made up their minds to make it happen. Toward this end, let's start right now, with your attitude.

How Iris Flowered

Recently a woman named Iris came to me for help. Four years before, out of the blue, her husband of many years dumped her for a younger woman. Iris was devastated and felt totally undesirable, really old and very unsexy. She hadn't had sex once since the dump and really wanted to have an active sex life again but didn't know where to start.

As we spoke we quickly came to see that for many years she had been enduring constant put-downs from her husband. Her self-esteem was eroded to the point where it had become nearly impossible for her to access her groove. Ironically, everyone around her saw her as sexy but herself. Although not a classic kind of beauty, she moved with a fantastic sensuality. She had such powerful erotic presence, in fact, that when she walked into a room, everyone looked. Truth be told, it was her sexual power that her husband couldn't handle, not her lack of it. He never felt he could match her, so he put her down.

After just a few sessions working together, Iris found a new, much better partner than her husband had ever been, one who could handle her sexual power—and then some. All we did to help this magical transformation was to examine and then change her negative thoughts about herself. All she actually needed was an attitude adjustment, and it worked wonders.

Negative thinking can clog and muck up your sex life big-time. It can cause you to become stiff, uptight, and fearful. When you're feeling like that, what's to enjoy?

Get ready for some plastic surgery! No, not on your body. We're talking about psychic plastic surgery—for the inside. Not only is it absolutely painless; it actually feels quite good.

Affirm It 'Til You Feel It

When I was a kid I loved to dance. I took tap and ballet lessons. I produced, directed, and starred in little shows in our family living room. Then, when I was thirteen years old, I started going to a "teen club," and, although shy, I would enjoy dancing whenever I was asked. One day, my friend Joan took me aside and told me that when I danced I moved my butt funny and it looked "weird." That one little critical remark led me to believe that I was a terrible dancer, and I thought everyone looking at me knew it as well. That was all it took to make me so self-conscious that I did not dance in public again for twenty years.

What happened to reverse this travesty? When I was thirty-four, I started going to a group called the New York Healing Circle, a group of about three hundred men and women who had partied hard until the early eighties and then, reeling from the devastating effects of the AIDS crisis, had come together to look for a way to cope. Different kinds of speakers and healers came to talk with our group and teach us things. One of them was Louise Hay, who wrote the book *You Can Heal Your Life*. That's her book right there, that small book with the rainbow on it, on the third shelf. It's hard to imagine that such a small book could carry so much weight to help a lot of us feel much better, but it did. Louise Hay suggested the use of simple positive affirmations to create change. Many of us started practicing this technique. A few nights later I was at a party organized by friends from the circle, and I really wanted to dance, but as usual I was too uptight to get out there on the dance floor. But when my friend Samuel Kirschner, the brilliant cofacilitator of the healing circle, asked me to dance, I could no longer resist. I adored Samuel, a beautiful man inside and out. So I started to dance. I was extremely uncomfortable at first, but then I began repeating over and over to myself, "I am a fantastic dancer." Negative thoughts came crowding in: "My butt looks funny, I look weird, I'm a bad dancer." Still, I stayed the course, and kept inwardly repeating the positive, affirming description of myself. "I love to dance. . . . I am a wonderful dancer. . . . I move like the wind. After enduring this excruciating mental exercise for a couple of songs, I actually started to have a good time. Samuel danced around playfully making up steps as he went. Finally, something clicked, and I just let go and started dancing all over the place. I became Ginger Rogers, and Samuel was Fred Astaire. Less than a year later, I had the confidence to tour the country (earning $5,000 a week) as a featured exotic dancer on the burlesque circuit. The only thing that helped me transform was that I changed my negative thoughts into positive ones.

When we think negative thoughts, they become the truth to us and often lead to a self-fulfilling prophecy. Could you be saying to yourself that you're not sexy? Or that you're just not a very sexual person? Or that you can't have a really great sex life because your husband or wife isn't into sex, or you've been married too long? When you say these things as if they are facts, you are presenting them as unchangeable, set in concrete. Better to think you can overcome any obstacles. If you can dream it, you can probably be it.

Now You Try It

Here are some examples of common negative beliefs and their flip sides, framed as affirmations. Read through them all. Then see what it feels like to say all the "before" statements. Then try saying all of the "after" versions to yourself—even if you don't believe them. It's even better if you do it out loud.

Before: My sex life is terrible.
After: I have a fabulous sex life.

Before: I don't feel sexy.
After: I feel really sexy.

Before: I had a really horrible experience, so I can't enjoy sex.
After: I had a horrible experience and I'm in the process of healing and open to the possibility of creating a wonderful, healthy, spectacular sex life.

Before: I'm not really interested in sex anymore, although I wish I were.
After: I'm becoming more sexually awakened and aware every day.

Before: If only I could lose/gain————pounds I'd be sexy.
After: I'm a magnificent sex god/dess exactly as I am.

Before: I will never enjoy sex the way my friend so-and-so does.
After: I deserve a spectacular sex life. I have a spectacular sex life. And so do my friends.

Before: I always end up sexually frustrated.
After: I expect my sexual life to be fulfilling and joyous.

Results: Check in. Notice how you feel. If you don't totally believe the positive thoughts, that's really okay. Just keep saying them to yourself anyway, and soon the affirmations will come naturally. It really works. You originally programmed your mind with negative thoughts; now you can reprogram your mind with positive thoughts. Just as it took time for the original, negative programming to affect you, so too it might take time to become reprogrammed. If you love yourself, then the rest will fall into place.

Put your positive affirmations somewhere where you can remember to read them to yourself often—maybe on the mirror in the bathroom, so you can say them whenever you look in the mirror. Or tape them into your daybook or diary. Or put them on your computer desktop or car dashboard. Read and say them at least once a day for a month, and you will be amazed at the results. Positive change will happen.

You can also make an audiotape of your personal affirmations and play it as you fall asleep at night. Record yourself reading your affirmations over and over while you play some nice instrumental music in the background. Fill up an entire tape. Each time you hear yourself saying the affirmations, they will become more and more real to you.

Another great way to use positive affirmations is while you are having sex, especially if you feel insecure or critical of yourself. You can do this the way I did my affirmations about dancing. So if, for example, you think you are not so great at giving your lover oral sex or have never even tried it before but feel ready to experiment, tell yourself:

"I am an oral-sex genius. I know exactly what to do, when and how! I'm so great at oral sex." Simply replace your negative thoughts with positive ones and watch how fabulous your oral-sex experiences become for you—and your partner. Try it!

TAILOR-MAKE YOUR OWN POSITIVE AFFIRMATIONS

What are some negative thoughts you have about yourself and your sex life?

1. _____

2. _____

3. _____

4. _____

5. _____

How can you make each of these into a positive affirmation?

1. _____

2. _____

3. _____

4. _____

5. _____

Expand Your Idea of What "Sex" Is

Remember the President Clinton and Monica Lewinsky episode when everyone in the whole country was debating whether oral sex was "sex"? It certainly behooved Bill to claim that oral sex was not sex. Despite endless discussions, the question was never definitively answered—because no one person or group has the final say on what sex is. But whereas Clinton, and others, wanted to narrow the concept of what exactly constitutes sex, in the interests of improving your sex life we are going to expand it. For your sex-life makeover, consider that everything that makes you feel erotically turned on *is* a form of sex. Expanding your idea of what sex is can make you feel that you are having lots of wonderful sexual pleasures every day, even if you aren't touching anyone. What if sex isn't just a physical act? Let's practice opening your mind to a whole range of erotic experiences, not just what we've been taught that sex is *supposed* to be.

Generally our culture largely defines sex as intercourse, and defines intercourse as penis in vagina, biological male in biological female exclusively. The way I have come (cum) to see it (pun intended), it's much more than that. Here are three categories of what I consider sex. I call them BodySex, EnergySex, and Body + EnergySex.

BodySex: This is the physical/genital–oriented kind of sex—what most people think of as sex. Some examples: oral sex, anal sex, manual genital stimulation, and penetration.

EnergySex: This is purely energy based—a sexual excitement takes place without any body-to-body touching. For example, getting superexcited when you're on the treadmill at the gym and there is someone supersexy sweating on the treadmill right beside you. Some other examples: heavy flirting, gazing into your lover's eyes, having a really juicy conversation with someone you have the hots for, riding on the back of a motorcycle being caressed by the wind, sucking ecstasy out of a chocolate-covered strawberry, swimming naked in the ocean on a hot sunny day, and having breath orgasms together (more on this in Step 13).

If only President Clinton and Monica could have enjoyed EnergySex, they might have avoided a lot of trouble!

Body+EnergySex: This is a combination of physical/genital sex with awareness of energy-based sex. Some examples: breathing energy into each other's mouths while grinding your hips together. Having intercourse while consciously orbiting energy through each other's bodies. Genital massage with conscious breathing to build energy. I'll tell you more about this kind of sex in later chapters.

If you have only BodySex, you might be limiting yourself. One of the ways to change how you think about sex is to allow everyday sensual pleasures to be part of your erotic life. As you embrace these pleasures as part of your sex life, you may find you are having more sex than you thought you were.

Begin to notice, pay more attention to, and eroticize/sexualize daily sensual delights, such as:

1. The sensuous feel of a silk scarf or tie on your neck
2. The caress of a soft breeze up your skirt on a spring day, or a hot breeze rippling the sweat on your skin in summer
3. The massaging of your scalp as you have your hair washed at the hair salon
4. The scent of jasmine on a humid night
5. Sliding naked into cool bedsheets at night
6. The newspaper tickling the crook in your inner arm as you turn the pages, giving you the chills

Over the next few days, try considering these kinds of sensations as part of your sex life and allow them turn you on even more. No one has to know you are subtly sexually aroused and having "sex." My motto is "Eroticize everything!"

Consuming Passions

Perhaps you have an idea of exactly the way you think a sexual encounter should unfold. The ideal sexual experience usually goes something like this:

You're with your lover with whom you are madly, passionately in love. Whenever you kiss, the world comes to a halt. You make exquisite love for hours, and then both of you come to orgasm simultaneously. Each time you make love you feel closer and closer to your lover. You are both always happy and satisfied until death do you part.

There is nothing wrong with having this, or any other ideal, as long as you don't let it get in the way of reality or let it hold you back from enjoying a whole smorgasbord of other erotic possibilities you might want. We have grown up inundated with lots of fairy tales, stories about falling in love, and sex being absolutely great every single time it happens, so we are often disappointed when sex is anything less than our ideal. Ask yourself, Who benefits from holding on to an unobtainable ideal? Do you?

One day I had an "aha! moment" when I realized that I could view sex in much the same way as I view food. This was very helpful, in that I realized I could really have different kinds of sex for different reasons and not feel dissatisfied if I didn't always end up with my "ideal."

Just as there are different food groups and qualities of foods, there are four basic types of sex we can enjoy: junk sex, health sex, comfort sex, and gourmet sex.

Junk Sex: This is the equivalent of junk food. When you are hungry and need something to take the edge off, and you don't have much time, junk sex perfectly fills the bill. It's a fast roll in the hay, maybe even rather mechanical, a quickie. It isn't particularly romantic, or like "making love," but it can be fun and sometimes quite hot. It's convenient.

Health Sex: Like health food or vitamins, health sex is nourishing and healing. If we have a headache, can't sleep, or feel tense, health sex can make us feel better. When you just need to be touched, or to get some stress relief, or want to get out of a funk, you are having health sex. It's good for you. Mae West once said, "An orgasm a day keeps the doctor away."

Comfort Sex: This is like comfort food—a nice, home-cooked meal. This is your meat-and-potatoes sex; it satisfies a hunger for love and intimacy. It's pretty standard, relatively easy to make, and predictable. Comfort sex is made from simple ingredients; you, your lover, and a bed.

Gourmet Sex: Like gourmet food for discerning adults this is what many folks consider the most delicious kind of sex, what people generally perceive of as the "ideal." However, it does take time to prepare, to savor, and to clean up after. Like gourmet cooking, it's a fine art; lovers need some skills, creativity, and experience in order to have gourmet sex. Gourmet sex can be absolutely spectacular, a religious experience, the delicacy of all delicacies. This is the ultimate romantic, earthshaking, mind altering, cosmic lovemaking.

Just as we have variety in the kinds of food we eat, so too is it good to have variety in our sex diet. For example, with gourmet sex, as with gourmet food, you don't appreciate it as much if you have it every single day. Besides, even the very best sexual relationships have their ups and downs. It just simply can't be earthshaking every single time. If it were, then even *that* would soon begin to seem humdrum. But if you don't expect it to always be earth-shattering and learn to accept what is, then you will never be disappointed. So drop your expectations when you drop your drawers.

Many things can affect the way a sexual encounter unfolds: your energy level, the time of day, the phase of the moon, the state of the world, and who knows what else. Comparing every sexual encounter with an ideal can create unnecessary disappointment. Entering into a sexual situation with an accepting mental attitude increases the probability of a positive outcome.

Paint with a Broad Stroke

To better understand human sexuality, yours and others' (indeed it can be quite a mystery), it can be helpful to compare it to art. Different kinds of people like, and dislike, different kinds of art, and the same with sex. Imagine yourself as an artist with a palette of pleasures. You will be adding colors, styles, and techniques to your pleasure palette as you go through the steps in this program, making you more versatile, more creative, and more skillful.

Sex, like art, has its genres. For example:

Romantic-art sex: This kind of sex is from the heart. It's sweet and lovely. Makes you swoon.

Tribal-art sex: This kind of sex comes from the hips. It's back to nature, sometimes animalistic, nonpretentious. Uninhibited. Unselfconscious.

Folk-art sex: This kind of sex is common sex. The kind people presume that most Americans have.

Outsider-art sex: Different from the norm.

Conceptual-art sex: This kind of sex is from the head. It's intellectually stimulating. It sometimes involves flirtatious game playing or creating unusual situations.

Pop-art sex: This kind of sex has humor. It's funny. Upbeat. Colorful.

Ancient-art sex: This kind of sex is old-fashioned, historical. It's influenced by past cultures.

Contemporary-art sex: Today's trendy sex, popular culture's idea of hot, good sex. In fashion.

Avant-garde—art sex: This is experimental sex, the sex of tomorrow.

Through self-expression you and your lover(s) can explore a variety of possibilities and, I hope, create masterpieces. Sure, absolutely anyone can paint a picture. And anyone can have sex. But to get good at either of them, you need to practice and take them seriously. Think of lovemaking as an art, and think of yourself as a "pleasure artist." *Voilà!*

View Your Sexuality As Fluid

Recently, after presenting a sex-education workshop at Vassar College, I asked one of the women students how she identified herself sexually, thinking she'd answer something like "straight, gay, bisexual, kinky, queer . . ." She said she was "fluid," and that most of her friends were "fluid," too. In that moment I had so much hope for the future, because what this young woman said meant that a new generation realizes they are likely to go through many different phases, and they were open to possibilities. That clever young woman, Chrys Curtis Fawley, ended up coming to work for me, and then went on to become a director of her own successful sex-education DVDs.

Considering yourself as fluid enables you to keep the door open to all kinds of possibilities. I also like my term *metamorphosexual,* a word I coined to describe those of us who feel we are in a state of sexual flux. I suggest that we all try to see ourselves as fluid, or metamorphosexual, in order to help welcome the changes we go through in our sex lives. The truth is, each of us is a magnificent, sexy work in progress, one that will never be finished. And you can never fully predict what will happen in your future.

Some people change in small increments, a little bit at a time, while some of us change often and dramatically. I'm definitely in the second category. Unfortunately, sometimes our friends, lovers, and communities aren't always supportive of our changes.

For example, I started out my adult sex life as a promiscuous *vanilla* (a word used to describe a nonkinky person) heterosexual. Then I became interested in kinky and fetish sex. People were shocked and disgusted! Some years later I discovered the spiritual side of sex and became interested in ancient Indian and Chinese lovemaking practices. My kinky friends thought I was way too "New Age-y." They smirked and put me down. Eventually I became interested in sex with women. Many of my straight friends were not happy about that. They'd hoped it was a passing phase. Then a big surprise I could never have predicted: I wanted to be celibate for a while. Wow, was that frowned upon in my social circle. Then, after being exclusively with women for several years, suddenly I wanted to have a male lover, and hey, did some of my lesbian friends judge me for that! Then I fell in love with a male-to-female transsexual and had a relationship with him, then her for three years. With every one of my changes I've had to face people's prejudices and resistance.

But through it all, my good friends stuck with me. I had to be true to myself and follow my muse. This process weeded out the people who didn't really care about the whole me, and my happiness.

Perhaps the reason you are interested in a sex-life makeover is that you have changed in some way and what you liked before just doesn't work for you anymore. Don't worry: When you change it doesn't mean that you have to change radically the way I did or that you have to switch lovers, social circles, environments, or wardrobes. Your life might look exactly the same outwardly—but you can't deny your inner changes. If you embrace them, you will ultimately become all the more YOU; more happy, beautiful, sexy, and satisfied.

To Thine Own Selves Be True

What does it mean to be true to your Self? You've probably heard the expression "Go with your gut." But what if you're not sure what your gut is saying? Or what if you feel one thing in your gut and you think differently in your mind? As you keep trying to seek your truth, the answers will become clear. When you tap into what your heart and soul deeply desire, it helps to begin to put those desires into action.

When practicing the suggestions throughout this book, check in with your body. How does it feel? What thoughts pop in and out of your mind? Even negative thoughts and feelings can be constructive. They signal there is something important for you to look at or avoid. You can learn a lot about your Truth from every thought and feeling. All these sensations, images, and intuitive thoughts add up to a holistic picture. Let's call that "Your Truth."

What's Your Current Truth?

Answer the following questions quickly. Don't think much about the answers; just write down the first things that come to mind. Go from the gut and your subconscious mind. Most important, be absolutely honest with yourself.

Sex is _____

When I was younger I thought sex _____

I used to feel sexy when _____

At school I learned that sex _____

My parents taught me that sex _____

My religion taught me that sex _____

The thing I used to be best at sexually was _____

The thing I'm best at sexually these days is _____

I used to love sex when _____

I used to dislike sex when _____

Today Mom and Dad basically think sex is _____

Today my spiritual/moral beliefs dictate that sex _____

These days society thinks sex _____

Today I love sex if _____

I feel most sexy when I _____

I'd have a better sex life today if _____

These days I like sex best when _____

These days I dislike sex when _____

I'd love to learn more about _____

I could stand to learn _____

I want a sex-life makeover because I'd like _____

What I'd love to do more of is _____

What I'd love to do but don't have the courage to is _____

In the future I expect that my sex life will _____

Eventually I would like _____

I wish _____

Now look over your answers and take a little inventory. Is there a time when what was the truth for you is no longer true? Has your sex life grown over time or withered? Can you gather any info from your answers about what Your Truth is at this moment? Has answering these questions given you insight into your sexuality and desires?

Spandex Your Psyche

When you see a wardrobe makeover on TV, they sometimes throw away the woman's entire wardrobe and she has to go get a whole new one based on their recommendations. Sometimes the woman being made over looks skeptical, gets angry and rebellious. Even though we the viewers can see how great she looks in her new clothes, she herself can't see it. But usually in time she'll grow to love and prefer her new look. As you consider new sexual personas and ways of thinking, you might feel a little uncomfortable. Mentally prepare for making some stretches and taking some risks. Try hard to keep an open mind. Tell yourself beforehand that it is possible that you might experience some discomfort, but that you're willing to endure it. Remind yourself that the discomfort won't last forever.

Think about other things in life that might make you uncomfortable, but that you endure for the benefits in the end. Some examples might be the physical irritations (mosquito bites, dampness) of camping outdoors; the anxiety before and during travel to a new country; taking on a higher-paying job that involves new skills. In all of these situations you go through a period of discomfort so that you can enjoy the rewards in the end. The same might be said of your sex-life makeover. At first you might feel uncertain when stepping outside your comfort zone, but if you remember the reasons you're doing all this and stick with it, you will eventually reap the rewards.

Start with Simple Baby Steps

If you think that creating a fresh, new sex life is overwhelming and too difficult, change that thought! It doesn't have to be that way.

Once upon a time I had a lover, Marco Vassi, whom many have dubbed the greatest erotic writer of this generation. Marco's great sense of humor was reflected in books like *The Erotic Comedies, The Stoned Apocalypse,* and a good dozen more. (I invite you to borrow one from my shelves and keep it on your night table.) Marco knew how to giggle at the absurdity of the universe. But when Marco got sad, he did it with the gusto of an

Italian opera. One day Marco found himself sitting in a Zen monastery with a Zen teacher and a group of disciples. The Zen teacher invited Marco to ask him a question, so he did. "In the morning when I wake up, I am totally depressed. Life is overwhelming. There's so much suffering in the world, and so much to be afraid of. I have so much I have to do and can't do anything. I can barely get out of bed in the morning. What should I do?" The Zen master said, "Get up and sweep the floor."

This might not help everyone, but it did help Marco. Why? Because the Zen teacher's instruction gave him a simple task to begin the day: He had to sweep the floor. It's a baby step, a very small thing to do, but once you take even one baby step, you've established some kind of momentum, and then more steps will appear before you. It can work the same way with your sex-life makeover. It might be overwhelming to imagine yourself going from A to B, but it is not overwhelming to, for instance, squeeze your legs together as tightly as you can right now for thirty seconds and notice what that does to your genitals. Just take baby steps, you'll get there.

Make Up Your Mind to Invest Some Time

Take a moment, close your eyes, and imagine you are lying on your deathbed. Look back over your life. What are you going to remember? Watching the weather channel? The dress you bought on sale at the mall? The newspaper you read? No, chances are you're going to remember the love you shared, and the romantic, sexy times you experienced. Wouldn't you like to have more of those kinds of memories?

If you live your life too fast you may miss your sex life completely. Besides cultivating positive thoughts, time is the best investment you can make in your sex life. If you don't have enough of it now, consider letting go of a hobby or activity, chore, or committee, or put something on hold for a while. Make up your mind to make more time for romantic adventure and sensual/sexual pleasure. Take time to smell the roses and other scintillating scents.

Create Support

There's nothing like support from others when you're creating changes in your life. It's natural to gravitate toward the familiar, the comfortable, but having company on your journey can allow you to risk a little discomfort and not lose your way. Often people think that they have to manage their sex-life challenges alone, that it all has to be private. Not true!

Ask your lover, if you have one, to support you and join in your process. Or you can follow along with this book with a pal. Do you have any trusted friends with whom you could share this process? For many years I have been a member of an amazing support group we call Club 90. The thing that brought us together was rooted in sex. The group—I, Veronica Hart, Gloria Leonard, Candida Royalle, and Veronica Vera—had all appeared in adult movies in the 1970s and '80s, and we wanted to explore how that unorthodox occupation had influenced our lives and to see where we could go next. By banding together we have created a network that has helped each of us to grow enormously, personally and professionally. You'll find Veronica Vera's two books in our sex-and-gender section. She created Miss Vera's Finishing School for Boys Who Want to Be Girls, the world's first cross-dressing academy. Candida Royalle went on to pioneer a whole new film genre, erotica for women and couples. She created the famed Femme Productions and recently authored the book *How to Tell a Naked Man What to Do,* which I highly recommend. Veronica Hart became one of the most respected director/producers in sex-film history, and did it all while raising a beautiful family. Her sons are now honors students in college. Gloria Leonard transitioned to paradise. She too raised a family and after her career in films and as a free-speech advocate, lives a life of luxury in Hawaii. You'll find all their works in your list of recommended resources at the end of this guide. These dear friends helped me transition out of mainstream porn and prostitution and into what has become a successful career in art and sex education. We all ended up wanting to stay in the field of sexuality, but on more of our own terms. Each of us would wholeheartedly agree that Club 90 has given us invaluable strength in matters of the heart, as well as in sex and relationships.

Why not create your own support group? Invite three, four, or half a dozen friends to come to your house every other week for about six months. Explain what you're doing and why, and invite them to take this journey with you—sort of like a book-reading group but with some personal sharing. Read a chapter every two weeks. At each meeting go around in a circle taking turns sharing what happened to you in relation to the chapter. Take an oath to keep what everyone says confidential. I promise it will be great fun, empowering, and you'll get to know your friends a whole lot better.

Are You a Victim, a Survivor, or a Thriver?

My heart goes out to you if you have been raped, abused, exploited, betrayed, or hurt in any way. If something horrible happened to you in relation to sexuality and you feel that it's getting in the way of your enjoyment and relationships, make healing a priority. If necessary, seek professional guidance and assistance on your healing path.

When it comes to your sex life, thinking of yourself as a victim is generally not helpful. That is why the recovery movement uses the word *survivor* to empower people as they heal. I suggest taking this a step further and consider using the word *thriver,* thinking of yourself as an explorer of love and sex, one who learns and grows from every experience. Hey, we can sure learn a heck of a lot from a terrible experience.

Considering how often I have courted danger, I have been extremely lucky in my life; however, I have certainly had some tough times. I remember once when I was eighteen years old and had just started appearing in porn movies, I had a difficult experience. I'd had a lot of fun doing the first four films, but on the fifth one, I hit a clunker. The director, the epitome of the phrase "sleazy pornographer," was bossy and controlling. He over-worked and underpaid the cast and crew, clutching us in his tight grip like the dollar bills he hung on to. By the end of the day, I was exhausted, hungry, and ready to go home. I had already performed three sex scenes, yet the director wanted one more, an anal sex scene, which wasn't agreed upon when I took the gig. I told him that I was exhausted and absolutely didn't want to, especially with the surly actor whom he cast me with. He pressured me into doing the scene, insinuating that he wouldn't pay me for my work that day if I didn't and offering me a measly $25 extra if I did, an amount, given my fatigue and state of mind, that was even more insulting than nothing. I finally gave in and just did it.

When the scene was over, I felt manipulated, taken advantage of, and used. When I got home I wept. The next day I thought of how I could have handled the situation better. I could have said no much more firmly and stuck to it. But at the time, I didn't know how. I realized that if I did say no I would have to say it convincingly. That was the day I learned to say no and stick to it. I made a promise to myself that I would take better care of myself from there on out. Today, I can look back and say it was a very empowering, educational day, and I can thank that awful creep for teaching me this valuable lesson. I went on to make over a hundred more sex movies, said no when I needed to, and never had a problem again; in fact, I always had a good time.

Occasionally you might feel bad after sex. (I hope this hasn't been your experience but if it has been, in other chapters I'll discuss this more.) Maybe you feel that you weren't true to yourself. Sometimes you have to take a risk to have a good sexual experience. The famous quote from an Alfred Tennyson poem "Tis better to have loved and lost than never to have loved at all" holds true for sexual experience as well. Without taking the risk of loss or of having "bad" sex, you may never know what fantastic sex is. Sometimes we overanalyze the past and use it to keep us from going forward. If you can, try to think of everything as useful—then you always come out a winner.

Plan It, Venus

Action creates change. Your decision to come to Dr. Sprinkle's Sex Life Makeover Center was an action. Now it's time to consider your next action. Are you ready to make a commitment? Creating a spectacular sex life doesn't have to be hard work, but it does take some focus and willingness. After you make a formal commitment to your sex-life makeover, you might be surprised at the magic that comes your way. You might notice that exciting coincidental events, important bits of information, and inspirational people suddenly cross your path.

It's important that the timing be right for you. If committing yourself to this process feels too difficult now, then put this book down and go do something else. You can come back to it at a later date. Another option is to read through this program guide without acting on anything in it. That's fine, too. But because you're reading this, I suspect that deep down something is pulling you toward a more spectacular sex life, and I encourage you to take the plunge. Please sign here.

Venus Contract

I, _____, understand that I will be undergoing a sex-life makeover. I will consider doing the things I deeply want to do and not do anything that I don't want to do. I take full responsibility for myself. I won't say "Annie made me do it!" I make my own choices.

I understand that I can always go back to my former sex life at any time. I am aware that perhaps some of my fears and anxieties about sex may come up. I will dare to take a look at my issues.

I promise to take good care of myself, emotionally, physically, and in every way.

I will aim to try some of the exercises and experiments Annie suggests. I want to release all the yummy sexual ecstasy inside me.

Signed _____

Date _____

Witness (optional) _____

The Think-About-Sex-for-Thirty-Seconds Experiment

1. Sit or lie down.
2. Take some deep relaxing breaths.
3. Check in. Mentally scan your body for a few seconds. Go inside yourself and notice how you feel, or don't feel, at this moment.
4. Now, for thirty seconds to a minute, close your eyes and think very intensely about sex. Think the most erotic thoughts that you possibly can. Fantasize about someone or something that really turns you on. Breathe deeply. Give it your complete mental attention.
5. When you are done, notice how you feel. Compare how you feel now with how you felt before you began thinking about sex. Do you feel a shift?

People usually answer that they feel things like "aroused," "more alert," "relaxed," "happier," "lighter."

What can you learn from this exercise? That there's a mind/body connection. That *just thinking* about great sex can actually change how you feel in your body and shift your consciousness.

Just thinking erotic thoughts can create positive psychological and physiological changes. Scientists have shown that just thinking about sex can even strengthen your immune system. So do . . . do . . . DO think erotic thoughts as much as possible! It's good for you. As Jerry Hall, the famous model and ex-wife of Mick Jagger, says, "The real fountain of youth is to have a dirty mind."

Step Two

Create Your Sexpot Profile

If you don't follow your bliss, how will you find it?

ollow me now to the Hall of Heroes and Sheroes. The large entryway is guarded by statues of some gods and goddesses. Venus, the goddess of love and sex, presides over all. From ancient to modern, whether real or imaginary, familiar or foreign, these role models are here to inspire you. What new version of yourself would you like to become? Since I believe that who you think and feel you are on the inside ultimately becomes manifested on the outside, let's begin by developing a clear vision of your "ideal inner sexpot."

Ladies, do you see her in this painting of a virgin waiting to be taken, or in these photos of a slut out on the prowl, a pent-up Victorian lady, a sixties flower child? Is she a shy southern belle or a horny housewife? Perhaps she's a butch biker babe or the heroine of a bodice ripper? Perhaps she's a seasoned porn star or a wicked dominatrix. Could she be *all* of the above and more?

Gentlemen, how do you see your inner sexpot? A rugged cowboy, a debonair playboy, or an energetic porn stud? Perhaps he's a satyr in the woods, a gentle sensual angel, a suave Casanova, or a skilled and sensitive sexual healer. Could he be all of the above and more?

I believe that we all have many different sexpots within ourselves and that these various personas can coexist in harmony with our everyday selves.

What has been your overall sexual persona in the past? Whatever you answered is perfect. You may not feel that way at this moment. But think about it. You made choices in your life based on where you came from, what you believed in, what your desires were, and how your life unfolded. Now, welcome to your future.

One way we can envision who we'd like to become is through the use of role models. The feminist movement enabled many women to see that what they wanted was often in conflict with who they were taught they "should" be. Seeing women who were doing what they wanted to do with their lives was liberating, and women looked to these role models for inspiration.

It's great to have role models. Even role models have role models! Actor Sigourney Weaver says that whenever she needs to make a hard decision she asks herself what Ripley, the heroine she played in *Alien*, would do. Halle Berry's role model was her fifth-grade teacher, Yvonne Sims. "She has inspired me to be the best I can be," says Berry. Alice Walker has eloquently stated that "role models in art, in behavior, in growth of spirit or intellect—even if rejected—enrich and enlarge one's view of existence."

You can gather helpful clues from your role models. Notice what you find sexy and attractive about them. Is it their confidence? Modesty? Wisdom? Intelligence? Flexibility? Energy?

Role models for our sex lives can be found everywhere: among movie stars, characters in plays or movies, artists, musicians, politicians, athletes, even our pets. (There's a reason the vulva is a "pussy.")

Discover Your Ideal Inner Sexpot

Part 1. Write down the names of any role models you can think of as examples of the way in which you'd like to be sexy. List what it is you admire about their sensuality/sexuality, presumed or actual. While in my office, be sure to notice the eight-by-ten glossies of some of my personal favorites. Here is a list and why I admire them. Read it, then make your own list.

EXAMPLES

Movie Stars

Queen Latifah—Large and sexy. Flaunts her big beautiful body and cleavage.

Jennifer Lopez—Walks with confidence.

Mae West—Not afraid or ashamed to admit she loves sex. A tough older woman with a strong sexual appetite.

Characters in a Movie or Play

Gypsy Rose Lee—Vulnerable and sweet. Had very low self-esteem but built it up. A sex worker without apology.

Erin Brockovich—Dares to wear the sexy clothes she likes. Uses her feminine powers for a good cause.

Artists, Musicians, Politicians, and Just about Anyone

Dolly Parton—Totally herself, unapologetically flashy, not afraid to wear false eyelashes and big hair.

RuPaul—A drag queen whose message is as much about love as cosmetics.

Superheroes

Xena—Extremely self-confident. Physically strong. Doesn't blab a lot.

Porn Stars

Georgina Spelvin—When having sex she exudes heat, lust, and passion.

Nina Hartley—The girl-next-door type but with great sexual skills and smarts. Extremely sex-positive.

Animals

My dog, Bob—He has no shame about sex and nudity.

A three-toed sloth—Moves slowly and deliberately, seemingly in a deep trance. Very focused.

Friends

Veronica Vera—Compassionate. Has a playful attitude.

People You Know Casually, or Have Seen

The librarian at my local library—Touches things very consciously and sensually.

Part 2. After you list all your role models, assemble their qualities into a legible paragraph, and read it through. Mine would read:

My ultimate inner sexpot is large and sexy. Flaunts her big beautiful body and cleavage. Walks with confidence. Not afraid or ashamed to admit she loves sex. Tough older woman with a strong sexual appetite. Vulnerable and sweet. Had very low self-esteem but built it up. A sex worker without apology. Dares to wear the sexy clothes she likes. Uses her feminine powers for a good cause. Totally herself, unapologetically flashy, not afraid to wear false eyelashes and big hair. Knows beauty is more than skin deep. Self-confident. Physically strong. Doesn't blab a lot. When having sex she exudes sexual heat, lust, and passion. The girl-next-door type but with great sexual skills. Extremely sex-positive. Has no shame about sex and nudity. Moves slowly and deliberately, seemingly in a deep trance. Very focused. Compassionate. Has a playful attitude. She touches things very consciously and sensually.

Now It's Your Turn

STEP 1

Write down one or two of your role models in each category, and list the
sensual/sexual qualities they have that you admire.

Movie stars: _____

Characters in a play or movie: _____

Artists, musicians, politicians: _____

Superheroes: _____

Porn stars: _____

Animals: _____

Friends: _____

Athletes: _____

People you know casually or have seen: _____

Other: _____

STEP 2

Now take away the names and keep the descriptions. You may need to adjust or tailor some words to fit into a cohesive paragraph.

My ultimate inner sexpot is:

_____

_____

_____

_____

_____

Use this description as a guide for the sexual person you'd like to become. Aim to nurture and embody these qualities that you admire. Affirm that these qualities are within you, because they are! Of course, you have to be somewhat realistic; I don't have Jennifer Lopez's gorgeous behind or Xena's superhuman powers, but I can certainly cultivate a confident walk and greater physical stamina. If I'm wondering if I should dare wear that outrageous low-cut fringe dress, I can ask myself "What would Dolly do?" and get the nerve to wear that daring dress that I really do want to wear but just need some courage. I can also aim to develop my sense of touch to be more like the librarian's. We *can* become more of what we aspire to.

Each day, take just one minute to imagine yourself becoming more like your ideal inner sexpot, and take some action toward achieving it. Do one thing each day that makes your inner sexpot a part of your personality. Kiss differently. Hug differently. Walk differently. Love differently. Dress differently. The more you act like your inner sexpot, the sooner you will become her. Of course, you probably won't want to be her at the office or the PTA meeting. Bring out your sexpot when it's appropriate, like out on the town on a hot date, or privately with your spouse.

It's helpful to use our role models for clues, but it's also important to be yourself, and you're unique, a one-of-a-kind. Allow your own personal sexual style(s) to emerge. Don't be surprised when others start seeing you as *their* inner sexpot role model. Maybe they already do!

Create and Explore Some Alter Egos

What's in a name? Plenty. The name you have carried for all of your life carries with it your entire history, and if you've been named after others, your name can carry even more. To use a new name and develop an alter ego or two can be really liberating and fun.

I first became aware of the beauty of having an alter ego when I was eighteen and I invented "Annie Sprinkle," who was the alter ego of Ellen Steinberg (my born name). Ellen was shy, insecure, and afraid of sex—the wallflower. Annie Sprinkle was outgoing, confident, and fearless—a star! When I turned forty I developed another alter ego, a more mature, wise, experienced woman whom I named Anya. These three personas (which are similar to the archetypal virgin, woman, and crone) are now each very much a part of me, and I draw from each of them at different times. Creating some alter egos really helped me to become more of how I wanted to be. Giving them names made it easier.

Sluts and Goddesses

For fifteen years I facilitated a workshop for women called Sluts and Goddesses, which was about creating and exploring two sexy alter egos. I did the workshop in countries and cities all around the world: from New York to Sydney, in Austin and Amsterdam, in Hollywood and Provincetown. Women everywhere told me they loved it and benefited from it.

We spent two full days together. On the first day of the workshop, we would introduce ourselves as we basically were, as our everyday selves. We'd talk and share, and together create a very comfortable and safe atmosphere. The rest of the day was spent exploring our "slut" alter egos. The slut archetype is basically a woman who is sexually wild, free. She could be a floozy, porn star, dominatrix, the French maid, stripper, hooker, party girl, nude model, can-can girl, biker chick, etc. She can be powerful and wise or very vulnerable and ditzy. I traveled with suitcases filled with slut gear of all styles, sizes, and fabrics, so that all the women could dress up like supersluts. Big wigs, tons of makeup, corsets, lingerie, false eyelashes, garter belts, high heels, fake fingernails—I had it, and they wore it. It was dress-up time, and over the top. Very fun.

Once we were in our slut gear and in character, each woman would choose a name for her slut persona: such as Peaches Delight, Luscious Lucy, or Elvira. Then we did smutty performances for one another, such as a striptease, a skit, a torch song. Whatever each woman wanted to do, alone or with a small group, she did. We all enjoyed the thrills of being both voyeurs and exhibitionists in a supportive environment.

We could hardly believe the amazing transformations each woman made; the excitement, the creativity, and the sexiness that were inspired by the costumes and the alter egos. Women were always shocked and amazed at how different each woman looked, acted, and felt and what a turn-on it all was. Susun Weed, who produced some of my Sluts and Goddesses events at her Wise Woman Center in Upstate New York, noted, "You can change your consciousness by changing your clothes."

Schemata Magic

On day two, when the women arrived they found that the workshop space had been transformed into a goddess temple, complete with candles, incense, sparkly canopies, altars, etc. The stage was set for them to create their goddess personas. This archetype can be the sexual healer, the powerful seductress, the tribal queen, the nature nymph, the flirty fairy, the oracle, the geisha, the sensuous princess, and the fertility goddess. She wears colorful, sensual, sparkly, flowing sarongs, saris, scarves, belly-dance costumes, shawls, beads, and grass skirts. (Goddesses travel lighter than sluts.) We would spend plenty of time adorning ourselves, decking ourselves out, and painting our faces to the point where each woman looked and felt like a real live goddess.

After everyone was fully attired and in character, we would form a circle. Each woman would choose a Goddess name, Kali, or Thea, Artemis or Isis or Sage Blossom . . . and as she declared it to the group we would bow to her and chant her name three times. Then we did drumming, rattling, breathing, chanting, and all manner of erotic goddess dances for one another with rubber snakes, swords, and finger symbols—for hours. The energy became ecstatic and divine. The goddess in each woman manifested in all her glory.

At the end of the workshop we would share honestly how we felt being our alter egos. Many women loved their experience in both personas. Some women felt uncomfortable with one persona or the other. The slut was just too not them and seemed ridiculous. Or the goddess just seemed too New Age or old-fashioned. Sometimes a woman was much more excited by one persona or the other. I found that when sex workers did the workshop many were bored with their slut persona and liked being their goddess persona better. Many others felt absolutely liberated by their slut persona and were far less interested in the goddess. Often women said how much fun it was just to play dress-up, and to be both voyeurs and exhibitionists. Most felt invigorated trying something new and taking some personal risks.

But most wonderful and telling of all was the feedback I got long after the workshop was over, months and even years later. Women would share with me that their alter egos lived on and continued to help them have more well-rounded and adventurous sex lives. They said that their husbands/lovers/partners enjoyed meeting and playing with their alter egos. Women said their alter egos continued to help them to be more fully themselves.

How to Create Your Own Slut and Goddess Alter Ego

Now I invite you to come with me to the Transformation Salon so we can create your slut and goddess alter ego. It's fun and easy. If you already have one or both, you can still add to your repertoire.

But wait! What if you learned that "sluts" were a bad thing and that you should never be a slut? Here at the Dr. Sprinkle Sex Life Makeover Center, we prefer to drop the word *should* so that you can be the woman you are. This is essential when creating your slut. You're going to create a slut whom you like, who is lovable and fun, and fabulous. One who is playful, desirable, healthy, and beneficial. What if you learned that a goddess was something from a faraway religion and had nothing to do with you? Not true. You are a goddess—a sex goddess here and now.

But wait again! What if you are a man reading this? Well, hey, guys, this one is really for the gals. But if you want to, you can still follow along. You can create some alter egos, too. Instead of a slut and a goddess alter ego, you can create a superstud alter ego. And, what the heck, a man can have a slut and goddess alter ego too!

What Can You Use These Alter Egos For?

- You can use your alter ego to say things you're shy about saying—or don't "sound" like you—to your lover. For example, you can write different kinds of love letters signed by your alter egos. (For example, I have a romantic-French-girl alter ego named Fifi. She's superaffectionate and lovable. I often sign love letters as Fifi.)
- You can step out of your everyday self and make love or get down, as it were, as one of your alter egos.

- You can buy sexy new things for your alter egos to wear.
- You can look to your alter egos for erotic inspiration.
- You can use your alter ego to develop parts of yourself buried deep inside.
- If you think you would never want to act out an alter ego, she, or he, could stay a figment of your imagination. Simply keep her or him inside you, just as people have their inner child, inner adult, and inner critic. Why not have an inner slut, or an inner goddess or inner stud? They could be helpful. Imagine what they would say to you.

Here's How to Create Your Alter Egos at Home

1. Put on some loose, comfy clothing like a nightgown or loose pajamas.
2. Look through your music and find the raunchiest, sluttiest, sexiest song you can.
3. Find a place where you can be alone and are able to play music.
4. Play the song, and let it move you to dance. Close your eyes. Dance the dance not to look good but to really FEEL your inner slut. Call upon your slut persona to come into your mind's eye. Let it be a slut persona that you love, that touches your heart.
5. As the song plays and your dance progresses, let your slut persona get clearer and clearer, and imagine everything you can about her. Take your time. (Play the song again if you want to.) Then see if you can answer the following questions:

What's her name? _____

What does she look like? _____

What is she wearing? _____

How does she act? _____

Does she have an occupation, hobby, purpose? _____

What does she enjoy, sexually or otherwise? _____

Does she have a sexual specialty? _____

Does she have anything she wants to tell you? _____

Does anything else come to mind about her? _____

6. To develop your goddess alter ego, find some goddesslike spiritual music that would inspire her to come to you, into your mind's eye. When you get a sense of her, then ask the same questions:

What's her name? _____

What does she look like? _____

What is she wearing? _____

How does she act? _____

Does she have an occupation, hobby, purpose? _____

What does she enjoy, sexually or otherwise? _____

Does she have a sexual specialty? _____

Does she have anything she wants to tell you? _____

Does anything else come to mind about her? _____

Note: When you do this dance, you might get a really strong, clear image of your alter egos, or you might not. If nothing comes to you, then simply make your alter egos up and answer the questions from your head.

Congratulations. Your alter egos are born. Love them, develop them, get to know them better, and enjoy them over the years to come.

Stir Your Sexpot—
A Look at Your Sexual Identity

What is your sexual identity today? In which direction do you want to move (literally and figuratively)? People tend to think of sexual identity as being merely a matter of the gender of one's sexual partners. But terms like *heterosexual, bisexual,* or *gay* are only about what kind of people you're attracted to. There are many other aspects to sexual identity that are equally or more defining.

As we go forward with your sex-life makeover you have the right to have your very own sexual identity. Challenges may arise when you want to share a certain part of yourself, but have no fear. Rising to that challenge is all part of your program and part of the fun.

Liberate Your Fantasies

Before we start, I want to point out that you can look to your sexual fantasies for hints about your future needs and desires. Paradoxically, we often fantasize about things we would never actually do; fantasizing or daydreaming about them is a way to explore what's scary or forbidden in a totally safe context. You may not want to do exactly what you're fantasizing—but maybe something similar to it?

Some women don't fantasize much at all. As with dreaming, though, it's usually just a matter of paying attention: Everyone dreams, and everyone fantasizes sometimes, but some people recognize and remember their dreams and fantasies while others don't. If you are one of those women who think they don't fantasize and you'd like to consider developing a stimulating fantasy life, you can start by reading about other people's fantasies. (Lots of folks love to write about their fantasies and share them in books and on the Internet.)

What If Your Fantasies Scare You?

Fantasies are beyond moral issues. While it's important to maintain a set of morals in life, when it comes to sex, our fantasies are sometimes morally incorrect, unhealthy, and even downright illegal. That's because fantasy is the place where we work out feelings we might never express in our "real" life. Again, as with dreams, fantasy is an area where our subconscious reigns freely, where we express and explore situations, thoughts, or ideas that we forbid ourselves from acting out.

But if you have fantasies that are particularly unwanted, and they make you feel bad about yourself or you are concerned about where they might lead you, then you can choose not to let yourself go there. For a while I found myself fantasizing about one of my best friend's husbands, but because this started making me feel very turned-on and uncomfortable whenever I was around him, I made a conscious decision not to let myself enjoy that fantasy anymore. After all, there are plenty of other fish in the fanta-sea . . .

Scary Movie

I used to be afraid of what might happen if I let myself have my most extreme sexual fantasies. Repressing them ultimately became more uncomfortable than exploring them because I was so afraid of what I might find. So eventually I made a conscious decision to let myself go all the way, deep into my psyche, to see what lurked in the darkest recesses. I had some real doozies: being attached to torture machines, being raped, having sex with a donkey onstage in a sleazy bar . . . I won't even tell you some of the others. Interestingly, after I let myself go all the way into my most extreme fantasies, they eventually melted away. It was sort of like getting bored with horror movies and wanting to see a love story. My fantasies totally changed at a certain point and actually became rather sweet and innocent. Some women enjoy the same fantasies for years and even lifetimes, and others find their fantasies change radically, as mine did.

On the other hand, some of my most delicious sexual fantasies led me to some wonderful sexual experiences, and led me into the next phase of my sexual life. For example, I started fantasizing about making love on the beach in the hot sun and ended up living in a house on the beach with my lover. I had fantasies of being part of a threesome and ended up having some excellent threesomes.

So take your current sexual fantasies or erotic daydreams (if you have them) into consideration as you answer the following questions. Only you will know which you want to try out in real life and which are strictly to be limited to arousal purposes only.

Okay, Let's Begin

In the following sections I am going to list a variety of possible sexual identities, styles, categories, and choices and explain a few things about them. Some you might be familiar with, and some might spark new interest. Some might turn you off. Others you may even object to. That's perfectly fine. Who you are *not* can also help define who you are. These are simply some options to consider.

However, if something does turn you off, try to honestly decipher if it's really a turn-off or if we've hit on something that actually excites you but that you're afraid of. If something makes you nervous and a bit uncomfortable but your mouth starts to water and waves of desire pass through your body, take notice.

What Are Your Sexual Orientations?

Sexual orientation doesn't necessarily mean whether you are simply heterosexual, gay, or bisexual. There are variations on these themes, as you will see when answering the following questions. Orientations can also change over the course of a lifetime, subtly or radically. Some people are born into one orientation for a lifetime, while others have nine (or more) different lives.

If you have been and plan to continue being in a committed, long-term monogamous relationship, some of these questions might not apply, but others will.

Circle as many answers as apply: male, female, other, or none. "Other" being a person who doesn't consider himself or herself male or female but hermaphroditic, intersexed, differently gendered, extraterrestrial, Big Foot, a tree—what or whoever doesn't necessarily fit into "male" or "female."

1. With whom have you had sexual activities? Men / Women / Other / None
2. With whom could you see yourself having sex in the future? Men / Women / Other / None
3. With whom have you enjoyed sensual, erotic activities that weren't overtly sexual? For example, a foot rub, flirting, or deriving erotic pleasure from looking at someone in a tiny swimsuit. Men / Women / Other / None
4. With whom could you see yourself enjoying sensual, erotic activities in the future that aren't overtly sexual? Might you want to be "bisensual?" Men / Women / Other / None
5. When you have sexual fantasies, whom are they with? Men / Women / Other / None
6. When you read or watch erotica or porn, which sex turns you on the most? If you have never seen erotica or porn, just imagine what might turn you on. Men / Women / Other / None
7. When it comes to romantic relationship(s), with which sex(es) does your heart lie? Men / Women / Other / None
8. Can you envision yourself having romantic relationships in the future with Men / Women / Other / None?

9. With which sex(es) have you been emotionally intimate in the past, sexual activity totally aside? Have you been emotionally close with both men and women? Or just one or the other? Men / Women / Other/ None

10. With which sex(es) could you envision being emotionally intimate in the future? For example, some women might prefer to be emotionally intimate with women but prefer being sexual with men. Or vice versa. Men / Women / Other / None

As you can see, orientations can be complex. Current research states that there is no simple explanation for why people make the choices they do. There are numerous biological and psychosocial factors that contribute to our choices and sense of erotic identity. Needless to say, some of the above choices can be . . . brave. The most compassionate thing is to aim to love your erotic self, regardless.

These days many new words are being used to describe people's sexual orientations: *Heterosexual, homosexual,* and *bisexual* are the most predominant. The members of the rock band Pepper Spray identify themselves as "quadrasexual," and they leave whatever that means up to our imaginations. Others say they are "omnisexual," meaning they're into an extremely wide range of possibilities. Then there are the "trisexuals"—they say they "will try anything." Cultural sexologist Carol Queen invented the term *absexual* for people who abstain from sex because of moralistic beliefs. *Asexual* is when a person is not interested in sex with anyone, including him or herself. *Cosmi-sexual* is when someone sees himself in energetic sexual union with the universe. And the list keeps growing as people evolve and times change. Perhaps you'll come up with a new one.

What Is Your Sexual Style?

Now I'm going to delve into the wide variety of sexual acts and sexual styles that can be part of a person's sexual identity. To illustrate these, I will share some of my own personal experiences with you. I hope this will give you insight into some areas of human sexuality that you might not have considered or quite understood before. And I hope you will still respect me in the morning. You can also look to see if you'd like to try any of the things I mention—if you haven't already.

Are You a Voyeur or an Exhibitionist? Some of Each, or Neither?

A voyeur is someone who gets turned on watching. An exhibitionist is someone who gets turned on being watched.

The "peeping Tom" engages in nonconsensual sexual behavior because his subjects are involuntary. He single-handedly (so to speak) gives voyeurism a bad name. The flasher does the same disservice to exhibitionists. I've been flashed a number of times by strangers on the street. It was unpleasant and extremely bad manners.

A Lid for Every Sexpot

Many adults enjoy being voyeurs and exhibitionists in healthy, fun, consensual ways. (When a voyeur falls in love with an exhibitionist, it's a match made in heaven.) Being a voyeur or an exhibitionist can be enormous turn-ons. Me, I can enjoy a bit of both.

Here are some ways I've enjoyed being an exhibitionist:

- A very sweet photographer once took one hundred very close-up Polaroid photos of every inch of my naked body and made a mosaic. It was an incredibly erotic experience. (I'd put this in the EnergySex category for sure.)
- Doing a smutty striptease with a raunchy floor routine while my lover watched.
- Once I went to the movies with my lover on a rainy night. As we stood in line he put his hand in my raincoat pocket, which had a big hole in it. He played with and stimulated my genitalia. No one else in line knew what he was doing, I'm sure. But it was very hot to be having sex in a crowded line at the movies.
- When I was staying in a hotel in Sydney, Australia, with my lover, we went to the rooftop pool and hot tub. No one else was there, so I slipped out of my swimsuit underwater, and my lover held me while I straddled a hot-tub jet, while we

enjoyed the view of Sydney. (It quickly became our favorite city.) The next day, when we were in the lobby we happened to notice a small television monitor at the front desk. Guess what was on that monitor? The rooftop pool and hot tub! Seems we had been on candid camera. Whether anyone watched or not, we will never know. I wasn't about to ask. It's not uncommon for the fear of getting caught to be part of the turn-on for an exhibitionist, but rarely is actual arrest very hot. The moral of the story is that if you are an exhibitionist, beware of surveillance cameras. They're everywhere these days. Be especially careful in elevators and stairwells.

- Appearing in all kinds of sex movies and nude modeling for dozens of photographers. (Not everyone's cup of tea, but it was good for me!)

Here are some ways I've enjoyed being a voyeur:

- Lying in bed and sketching my lover's genitals, with a pencil on paper, while my lover posed with legs spread.
- Watching my lover masturbate to orgasm. Delightful.
- Going with my lover to Salambo's in Hamburg, Germany, to watch a live sex-show revue.
- Taking an erotic massage workshop and looking around the room to see the other people enjoying their erotic massages.
- Watching a porn movie by myself in my hotel room when I was alone on the road.

If you're a budding exhibitionist, I recommend you check out Carol Queen's book, *Exhibitionism for the Shy*. Dr. Queen, cofounder of San Francisco's Center for Sex and Culture, financed her Ph.D. by working at the Lusty Lady Peep Show doing "private shows" in a booth. If you're interested in voyeurism, you might enjoy the photos and essays in David Steinberg's book *Erotic by Nature* or Jill Posener and Susie "Sexpert" Bright's *Nothing But the Girl*. These are just some of the wonderful resources that can be added to your erotic library, to keep your makeover fresh.

Studying the Classics

Many (probably most) women are perfectly delighted and satisfied with the more standard forms of lovemaking: kissing, hugging, sensual touching, manual stimulation, oral sex, intercourse, and cuddling—often in that exact order. Perhaps you are the kind of woman who loves romance, and you delight in the connection you create with your partner. Do you seek that intimacy and engagement?

This is sometimes called *vanilla sex, meat-and-potatoes sex, pedestrian sex, straight sex, vintage sex,* or *nuts-and-bolts sex*. Unfortunately, these terms are rather derogatory. I can only imagine that perhaps they were created by people who wanted to feel superior for being outside the norm because they had previously been judged for being outside it. In any case, I call it *classic sex*, and it can be absolutely divine and can certainly provide abundant delicious possibilities, spectacular adventures, and deep satisfaction.

So if you are a vanilla kind of gal, with no interest in any kind of experimental or kinky sex, be proud, be strong, and enjoy. You need not try another thing.

But then again, perhaps you'd like to expand your repertoire?

Do You Like to Play with Gender? Or Not?

Yes, you are a genetic woman, or a genetic man, but have you ever done anything that made you feel sort of like another gender? Or something in between? The ancient goddesses shifted genders, even shifted species, all the time, and it's never gone out of style. Playing with gender is one of the hottest, trendiest kinds of sex play today. You can reach new heights of self-discovery by stepping out of your pumps and walking a mile in someone else's wingtips (or boots, or whatever suits you).

Perhaps gender play is a new concept to you, but in recent years it has permeated the culture all around us: in fashion, music, art, and television. Basketball celebrity Dennis

Rodman, who is known for his ball gowns as well as his hoops, is one example among many. Perhaps you feel confined in your gender role. You might want to explore breaking out of your usual gender role, if just for a night. Here are some lighthearted ways in which I have enjoyed gender play over the years:

- I sat on top of my guy's penis and rode him very aggressively, as if he were the woman and I were the man. Very enjoyable.
- After sex I put on my lover's boxer shorts and T-shirt and assumed a butch persona.
- I used a strap-on dildo on my boyfriend. (One of the most popular and biggest-selling classic sex films is *Bend Over Boyfriend*, which is about women strapping on dildos and penetrating their men. Believe me, men enjoy far more anal pleasure than many people realize. Right, guys? Don't knock it until you try it.)
- When I lived in Provincetown (a very gender-fluid community) I once dressed up like a man wearing female drag and went out for the evening. Everyone really thought I was a man dressed as a woman! That's called a "faux queen." It was great fun—although if you live in a conservative little suburb, I might not recommend this except on Halloween.
- I sucked my girlfriend's clitoris like it was a penis.
- I've been with several transsexual lovers, people whose change lasted a lifetime and made it possible for them to access feelings, including sexual feelings, that they could not reach prior to making a change. My video *Linda/Les & Annie— The First Female-to-Male Transsexual Love Story,* documents one of these relationships. It is far from a scholarly take on the subject, just two people going beyond borders to make love—and sometimes that is what it takes.

Heavenly Bliss—Sacred Sex

Our lovers' round bamboo hut and the adjoining hot tub in the orchid garden are the perfect environments for you to explore the spiritual aspect of sexuality. That is, if you are interested in "sacred sex."

It wasn't until my thirties that I discovered the spiritual aspects of sex, although I thought sex was heavenly from the night I had lost my virginity on. When I was working as a journalist for *Penthouse* magazine, I was assigned to cover a Tantra workshop being taught by a beautiful woman named Jwala. All I knew was the little bit I'd heard about the *Kama Sutra*, an ancient manual from the Far East on the art of making love. I expected to find the workshop rather silly and woo-woo, and I thought I knew a lot about sex. But by the end of the weekend I realized there was a lot more to learn, and I became a convert to Tantra and "sacred sex" and committed to doing more of it.

Tantra originated around 5000 B.C. in India as a yogic path to enlightenment. Popularly, Tantric lovers focus on exchanging energy, breathing together, and making love very slowly for a long time. They use sex as a meditation and as a way to experience God/ Goddess. Tantra can deepen the experience of love and nourish the spirit with its emphasis on sensuality and beauty.

Jwala and I became very close friends and housemates. She had made herself over from a suburban northern California girl named Kathleen into Jwala, a world explorer who called Poona, India, her real home and an internationally acclaimed teacher of the arts of love and author of *Sacred Sex*. I learned much from Jwala and went on to learn all I could from other ancient sex-positive spiritual traditions. I studied some Chinese Taoist sex practices as taught by Maneewan and Mantak Chia. I rode the ecstatic wave of "Oceanic Tantra" taught by Kutira Decosterd and Raphael in their Hawaiian paradise. From Swiss teacher Margo Anand I learned about her "Sky Dancing Tantra." Then I participated in ancient pagan menstrual blood rituals with famous witches, sweated through Native-American teachings and fire breath orgasms with medicine man Harley Swiftdeer, and did the "rites of pleasure initiations" led by English psychotherapist Allan Lowen. I received an initiation in the cobra breath orgasm from African-American teacher Sunyata Saraswati, studied mystical Sufi-style love with German Sufi master Dieter Jarzombek, and learned many more wonderful things from some of the world's top sexuality teachers.

I had always believed sex was a powerful force, but learning about all these traditions gave me another context for my experiences and taught me tools and techniques that have been really useful, some of which I'll share with you later on in this program.

Have you sometimes felt that sex was a meditation, felt moved to express gratitude, and felt connected with everything and everyone in the universe? If you are the kind of person who loves making sex last a long time and likes going into deep trance states, then this is all part of your sexual identity.

Here are some ways I've experienced spiritual sex over the years:

- There were moments in the throes of ecstasy when I felt as though I were in a dream, and there was no past and no future, only the present. I went into what Australian aboriginals call the "dreamtime."
- When I was in Jamaica I was making love with my then-fiancé Joseph Kramer in the rain and thunder. We felt the earth's sexual power come through our bodies.
- On the anniversary of my domestic partnership, I created a special lovemaking ceremony. It took me the entire day to prepare: cleaning, shopping, primping, preparing exotic drinks, etc. Then from about five P.M. until sunrise, we didn't leave the bedroom, or sleep. We made love in various ways, without any rush, and expressed gratitude for each other while basking in the afterglow. We dedicated our lovemaking session to another wonderful year together.
- One day when I was masturbating on my bed, I looked out the window and noticed a particularly beautiful puffy white cloud. I imagined that I was making love with that cloud. Just as I was about to come to orgasm, a helium balloon came from nowhere and floated up into the cloud. It moved me to tears.

If you are interested in learning more about "sacred sexuality" but you find a lot of the books, DVDs, or workshops out there too "New Age" for your taste, check out Barbara Carrellas's book or workshop called Urban Tantra. She teaches sacred sex with humor and an edge. It's a fabulous fun read.

Do You Enjoy Erotic Power Play?
Do You Enjoy Being Dominant, Submissive?
Or Are You Switchable? Or Not?

In the bedroom, tops and bottoms can mean more than pajamas. Some sex researchers and educators feel that elements of power are always present during sex between partners—for example, when one partner simply surrenders to the strength or desire of the other. There is a variety of ways to explore these dynamics, some subtle and some not so subtle. You can choose to be a "top"—the aggressive, or dominant, partner—or the "bottom"—the receptive, or submissive, partner. Or, you and your partner can switch roles, depending on your mood, your partner, and the position of the moon.

There are women who feel threatened playing with power in a sexual context, as it can bring up memories of being powerless. It is also possible to feel afraid, or mentally turned off, yet still be sexually excited by power play—and then feel ashamed and guilty for these feelings. It's important, if you do want to explore erotic power, that you give yourself permission to do so without beating yourself up for your desires. If you find that you cannot overcome such feelings, then playing with power could turn out to be too much of a conflict for you. Or it could be just the ticket to your empowerment and growth.

It is important when doing power play that you and your partner trust one another. You might need to have some conversations before, during, and after engaging in these activities. In fact, some aficionados of power play say that one of the benefits of playing with power is an increased level of communication with their partners in general. You need to know that she or he will not do anything that you don't give explicit permission for. You also need to feel confident that he or she will not use whatever you do in bed in other areas of your relationship; for instance, if, at the height of sexual excitement you tell your lover you'll do anything s/he asks, he or she needs to honor that this is a sexual moment only and not expect a permanent slave girl.

Power play can take many forms. It can be simple, innocent, and fun. It can be a straightforward situation in which the dominant partner tells the other what to do while the submissive partner obeys; it can involve playing stereotypical power roles such as secretary/boss, nurse/doctor, or student/teacher; or it can go so far as to incorporate spanking, slapping, sensual whipping. If you are interested in this kind of erotic play I recommend that you read one of the many excellent books available on the subject. (See the Resources.)

Here are a few ways I've enjoyed being dominant over the years:

* I gave my lover very sexy birthday spankings with a Ping-Pong paddle at the stroke of midnight.
* In the heat of passion I got on top and gave my lover a big hickey, as if I were a thirsty vampire.
* At a thrift shop I found a nurse's uniform, which I hemmed very short. Then I went to the drug store and bought one of those disposable enemas. That night my lover was watching TV, I donned my nurse uniform, went and turned off the TV, and commanded, "Turn over, it's time for your enema!" First we had a really good laugh; then we had some very sexy fun.
* Someone once gave me a gift of a really beautiful black leather blindfold which had soft fur on the inside. Sometimes I would put that blindfold on my lover, lie her down and hold her arms gently back. She surrendered and could only imagine where I was going to kiss and nibble her next.

Here are some ways I've enjoyed being submissive over the years:

* After reading the classic erotic book *The Story of O* when I was eighteen, I imagined myself as the character of O and being someone's willing sexual "slave." It was one of my hottest masturbation fantasies for many years.
* Sometimes my lover would bite my nipples quite hard, and I would totally surrender and enjoy it.
* My lover once tied me to the dining-room table, then pulled up a chair and ate me for dinner.
* When I was giving a particularly hot sexy lover oral sex, he held my hair really tightly in his fists and pushed and pulled my head around, and I just went with his movements. It was very exciting for me, and I could tell it was for him as well.

Here are some ways I've enjoyed being a switch:

- I totally surrendered to my lover, 100 percent. Then after he had his way with me, I would turn the tables and have my way with him 100 percent. I have found there is an exquisite beauty in experiencing both roles back to back.
- Play wrestling. It's great foreplay. Sometimes I win, and sometimes I let myself lose.
- Sitting dominantly upon my lover's face, then turning over and totally letting go, and surrendering to the powers of my lover's tongue.

Do You Have a Fetish, or Two or Three? Or Not?

Fetishes have gotten a bad name because occasionally they involve criminal behavior, such as a shoe fetishist who steals women's shoes or a panty fetishist who swipes ladies' panties off a clothesline. Fetishes can also be troublesome when they interfere with a relationship, or with everyday life. But as long as playing with a fetish is totally consensual, non-exploitative, safe, and legal, there is nothing wrong with indulging in it. Over the years I have met all kinds of people with all kinds of interesting fetishes, especially when I worked as a professional dominatrix for a year and a half. In my experience, fetishes can be good, clean, healthy, erotic fun.

The textbook definition of a fetishist is someone who has a fetish that is all-consuming, in that the fetishist can only get turned on by a particular inanimate object (i.e., leather gloves) or a particular body part (i.e., feet) and nothing else. But people also use the term *fetish* more loosely to describe something that simply turns them on. I'd call this a "mild fetish," versus a "true fetish." I've greatly enjoyed exploring other people's fetishes (both mild and true) with them as well as delving into a few of my own, from wearing black seamed stockings, to playing with bondage, to piercing my labia and wearing a gold ring.

Are you a butt woman or a chest woman? Are you a breast man or a leg man? Do you have a thing for athletes, or construction workers, or a man or woman in a uniform? A fetish can be for Asian (or any ethnicity) women or men, amputees, cowboys, or a bodybuilder's biceps. Is your fetish wearing sexy shoes or seamed stockings? These kinds of turn-ons are also part of your sexual identity.

Some people might argue that it's oppressive to fetishize people, body parts, nationalities, or skin colors. (Just about anything or anyone can be a fetish!) But hey, as long as it's in the spirit of appreciation, and respect, and you're polite about it, it shouldn't be a problem.

Having a fetish doesn't make you a "deviant" or a "pervert"—unless, of course, you would enjoy identifying yourself that way. Remember, at one time oral sex and anal sex were considered deviant, but now many people enjoy these as common sexual activities. An excellent and fascinating book about fetishes is Katharine Gates's *Deviant Desires*.

Kinky Capers

Here are some ways I've enjoyed fetishes over the years:

- I had a boyfriend who got totally turned-on seeing women wearing very high heels. So I wore them often, both in and out of bed. He literally let me walk all over him. I got excited knowing he was excited.
- My friend Antoinette designed and manufactured latex fetish clothing and underwear. My best friend, Veronica Vera, and I hosted a party and dressed everyone up in Antoinette's latex clothes, powdering them first before encasing them in rubber. Latex looks fabulously sexy and feels like a second skin. It makes you sweat and feels like a return to the womb. It was a fabulous party.
- I once met a handsome man who had a very serious foot fetish. He actually worked as a professional pedicurist but rarely admitted to his fetish to his clients. He offered to give me a professional pedicure (which was the best I'd ever had) in exchange for letting him get to give me his favorite kind of kinky pedicure, which he called "the Chinese pedicure." He put four chopsticks on each foot between my toes, and then tied them together with string. He would then pull the

string to tighten the chopsticks and squeeze my toes while using a hairbrush to spank the bottoms of my footsies. It wasn't as painful as it might sound, especially with my trusty Hitachi Magic Wand fast against my clit. It was truly bizarre, and truly fun and sexy. I admit I got very aroused. But he wasn't interested in any sex above the ankles.

Are You Interested in BDSM? Or Not?

BDSM stands for bondage, discipline, sadism, and masochism. Some people interpret BDSM simply as sex that involves "pain." But is it really "pain" if it really feels pleasurable? After all, it's not like dental surgery. Maybe it's better to think of it more like "a very intense form of touching," involving anything from nipple pinching, neck biting, butt spanking, to back scratching or whipping and more.

One reason some activities like these can be superexciting for some people is that they can increase the flow of endorphins in the body. BDSM can induce trancelike states that help lovers surrender and relax, and transcend everyday reality. It's a form of self-expression and self-exploration. My friend Jim Ward, who is largely responsible for the popularity of piercing as body decoration, once said to me that "BDSM is simply cowboys and Indians for adults." It's adult play, and it usually has its origins somewhere in childhood. Some people are simply wired to deeply desire BDSM.

S/M gets a bad name when it's unsafe, nonconsensual, and exploitative. Then it becomes either a horrible accident or a crime, such as kidnapping, rape, or torture. These crimes make the nightly news, so then kinky sex is almost always presented as nightmarish and criminal. The press thrives on sensationalism, ignorance, and sexploitation. These sensational headlines make it seem as though all S/M is dangerous and evil. But one way to try to understand the absurdity of this is to see it as similar to marriages that start out loving and equal but end up becoming horribly abusive. It's not marriage that leads to abuse, and it's not S/M that leads to criminal activity.

The world of psychiatry and psychology sometimes sees S/M play as dysfunctional, as something you'd want to get rid of if you could. But one research survey done in 1990 showed that 25 percent of the people surveyed engaged in some kind of S/M activities. That figure is probably much higher today, as kink and fetish communities have grown much larger and more visible. In my experience as a sex professional, even people with the most outrageous kinky desires just seemed to be like grown-ups playing a fun game. Lots of folks of all kinds are enjoying kink. Again, as long as it's safe, totally consensual, and nonexploitative, there isn't anything wrong with this kind of sex play. When the activities have been undertaken in order to give and receive pleasure, and have been enacted with love and in the spirit of playfulness, they can be deeply intimate, moving, healing, and joyous. Even humiliation can be uplifting—like when your lover teases you that you are so "dirty" or "bad" or "horrible" It's the intention that counts.

Where Do You Go from Here?

We have fleshed out your inner sexpot, and we have looked at some possible sexual identities and options. Maybe after reading this you're shaking your head and thinking, "I'm not kinky. I have no fetishes, I don't want to switch genders, and I don't want to explore Tantric sex." Maybe you've already been there and done that. Maybe you're thinking, "I'm happy having regular, old-fashioned, vanilla sex." If that's the truth for you, embrace it. It seems that the more sexually "liberated" we become as a culture, the more pressure is placed on us to "get with it." Please don't interpret anything I've said as pressure to try or do something. We're just looking at options here. It's your prerogative to change your mind whenever you feel like it. You are never locked in. Just never say "never!" or one day you might have to eat your hat . . . or latex garter belt.

Perhaps you feel apprehensive and choose to cling to the past. Or you realize you actually prefer your status quo to any new choices. Or maybe you realize that it's time for a stretch. If you get a few butterflies in your stomach when you think of modifying or changing your sexual identity(s), don't worry! You are stretching and growing, and on a new adventure. It could be possible that you may need to mourn any part(s) of your self that you are letting go of before you can move onto becoming someone new. After all, your former self probably served you well, for a while.

Perhaps you're totally up for trying some new things now, or exploring some previously hidden side(s) of yourself. If so, then just go for it! It's highly likely that you'll find any personal stretches well worthwhile. As my friend sex educator Felice Newman so eloquently wrote in her excellent *Whole Guide to Lesbian Sex*, "Once you feel the exhilaration of self-expression, your energy and enthusiasm will increase. When we make personal choices based on self-knowledge and self-love, not on guilt or self-consciousness, we feel more contentment."

Step Three

Confront Your Party Poopers

It's my sex party, and I'll cry if I want to.

Let's you and I have tea on the terrace. It's lovely and quiet out here, the perfect place for an intimate tête-à-tête. Now is the time that I must warn you about some uninvited guests that might show up and try to distract you from your sex-life makeover program. Sometimes, no matter how well we plan or how far we travel, there are those who want to spoil our good time. So, let's take a look at some of them together and expose them to the light.

The Party-Pooper Parade

Imagine that you have meticulously planned a gloriously sexy evening with your lover. You're filled with anticipation. Finally the party begins and . . . uh oh! You find yourself feeling out of sorts. Which of these "party poopers" is whispering in your ear? Put a check next to each one who seems familiar, even if only a tiny bit.

If you're a man, you will likely relate to many of these female party poopers. Just change the female names into male names. But mostly take this opportunity to try to understand what women are facing and dealing with. This part of your program can help you to become more sympathetic and understanding, and that will certainly make you a better lover. Plus I'll give you some ideas of how you can be supportive of your partner.

_____ *Self-loathing Sally*—She thinks, "I'm not good enough. I'm not doing it right. I don't deserve it." She's often hard on herself. She can be shy, insecure, and scared. She feels sexually inadequate.

_____ *Sex-Negative Nancy*—She thinks sex is animalistic, uncivilized, dirty, and disgusting. Because of these negative beliefs about sex she has a hard time accepting her sexual side, her animal nature. She's uncomfortable surrendering to her desires.

_____ *Sinful Sarah*—She expects herself to be a "saint," and if she has any "impure" thoughts, and she has many, or engages in any "impure" activities, she feels guilty and figures she's doomed to eternal damnation. No matter what she does, she's a bad, bad, bad girl.

_____ *Germ-Phobic Gerry*—She's afraid of all the diseases and infections that she might get, or pass on. She can't let go sexually because she's afraid she will lose control and take health risks. Rather than learn how to have sex safely, and take responsibility for herself and her lovers, she simply avoids sex.

_____ *Lulu Low Libido*—She likes sex but doesn't have it much. She keeps waiting until she's in the right mood, rather than making it happen. But she's rarely in the mood. Sex seems like too much of a hassle. She doesn't have much oomph. She lost her groove.

_____ *Miss Goody Two-Shoes*—Even though she's an adult, she's still living her life to please her parents, neighbors, friends, and peers. She's worried about what people think of her and terrified of gossip. She "shoulds" all over herself.

_____ *Victim Victoria*—She had some painful experiences related to sex, so she thinks that she's absolutely incapable of ever achieving a spectacular sex life. She's gotten past the posttraumatic-stress phase, but sex still can make her feel very uncomfortable. She feels hopeless.

_____ *Paranoid Polly*—She's afraid that if she really explores and expresses her sexuality, something terrible will happen. She'll be raped, lose her job, her life will just fall apart, or change dramatically. Sex is simply too dangerous. She has little trust in herself and in others.

_____ *Controlling Connie*—She thinks that if she lets herself surrender to her desires, she'll lose all control. She's uncomfortable with abandon and letting loose. She always has to feel in control of a sexual situation. She has a difficult time being in a relationship and receiving love and pleasure.

_____ *Fear of Success Frieda*—She fears her own sexual power and her true desires. Afraid that if she has a wonderful sex life other people might judge or resent her and not want to be her friend anymore. Her life might change radically. If she became the really sexy and juicy woman she is inside, then people would notice her more, be attracted to her, and she couldn't handle that.

_____ *Heartbroken Hanna*—She's afraid she'll get her heart broken . . . again. So she avoids intimacy. She can't possibly go through the pain of love anymore. She feels weak, vulnerable, sad, and unlovable.

_____ *Cathy Comparison*—She constantly compares the way she looks to women in magazines, on TV, and in the movies. She dislikes most everything about her body. Every sag and wrinkle is cause for embarrassment. She's ashamed to let anyone see or touch what she considers her imperfect body. She thinks she's unattractive.

_____ *Judgmental Judy*—She's critical of others. No one is good enough for her, no one does it right, and no one can really fully please her. She has extremely high expectations, and they're rarely if ever met. She's rather bored, disappointed, and or frustrated with her sex life.

_____ *Barbara Too Busy*—She's on every committee, volunteers to do everything, and takes care of other people and perhaps kids. She has no time or energy left for sex. There are dozens of e-mails to answer, she's got shopping to do, and that new project she started has to be done right away. She puts taking care of herself and her needs last.

_____ *Chronic Condition Carla*—Yeast infections, bacterial vaginosis (BV), pelvic pain, vulvadenia, vaginismus . . . The list goes on. She suffers from one chronic condition or another, so she doesn't really like to have sex much. She feels like abnormal and damaged goods.

So, how many of the party poopers did you check? I'd venture to say that we all have a little bit of all of them inside us at various times. Some folks might also run up against these guys: Premature Perry, I'm-Too-Tiny-Tony, Must-Be-Macho-Man Mark, Mr. Softie, Performance-Anxiety Andy, and Goal-Oriented Gary.

Once I participated in a weeklong gathering of sex educators and sex therapists, and I was rather surprised to discover quite a few party poopers lurking. So, if you have some challenges in your sex life, you are absolutely normal. Even "party-pooper busters" do, too. Sometimes those party poopers can be tough to shake.

Where Do Those Party Poopers Come From?

Let's take a look at how the American Psychiatric Association views sexual challenges. They label them "disorders" and have identified four categories: "sexual desire disorders, sexual arousal disorders, orgasmic disorders, and sexual pain disorders." Men and women's "problems" are lumped together—as if their issues are the same(?) When it comes to sex, sometimes maybe, but certainly not always. I know of no men who are afraid they will get impregnated or who have a chronic vaginal yeast infection.

Sex researchers Ellyn Kaschak and Leonore Tiefer are doing fantastic pioneering work examining women's sexual problems from a much broader, deeper, and more feminist perspective. Kaschak and Tiefer, along with a group of sex researchers, created a new classification system for women's sexual problems. Our party poopers all can be traced to four primary causes (paraphrased somewhat here):

1. Sociocultural, political, or economic factors—such as lack of information about sexual trauma, domestic violence, or biology; and inadequate access to information and services for contraception and STD prevention and treatment.
2. Sexual problems relating to partner and relationship, such as distress arising from betrayal, dislike, fear of partner, and negative patterns of communication. Shame about one's sexual orientation or identity, or about sexual fantasies and desires. Lack of interest, fatigue, or lack of time due to family and work obligations.
3. Psychological factors, such as unresolved problems with attachment, rejection, or emotional abuse. Sexual inhibition due to depression or anxiety. Sexual inhibition due to fear of sexual acts or their possible consequences, such as pregnancy, loss of partner, and loss of reputation.
4. Medical factors, such as side effects of medications, medical treatments, pregnancy, sexually transmitted diseases, or neurovascular problems.

What might be holding you back from the ecstatic, juicy, pleasure-filled life you desire and deserve? Some concerns exist for a good reason, to protect us from danger. But other concerns are unjustified and yet can still be absolutely paralyzing. Let's explore what kinds of concerns are real and which are irrational, and look at some ways to keep the party poopers from shouting over the music.

Parents, Religions, and Schools, Oh My!

Think about where your basic ideas about sex come from. Is it the culture in general? Did something scary happen to you? Did someone tell you that certain types of sex were bad? Did you see television shows or movies that implied sex was bad? Did you do something you felt guilty about? Or were you raised to believe that sex was beautiful, pleasurable, and a great gift? Were you made fun of for having a crush on someone, or for wanting to do things that people thought didn't correlate with your proper gender role?

Where we come from and what we've been through have all set the stage for us as sexual beings. In order for your makeover to really take root, it *will* be necessary to uproot some old ideas.

Most of us got our first ideas about sex from observing our parents. Were your parents uptight about sex, bodies, and bodily functions? Did they give you the message that sex is dangerous, dirty, or otherwise bad? Maybe they were so uncomfortable about the subject they gave you the same sex education they got as children, silence. Was your hand slapped when you touched your genitals while being diapered? Were you punished for playing doctor or staying out late with a boy? You're a big girl now, and it's time to speak up for your sex life.

If you need to, a very effective thing you can do is write a letter to your parents informing them that you are going to have a great sex life. Don't worry; you're not going to mail it. Get all your feelings out! Thank them for protecting you, but let them know that you're grown-up now and you intend to derive pleasure from grown-up sex—your way. Take all the time you need to do this. For extra impact, read it out loud as if you were reading it to your parents. Doing this really can help.

Religion certainly can have an effect on our attitudes about sex. For example, if your religion told you masturbation was a sin but you still masturbate often and feel horribly guilty about it, then maybe you might want to examine what the truth is for you. You can choose to follow your religion and not masturbate, or you can masturbate and feel horribly guilty about it (then hopefully guilt is part of your turn-on), or you can choose to disagree with your religion and enjoy masturbating guilt-free. The important thing is that you know that you have the power to choose what is right for you, and feel good about what you choose.

Religion and sex need not be unhappy bedfellows. There is good reason why so many people cry out to "God" during sex. Both religion and great sex can put us in touch with our soul, our sense of wonder, our awareness of the gift of life and spirit. You can certainly regard sexuality as a spiritual gift meant to help you cope with the hardships of life and to teach you lessons. Some religious faiths promote a lot of sexual guilt and set impossible standards for many people to follow. Maybe the religion you grew up with no longer fits who you are and what you feel and believe today. Don't despair; there are plenty of other wonderful religions from which you can choose.

The Lady Is a Tramp

Another place we receive early impressions of sex is at our schools. Perhaps you learned that being labeled a slut would be a horrible burden to bear. Many girls, often no more sexually active than their peers, suffer greatly from this tradition. Ironically, the girls not labeled suffer too, curtailing their behavior so that people don't get the "wrong idea."

Sex and danger are paired early in our collective imagination. In popular movies, highly sexual women often end up being punished for their sexual desires with rape or murder, or being made just plain miserable. Scaring women into being less sexual with the threat of violence is one of the ways that our culture keeps women from fully exploring their sexual power. The sexual rebel must always pay for her sins. Let's not forget what a power we have. We have the power to populate the planet. No wonder for centuries various forces have tried to harness that power.

Girls and women are taught that sexual energy must go hand in hand with love and marriage to be "respectable." Otherwise, very bad things will happen to us. Being cautious about sex isn't a bad thing. Sex *can* be dangerous. But when fear of what might happen rules your life and prevents you from having a satisfying sex life, it's time to step back and take a reality check.

One of my concerns when I started modeling for sex magazines was the possibility of being harassed on the street by people who might recognize me. I lived in Manhattan, and the streets could be dangerous. Interestingly, though, whenever I was recognized it was with great respect, even by hardened ex-convicts who would bow down at my feet and treat me like a queen. Still—I was always careful. But fortunately I didn't give up my dream of being a pin-up model because of my fears.

We as human beings are equipped with intuition and a survival mechanism that goes into action before we're even consciously aware that we're in danger. You need to learn to listen to that part of yourself and to trust that when you really need to be afraid your body will usually tell you. Cultivating that inner voice will go a lot further toward self-protection than trying to avoid all potentially dangerous situations. By all means, take a self-defense course if you are so inclined. Take an assertiveness-training class if you have a hard time saying no when your gut says to. Take good care of your precious self, and at the same time, dare to live your life fully.

Stereotypes, Aging, and Bodies, Oh My!

In this youth-and-beauty–worshiping culture, we are constantly exposed to tall, thin, flawless bodies everywhere: on billboards, in magazines, on television, in the movies. We are made to believe that if we don't fit the supermodel type or the porn-star pin-up model type, then we aren't any good. Many women deal with the overwhelming feelings of inadequacy by distancing themselves from their bodies, which creates a great big obstacle to having a fabulous sex life.

Imagine how wonderful it would be to grow up learning that our bodies are all perfect in their own ways; that our vulvas are sweet and pretty and that you can swell with pride that you have a unique one of your very own; that all our breasts and butts are the perfect right size and shape for us. Imagine if guys were taught that their penises were all the right size for them and that their bodies were all quite lovable as they are.

You must come back into your body, and love it—no matter what. (How to do this is addressed in the next step.) Treat it with kindness and reverence, because that's how you will find your freedom and happiness.

Croning Glories

Our youth-obsessed culture provides few images of older people being sexual, except as jokes. We must find sexy older role models. One of mine is sex educator Betty Dodson, who at seventy-three years old is fabulously sexy and has a spectacular sex life, which she writes freely about in her book *Orgasms for Two*. One of my fellow porn-star buddies, Juliet Carr (who became a porn actress at the age of forty!), recently produced a video called *Ageless Desire*, which shows couples over sixty having great sex. This video seriously challenges our prejudices, then gets us beyond them, to where we can see what wonderful, skilled lovers people over sixty can be.

Many older women report that sex became more enjoyable later in their lives—albeit sometimes of less quantity, but more quality. From everything I've seen, heard, and experienced, older women are far better, more skilled lovers. Young women do have their charms, but older women have developed their sensitivity and have far more knowledge and awareness. They're much more advanced and powerful sexually. Perhaps society puts down the vintage Venus because she is so much more sexually powerful: a beautiful, savvy queen. The vintage Venus is exquisitely beautiful and sexy. Believe it!

You will likely go through, or have gone through, profound changes in your sexuality with menopause. It's true that our desires change and the ways we make love can change radically. But that certainly doesn't mean it's over or worse than it was; it's just *different*, sometimes just a little bit different and sometimes radically different. I've noticed that some older women find they want to take a break from sex for a while and desire a period of celibacy. I call this the "postmenopausal afterglow phase." But then they come back to having sex in a big, new, beautiful way. There's absolutely no reason why older folks can't have a much better sex life than when they were younger—but it will likely be different.

Aim to stay in and enjoy the present and not constantly long for whatever it was you enjoyed in the past, and then you will likely be happier. If you're in a long-term committed relationship, I hope your partner will be in tune with and supportive of your changes and phases. If not, then you have to face this challenge and work things out between the two of you.

Hormones can certainly play a huge role in our changes. Perhaps you might choose to use some hormone-balancing treatments. Be patient until you find what works for you. Every woman is so different.

There is talk among the postmenopausal women I know that they are "learning the difference between arousal and desire." Some say they don't get as " horny" as before, that there's not the driving desire for sex, but there is still plenty of arousal when stimulated, and the arousal starts more at the heart than before and then flows down into the genitals. This kind of sharing is so helpful to many of us more mature gals.

We have lots of socially conditioned stereotypes about what kinds of people have good sex by the way they look. My friend Amanda told me how she always thought that people who looked kind of nerdy or conservative or old had very boring sex lives. After working at Good Vibrations sex toy boutique in San Francisco and helping many people find the right sex toy or erotic book, she had to revise her opinion. She found that people's appearance and demeanor had absolutely nothing to do with the quality of their sex life. The tall, slender, busty, young Penthouse centerfold type admitted to a boring and problematic sex life, while the short, stubby, flat-chested gray-haired woman was having an absolute ball.

Fortunately in some parts of the country there is a growing acceptance by the nursing-home industry of the sexual needs and rights of the elderly. If I ever have to check into a nursing home, you can bet it's going to be one where sexuality is respected. What greater benefit of being retired? More time for snuggling and making love.

Diseases, Germs, Safe Sex? Oh My!

One big thing that really can hold us back from enjoying sex can be the fear of getting and/or spreading sexually transmitted infections. Even people with the best self-images cannot escape the reality of HIV, herpes, hepatitis, and the rest. If you are newly single, infection prevention or transmission may be all the more daunting.

If you are holding yourself back because of this fear, the thing you need to know is that knowledge is power. Learn whatever you can about safer sex. There are many ways to express your sexuality and have great enjoyment without risk. The information is widely available, and these days it's better than ever. It's free at city clinics, on the Internet, and in libraries. Chat with your gynecologist or medical doctor. Find out which organizations in your area are teaching safer sex, and

(a) Perhaps get a knowledgeable safe-sex coach for an hour to discuss how you can have safer sex tailored to your specific situation(s).
(b) Or throw a safer-sex-education party/brunch at your home. There are some great safe-sex educators who have really creative ways of teaching, including having you and your guests play funny, educational games.
(c) Practice!

Don't Be a Stupid Cupid

Knowing how to have safe sex and how to do risk assessment are the best ways to go. Denial and ignorance are the biggest risks. Use the safer sex book and Internet Resources in the back of this guide. I encourage you to learn all you can, and practice safer sex. Don't fight it. Handy is healthy—so keep some condoms and other needed supplies in your purse or pocket. Total acceptance of the fact that you are living in the rubber age is the least frustrating way. Safe sex can be fabulous, hot, satisfying sex. You need only to learn how to do it, how to seductively talk someone else into it, and/or to teach them.

Bodies. Ya Can't Live with 'Em, and Ya Can't Live Without 'Em: Pain and Chronic Conditions

If you have any chronic conditions that affect your sex life, the best way to deal with them is *acceptance* and self-love. All of our bodies have their vulnerabilities and quirks, and we have to work with the situations at hand. Kicking, screaming, and complaining about them constantly, or avoiding or ignoring them, doesn't help. Avoiding sex can also be detrimental.

For example, if you have chronic pelvic pain and you want to make love, then talk in detail with your lover to find things that work for YOU. Focus on what you *can* do, not on what you *can't* do. What time of day is the pain lessened? Perhaps you can develop doing EnergySex together, or focus on what does work well. Above all, aim to maintain a positive attitude.

There was a period of about two years when I had chronic yeast infections. Yes, it was sometimes a frustrating drag when I couldn't have any vaginal penetration. But those yeast infections forced me to be more creative, which made for some really good times for other areas of my body. And for my partner. We have to learn to accept our limitations. There are always some options and ways to manage and to thrive. There is a wonderful new book that addresses many of these kinds of challenges: *The Ultimate Guide to Sex and Disability—For All of Us Who Live with Disabilities, Chronic Pain and Illness,* from Cleis Press.

When an ex-boyfriend of mine lay seriously ill in a hospital bed, sex was certainly the last thing on his mind. But he had always loved sex and loved to be touched. So when I went to visit him, I put together a bag full of sensual delights: two different types of vibrators, a piece of fur, a feather, a scratchy mitt, some things to smell, taste, etc. I tickled, teased, vibrated, and scratched his lifeless body, and from the moans of pleasure and the smiles on his face I knew he sure did enjoy and appreciate it. As did I, to feel close to him in this erotic way.

If you've gone through a serious illness or a major surgery like a hysterectomy, mastectomy, or colostomy, if you have or had cancer, you **must forgive your body and love yourself** all the more. It's perfectly okay to give yourself a break from sex if you need it, for as long as you need it. Perhaps your sexual energy is all being used toward your healing. These are life-changing events, and you will likely be a somewhat different person sexually than before. Try not to hold on to the way things were in the past and learn to accept and love the new you. What new turn-ons does the new you like? If you try, you might find that you grow to love the new you even more than the old you.

Sexual Healing After Sexual Abuse

Few of us have escaped the "sexual abuse" woven into the very fabric of our culture. Unfortunately, many of us also know sexual abuse in a way that's closer to home, and the abuse can have devastating, long-term effects on one's life and sex life. This can happen to anyone. We all have heard about the extraordinarily high percentages of children, adolescents, women, and men who have been sexually harassed, abused, exploited, raped, and molested. It's incomprehensible and makes me cry just to think about it.

If something traumatic happened to you, find some ways to heal that work the best for you. Compassion is the foundation for healing and the place to begin. There are several new, innovative, and very good resources available if you need them. I recommend that you read either Stacy Haines's book, *The Survivor's Guide to Sex,* or watch her DVD *Healing Sex,* from SIR Productions. Work with a good therapist or a support group, if you choose additional support. If you are the partner of someone who has been abused or of an abuser, that can be really tough, too, and you might need to gather strength, patience, and support as well.

The good news is that healing is absolutely possible. I've met many women and men who have come from horrifically abusive pasts and have become supremely happy and brilliant lovers. In fact, some of the most gifted, divine, spectacular sex goddesses and gods come from abusive pasts. It takes some effort, some time, and support. But we *can* overcome. And come and come.

Relationships, Heartbreak, and Ex-lovers, Oh My!

Although sex has its dangers, love, which does indeed often go hand in hand with sex, is perhaps the most desired and risky part of the package. Are you afraid to love again? It's a painful truth that heartache helps your heart grow, expanding your capacity to give and receive love. But if you're on the dark side of love now, you probably couldn't care less about growth and expansion. That's okay. I understand.

Having your heart broken or being rejected can be an intensely physical feeling; it can actually make your chest ache inside. The pain can go on for a relatively long time. It doesn't matter to you now that you've gotten over heartbreak before and come through it. It doesn't matter that human beings get their hearts broken all the time. It doesn't matter to you that without heartbreak the world would hardly have any art. Surely, no one else has ever felt *this* bad.

If your heart has recently been broken, you must keep telling yourself that what you're going through *will* pass. Healing has its own time line and must be respected. Sometimes, though, we sabotage our own healing and unnecessarily prolong our suffering. If you think you're going down that road (be superhonest with yourself), you can reverse course and try to help yourself along. Start to force yourself to think positively about the future. Indulge in good self-care: Get massaged, take walks in nature, scream into a pillow, etc. Instead of thinking of your heart as "broken," try to think of it as "broken open." Try to find the ecstasy in the agony. Enjoy crying to all those sad country-and-western songs while you can.

Drown Your Troubles

It can do wonders to write a letter to your ex, which you don't send. Tell him or her everything you didn't say or couldn't say during the relationship and breakup. Tell everything you've felt since you two broke up, whether it's good or bad, angry or sad, reasonable or unreasonable. Let yourself feel it all, and put it into the letter. You can do this over a period of days, returning to the letter whenever you think of something you want to add to it. When the letter is done take it down to the ocean, lake, or riverside, tie the letter to a rock, and throw it in the water. Doing this will help let your psyche know you are finished with this phase of your life.

If you are in a lover relationship now and are having difficulties with your partner, hang in there. I will address many more relationship issues and give you many more solutions in future chapters. You also need to be aware that your partner has a whole bunch of party poopers, too, that you might have to deal with as well.

You Can Do It!

We all have baggage, issues, difficulties, and challenges. It can take some courage to be honest with yourself about what's holding you back. But I assure you; it's worth it. There's virtually nothing you can't overcome if you set your mind to it and if you follow along with the upcoming steps in the program. Miss Goody Two-Shoes can become Miss Feels Really Good (and is good). Paranoid Polly can become Sensible Polly. Heartbroken Hannah can become Heart Full Hannah. Sally Self-Loathing can become Sally Self-Loving. Premature Perry can become Pleasurable Perry. Too-Tiny Tony can become Tony the Tiger. Must-Be-Macho-Man Mark can simply be Mark. Goal-Oriented Gary can just chill.

Strive to get all your party poopers in check, and no one need rain on your parade.

Rituals for Self-Healing and Makeover Magic

An excellent way to heal and make positive changes in one's life is to perform some simple personal rituals. It wasn't until I was thirty-two years old that I learned about the power of personal rituals. I was taking a workshop at the Wise Woman Center in Upstate

New York, taught by the world-famous herbalist Susun Weed. She invited everyone in our group to think about a role in our life we wanted to let go of, and what role we wanted to take on next. I was bored with being the carefree party girl, and I wanted to take on more responsibility and become a teacher. So together we walked in a procession out to the top of a hill and stood around a big bonfire. One by one we stated our "let go" and our "take on," each bearing witness to the other. It was a powerful action. Later at dinner, after the ritual, Susun Weed walked up to me and asked me to teach my first workshop at her world-famous center! After that ritual, I performed many other rituals over the years, and they always had a positive and profound effect.

Results aren't always so quick to manifest themselves, but sometimes they are. In one episode of *Friends*, Monica, Rachel, and Phoebe had a similar ritual, to burn mementos from old boyfriends. They wound up setting a fire in the wastebasket, and three hunky firemen arrived.

Rituals Demystified

Here's why rituals work. Your subconscious mind is coaxed into believing something is actually true. So, for example, if you have a ceremony to renew your marriage vows, then your vows do indeed feel and become renewed. When you take a moment and give gratitude for the food you are about to eat, then you feel more grateful for that food. Putting out into the universe what we want to create helps create it.

Rituals can be powerful, moving, and feel wonderful to do. When we put some energy and focus into what we want to have happen, it can be absolutely magical. So now, I invite you to try two different rituals. Feel free to modify them however you'd like, to fit your needs, interests, and desires. You can also do these as a couple.

The Burn-Your-Troubles-Away Ritual

Intention: To set yourself free of limiting habits, ideas, fears, and roles that no longer serve you. To get rid of whatever is in the way of your having the pleasure, joy, happiness, and spectacular sex life you desire. To free you up and release the past.

Where to do it: Somewhere private, preferably outside in a lovely, natural setting. However, you can also do it on an apartment terrace or on your porch. In a pinch, do it in your kitchen or bathroom.

What you will need: A writing utensil and some pretty paper. You will need to make a fire; for example, you can dig a small hole in the dirt, or use a skillet on your stove, or use a large bowl filled with sand. Be sure you have good ventilation if you do it inside. You'll need some matches or a lighter.

What to wear: Wear something that you feel is special and makes you feel powerful and beautiful. Create a ceremonial feel for yourself. For example, wear something that you wouldn't wear on a normal day, and perhaps do some special makeup, or put on some special jewelry.

What to do

1. Go to your special place and make your fire.
2. Gaze into the fire for a while. Allow the flames to take you into a contemplative head and heart space. Feel the warmth, glow, and power of the fire.
3. When you feel ready, write down whatever you'd like to release and let go of. For example: my need to control, my negative belief that _____, my fears of intimacy, my attachment to so and so, my anger toward so and so . . . If you did something you feel bad about, write that on your paper, too. Contemplate your list for some moments, or better yet, read your list out loud, saying "I release _____," or "I forgive myself for _____." (Fill in the blanks.)
4. Close your eyes. Take some deep breaths. Hold the paper in your hands for a minute and really feel the emotional weight of what's written on the list.

5. Put the paper in the fire and watch it burn. Let the fire cleanse you. Imagine whatever is inside you that you don't want, burning away with the paper.

6. Feel whatever it is that you had on that paper actually leaving and your spirit lifting. Take some deep breaths.

7. Put your hands on your heart. Feel the possibility of change. See your life with new, soft, compassionate eyes.

8. The end of the ritual can be when the fire burns out or when you put the fire out.

The Bed-Bath-and-Go-Beyond Ritual— To Help Birth a New You

Where: In a bathtub. (If you don't have one, use a shower.)

What you will need: Flower petals, matches, one candle, incense (preferably some you have never used before), a seashell, beautifully scented bath oil, beauty clay (sold in health food stores or drugstores for clay masks), dental floss, comfy pajamas, a soft towel, pen, and paper.

1. Run a hot bath. Put flower petals into the water to help make this a very special bath, like none other you've taken before.

2. Light the incense and spread the smoke around throughout the bathroom (smudge), especially in the corners. Imagine the smoke clearing out any old, stale vibes and bringing in new clean vibes. You are creating a sacred space.

3. When you light your candle, make a wish. Think about what you want to create in your sex life or life in general.

4. Turn off all electric lights in the bathroom.

5. Put the seashell into the bath to help bring the cleansing, purifying powers of the ocean into your bath.

6. Pour the scented oil into the water and really enjoy the aroma.

7. Take off whatever you're wearing and spread the clay all over your whole body,

including your face, in your hair, on your palms, and the bottoms of your feet. Sit on the toilet (seat opened or closed) and imagine receiving nourishment from the clay, from Mother Earth. Let the rich clay nourish you on all levels for a few minutes.

8. Get into the water in the tub. Soak, relax, enjoy, and float on both your front and your back. Close your eyes. Give yourself love. Imagine there is no such thing as time as you soak in the bath. (Do not do any normal bath chores like washing your hair, shaving your legs, or even scrubbing your fingernails.)

9. Open the drain to let the water flow slowly out of the tub, but stay lying in the tub until all the water is gone. Let it be as if the tub were giving birth to a whole new you. Gently wipe away any leftover clay from your body as if you were a newborn just coming out of the womb. Let it be gentle and sensual. Shower off remaining clay if needed.

10. Dry off with a soft towel.

11. Brush and floss your teeth. (It's important to take care of your gums.)

12. Put on your favorite comfy pajamas.

13. End the ritual by blowing out the candle while imagining your dreams and wishes coming true.

14. Then go celebrate your life!

Shrine Your Light
Create a Love-Life Altar

Making an altar can be a helpful ritual because it manifests on the physical plane what is inside your mind, heart, and imagination. Feel free to do this in your personal style and way.

1. Find a place to put your altar. It can be in your bedroom, kitchen, garden. Preferably a place where you spend a lot of time. One of my altars is on my car dashboard.

2. Gather some tchotchkes (knickknacks) that have special meaning for you: things like statuettes, treasured photographs, a snippet of your lover's pubic hair, a sexy flower, or anything that strikes you as worthy or desirable to put on your altar.

3. Find a pretty little jar or pot or box and put a copy of your inner sexpot description that you wrote in step 2, where it can brew on your altar. And write down what your wishes/desires/prayers are for your love life.

4. When everything is assembled, put a candle (in a container to keep it safe) on your altar and light it.

5. Imagine the light of the candle bringing your inner sexpot and love-life wishes more into the light.

6. Over time you can revamp your altar as you please.

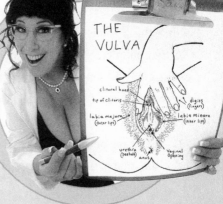

Step Four

Fall Madly, Passionately in Love with Yourself

No one can make you feel inferior without your consent.

ELEANOR ROOSEVELT

Reflections

Almost every room at the Sprinkle Sex Life Center is equipped with large ornately framed mirrors. We spare no expense in having beautiful frames for you to see yourself reflected within. But even the loveliest frames can go only so far. It's not what you see in front of your eyes that creates how you view yourself; it is what is behind them.

Did anyone tell you negative things about yourself when you were a kid? Like you were ugly, your belly was too big, legs too hairy, you weren't tan enough, and if you didn't learn to spell you'd never amount to anything? I hope not. Well, they did say such things to me, and I believed them. As a result, for a long time I didn't like myself very much, and I didn't think I was sexy (or smart) in the least.

Other people could see the lovable and sexy side of me long before I could. Fortunately, I eventually did learn to love myself—and what a relief and aphrodisiac it proved to be. Improving my self-esteem was key to my own entire life makeover, and it didn't require a single surgery or an expensive fat farm—though a razor and spell check did help.

If you are a person with great self-esteem, then you are one of the lucky ones. But if you're like many of us, you could use a boost. Certainly many, if not most, women have work to do in this area.

How can you tell when you love yourself? If the concept of self-love seems a bit vague to you, think of love as a verb. What do you do for yourself to help you feel good? Some examples might be that you avoid people who are critical of you, you don't let someone talk you into having unsafe sex, you wear clothes that make you feel good, you eat well, you take care of yourself. In other words, when you make good self-loving choices you are, in fact, loving yourself.

You know how when you first fall madly, passionately in love with someone else, you feel so much adoration and desire toward her or him? The same thing applies when you fall madly, passionately in love with yourself. You can actually fall in love with yourself, just the way you can fall in love with others. It feels every bit as wonderful. As the Whitney Huston mega-hit song "Greatest Love of All" (written by Michael Masser and Linda Creed) says, "I found the greatest love of all, inside of me. Learning to love yourself, it is the greatest love of all."

Mirror, Mirror

Remember what a crime it was in junior high school to be "conceited"? Fall in love with myself? Well, you might ask, isn't that a crime? If someone would pay me a compliment I couldn't accept it or believe them. I had such a low self-image. Enlightenment can be found in surprising places. When I started modeling for pinup magazines in my early twenties, one of my modeling gigs involved a photographer I'll call Mr. M. He was a horny senior gentleman with a thick European accent. He lived alone except for his beloved dachshund, Natasha, who scampered around the studio at Mr. M's heels. During the modeling job Mr. M. asked me to pose primping and preening in front of a mirror. I told him that I thought this would make me seem haughty and vain. I had been taught that you weren't supposed to worship and adore yourself. M said that he felt the sexiest thing in the world was to see a woman gaze lovingly at her self-image. Doing this, he said, showed that she felt good about herself. He basically gave me permission to look lovingly at myself in the mirror. I tried it and discovered he was right: The more I looked lovingly, the better I liked what I saw. Thanks, Mr. M.

When you look at yourself in the mirror, do you focus on what you like about yourself or what you don't like? Do you see only the surface you or a deeper you? The more you see yourself in a positive light, the more likely other people will as well.

Maybe you've already worked on your self-esteem in the past and are wondering if you're missing something because you still don't feel 100 percent great about yourself. I understand completely. Perhaps a few people have had lightning-bolt self-esteem awakenings, but that's exceedingly rare. For most of us, building our self-esteem and keeping it strong is usually a project that lasts years, or even a lifetime, with two steps forward and one step back.

Practice daily care. Start by putting yourself first whenever possible. By all means, love others as well, but speak up for your needs. You'll have much more to offer others if you're coming from a place of strength, fullness, and honesty.

EXERCISE: REWRITE HERSTORY

If someone has told you negative things about yourself, especially regarding your body or your sexuality, write a few of them down.

1. _____

2. _____

3. _____

4. _____

5. _____

Now take your pen or pencil and simply scribble over the above judgments and criticisms. Just cross them out! They were simply not true. Or if they were true, compared to what or whom? So maybe your nose is bigger than most, but that doesn't mean you have to think it ugly or unsexy. Certainly there are other people with much bigger noses, and big noses can be very sexy. So you have twelve toes. Who said that can't be exciting? Later, if these criticisms come up again or new ones appear, notice them and imagine yourself crossing them out again.

If someone did say something mean to you about your body or gave you negative messages, then isn't your happiness and scintillating sex life the best revenge?

Disabled or Don Juan?

Self-acceptance and a healthy body image are crucial to liberating yourself from the shackles of low self-esteem and finding the freedom to be fabulous and sexy. People of all physical types have great sex lives. One of the most remarkable sexpots I know, who is a great inspiration to me, is performance artist Frank Moore. Frank was born with cerebral palsy. It affected his body but not his libido. He cannot walk or feed himself. Frank communicates by grunting and forming letters with his tongue. Determined to have a sexy life, Frank created "eroplay," which, as it sounds, is a form of erotic play. Eroplay performances involve Frank lying naked in a tent while members of his audience, a bevy of naked beauties of all types, enter the tent and roll around with him.

Frank's art is quite political, and also critically acclaimed. Yet he has a great sense of humor and can laugh at himself. He says he has the perfect body for a performance artist.

His full-time partner/caretaker, Linda Mac, adores him exactly as he is. Privately she praises his prowess at oral sex. Apparently spelling out all those words has really built up his love muscle.

Learning to love your body can be a challenge. One study showed that 80 percent of women are dissatisfied with their appearance. Our bodies can be a tremendous source of pain and suffering, and also a tremendous source of pleasure and bliss. Your body is not your enemy or slave. Lest you forget, think about all the delicious and amazing things your body can do and feel. Why not become your body's fan-club president? Let your body know you appreciate it.

Body Cheer

Rah, rah, rah!
Sis boom bah.
My body is great,
No matter what weight.
Yum, yum, yum,
Yum, body, yum!
GO, BODY!

If loving your body as it is still seems a challenge, go back to step one: Reread the section on affirmations and create some body-focused affirmations like "My body is beautiful and sexy." Or "My body is fully capable of giving and receiving pleasure just the way it is right now." Or the classic "I love my body" works well. Say them often. Over time, it really helps.

(Self-) Hate Is Blind

I struggled with disliking my body starting at eight years old, mainly because I had a little potbelly. I felt horribly defective next to my flat-bellied girlfriends. Later, when I became a porn star, I thought I was the fattest girl in the biz, if not in the world. Looking back at those old movies, I now see that I wasn't fat at all! What a shame that I couldn't see the lovely me all those years, and couldn't enjoy my youthful beauty. Eventually when I hit forty-seven, I gained fifty pounds and I really freaked out. Here I was, a sex symbol of sorts, and I felt completely unsexy. For months I avoided sex, because I felt so horrible about myself.

Of course I had tried all the usual diets and weight-loss programs. Try as I might I couldn't keep the weight off. Eventually I approached the weight issue as one of improving my self-esteem. I joined a wonderful support group called Beyond Hunger, based in San Rafael, California. (The founders have a wonderful book called *It's Not About Food*. See Resources.) What we did was simply to practice loving ourselves more. At the end of six months, according to the scale I hadn't lost a single pound, but I literally felt as if I'd lost a hundred pounds. And when I broke my sex fast, the sex was even better than when I weighed fifty pounds less, because my self-esteem was so strong. Once I began feeding myself more love, I then also stopped a lot of my compulsive overeating.

On occasion I still find myself criticizing my body, especially when I'm clothes shopping. But I can honestly say that I love and appreciate my body now more than I ever have, because I stopped being so hard on myself and gave myself some much-needed unconditional love.

Fake It 'Til You Feel It

Being unhappy with your body can be a good excuse to avoid or postpone a sex life. Are you avoiding underlying issues by obsessing about dieting, plastic surgery, or that new wardrobe? If so, your issue may not be so much your body but the *feelings* you need to face and overcome. Being or looking a certain way is a fact. But believing you can't have a fabulous sex life because of how you look is only a *belief*, and it can be changed. I'm going to show you a few ways to throw off those low-self-esteem shackles and celebrate your magnificence—exactly as you are. Many people are so incredibly critical of their bodies that they can barely enjoy them. Please don't do this to yourself. *Sexy is not how you look; it is, in fact, an attitude.*

Exercise: Just for a Day

For just one day, try to notice and count the number of times you say something negative about yourself to yourself, or don't take care of yourself, or don't really love yourself in some way. If you've lost count before lunch, don't be surprised.

The next day, try to begin loving yourself just a little bit more. Compliment yourself a few times. Be a little nicer to yourself. Try it again one more day. At least try to get to where if you have nothing nice to say about yourself, you don't say anything at all. I guarantee that you'll start to feel happier and sexier. It's so simple and yet so effective.

Pinup Photo Therapy

Do you ever wish that you looked sexy like a pinup model? Well, did you know that most pinup models don't look like pinup models either? They really don't look the way they do in the magazines, I can assure you. I know because, besides being a pinup model myself, for many years I worked as a professional photographer for almost all the major sex magazines. (I majored in photography in college.) When a model showed up at my studio door, I would take a "before" photo of her. Then I would do an "after" photo, once she was made up, costumed, and well lit. This became my "Before and After" series of photographs of pinup models, which I displayed in numerous art galleries. People were fascinated, because they got to see behind the façade, so to speak, and learn the ways that the glamorous "after" images of the women were created with lighting, costumes, attitude, good angles, makeup, hairdos, etc.

No doubt you've seen how celebrities look so different without their makeup when snagged by a paparazzo and published in the tabloids. We can't help but gasp and marvel.

After every photo shoot that I did, I noticed how a professional photo shoot made a woman feel good about herself. When she saw herself looking like a pinup model, it boosted her self-confidence. So I started offering boudoir photography to all women who were interested.

Picture-Perfect—Things-I-Love/Hate-About-My-Body Art-Therapy Session

Get ready for some transformational art therapy. Don't worry; you don't need any artistic skills to do this. You are going to make two sketches. The first sketch is of your body, which you don't like; the second is of your body, which you do like.

1. Get yourself some paper and some writing and drawing utensils of any kind.

2. Without thinking or listening to your inner art critic, sketch a simple drawing of your body, from head to toe. Let the drawing flow out of your subconscious. It can be very abstract if you want. Draw your body from a place of not liking it. Be extremely critical—just this one last time.

3. Next, draw lines from any body parts that you don't like and write down what you don't like about those body parts. Think about where those thoughts came from. See what you can learn from this drawing.

4. Take some time to analyze your drawing. Do any thoughts, feelings, or realizations come to you? Which body parts stand out or aren't there?

5. Now make another drawing of your body from a place of really loving your body. This might actually be harder for you, but try your best. Get into feeling that you have an absolutely wonderful body, and sketch it with glee. Accentuate the positive. Draw all the parts of your body you really appreciate, for any reason.

6. Draw lines from the individual parts you like and make notes as to what you like about them, even if it's just a little bit. Take a moment to think about what pleasures you have had through those body parts. For example, draw a line from your ear and write that you enjoy music with it. Or draw a line from your nipples and write that you like the way they feel when they're touched. Or that you like the way your calves look. Write as many positive notes as you can.

7. Now compare the two drawings and notice how they each make you feel.

8. Think about how it really doesn't help to criticize your body. You are just making yourself feel worse. You might argue that the self-criticism is what gets you to make change. But when you think about it, self-criticism probably hasn't really gotten you as far as the times when you came from a place of self-love and self-care.

9. Now, ceremoniously rip up the negative body drawing, or fold it up and bury it in a file drawer. You don't need it anymore. Then hang the positive body drawing somewhere where you will see it, to remind you what you do like about your body.

10. Make a promise to yourself that you will try to focus on what you do like about yourself. If you forget what you like, just take a look at that drawing. Doesn't that feel GOOD?

Tricks of the Trade

Whenever a "regular" woman came to my photo studio, she was usually quite nervous at first. I'd have her makeup professionally done, then costume her in something fabulously sexy. Put her on a sensuous set and then coach her in doing pinup-style poses. Being quite sure to add lots of backlight on her big hairdo. Often we added things like corsets, high heels, garter belts, lingerie. She'd pose for a couple of hours, and by the end she was always totally relaxed and felt she had had tons of fun. Later when the woman saw the photographs of herself, she would marvel and light up. Seeing herself looking like a sex star always had a very healing and empowering effect.

A woman named Marsha was astonished at the photos from our photo shoot. When she saw herself through my eyes, she said, "I can't believe how gorgeous and sexy you made me look." I pointed out that her gorgeousness and sexiness were there all along.

So I highly recommend that all women have a professional boudoir photography session if they can. It doesn't have to be nude or very risqué. "Glamour" shots are even offered in some shopping malls, where they fix up you and the environment to make you look like a model or movie star. It's wonderful to see yourself all dolled up, with professional makeup, styling, lighting, etc. You don't even have to show the photos to anyone if you don't want to. Just do it for yourself. It's fun and a great experience. Another alternative is to have a photograph you like of yourself professionally airbrushed. In the Resources I've given two photographers who do erotic photography, for men and women. One of whom did the shots of me for this book.

Instant Gratification

If you don't want to have a professional photo session, almost as good is the Polaroid camera or a digital shoot at home. If you use a Polaroid camera, get lots of film, at least fifty or sixty shots, and ask your lover (or friend?) to photograph you. Camp it up. The flash of a Polaroid is generally very flattering. Stay pretty close up. You'll look best at no farther than four feet away from the lens. Both Polaroid and digital cameras give you immediate results. Pick out only your favorite photos and trash the rest. Polaroid offers the most privacy since each shot is one of a kind. Go wild, you sexy thang!

I'm absolutely not advocating that women should aim to look like airbrushed pinup models from a men's magazine. Not at all. Personally I find other kinds of looks and styles much sexier. Our "before" images are no more or less sexy than the "after" ones. Both are beautiful and sexy in their own way. But sometimes to embrace our childhood dream of being Marilyn Monroe (or whomever was *your* childhood sex goddess), if just for a day, is better than to resent her. For a moment, if you can't beat 'em, join 'em. Then go on with your life.

Another reason for taking these kinds of photos of yourself is to learn, on an experiential level, the way that the pictures of beautiful women in magazines and on television are created. When you learn on a gut level that you yourself, given the right lighting, makeup, and costumes, can look as fabulous as they do, you need never compare yourself unfavorably with them again. You also don't need to feel hostile toward them, or wish them gone. Rather, once you see them for what they are, you can accept and enjoy pictures of "sexy" women in the same way you might enjoy a painting by Matisse.

Interestingly, there are all kinds of sex magazines that feature all kinds of women. I worked as a photographer for one sex magazine that featured only women over fifty and another that featured only women who were over two hundred pounds. Regular mainstream magazines rarely, if ever, feature older or heavier women in their pages or on their covers. I worked for those magazines because I liked that they appreciated different types of women as did I. Our culture so needs to expand its idea of what can be sexy. Let it begin with us.

Nip and Tuck and Suck and Fluff

If you've done your self-esteem work and still feel like there's something you really want to change, plastic surgery, Botox, gastric bypass, or other medical interventions are indeed options, if you can afford them. Clearly, for many people, these kinds of makeovers are and can be helpful. The procedures are better, safer, and less painful than ever before. I've seen people joyously happy with the results, and they actually seemed to enjoy going through the process of their surgical transformations. Just be sure that you realize the risks involved and are realistic about the recovery period. I've seen botched jobs and terrible complications, such as chronic pain for years. In the worst-case scenario, a lovely stripper friend of mine, Joey Carson, died tragically from her leaky, toxic breast implants at age thirty-two. Olivia Goldsmith, the writer of *The First Wives' Club*, died during a "routine" liposuction procedure; she was only in her fifties. These outcomes are very rare, but they illustrate the fact that plastic surgery IS surgery. Most of my friends who have had plastic surgery stated they were shocked by the intensity of the pain following their procedures; three of them said if they had known how long and painful the recovery period was they would not have had the procedure. So thoroughly educate yourself before going under the knife, and be sure the benefits outweigh the agonies. Also know that there are many other ways to make changes as well.

Perhaps you've already had some plastic surgery and/or medical makeovers, such as with Botox. I hope you are happy with the results. These modern procedures certainly can make big changes in how people look, and afford such jaw-dropping television entertainment!

Lately vaginal surgery is becoming more prevalent: tightening the vaginal muscles, liposuctioning the pubic area, and shortening the labia. Much of this makes me pretty sad, because these procedures can actually hinder sexual functioning, severing nerves, making a woman less sensitive, sometimes creating pain where there wasn't any before. All in the name of looking "normal." I've seen hundreds of vulvas in my time, and not one of them looked ugly or abnormal to me. And I'd venture to say that virtually no men are concerned with the size or symmetry of labia.

It's always best not to be judgmental about (or jealous of) other people who have had plastic surgery—whatever it takes to boost our self-esteem can ultimately work wonders in people's lives. And some people, such as those who work in the entertainment industries, are under enormous pressure to stay youthful looking. But it does seem to me that if you can avoid major cosmetic surgeries you're better off. Here again, only you can decide what's best for you.

A Pussy Is a Woman's Best Friend

Once I was a guest on Joan Rivers's daytime talk show. We were discussing how important it is to love your body—including your genitalia. Joan Rivers reached into her purse, pulled out her powder compact mirror, held it between her legs, and pretended to look at her vulva. She made an awful face and screamed in horror, *"Eeeeekkkkk!"* It was great for a huge laugh, but it was also sad—because so many women actually feel this way.

A supreme sex goddess knows and loves her mound of Venus inside and out. If you haven't done so already, take a good long look at your pussy in a mirror. Do this when you know you'll be alone and won't be interrupted. If you've never done this before because you were told not to look "down there," then think of this as a stepping out of your comfort zone, which I discussed in the first chapter. It's really okay to look at her. Learn everything about her anatomy, and see if you can identify all her parts by name. Tell her she's beautiful. Pay particular attention to your magnificent clitoris. As far as is known now, it's the only human organ entirely devoted to pleasure and fun. Did you know that your clitoris has long "legs"? I like to call them "roots," which branch into your vaginal walls? Find your clitoral hood (like a female foreskin). Can you see your urethra (pee hole)? Some women can see part of their urethral sponge if they push out, which is the protective padding surrounding the urethra. Do you have any hymen tags when you pull your labia open? They look like tiny labia inside your inner labia. Some women have them

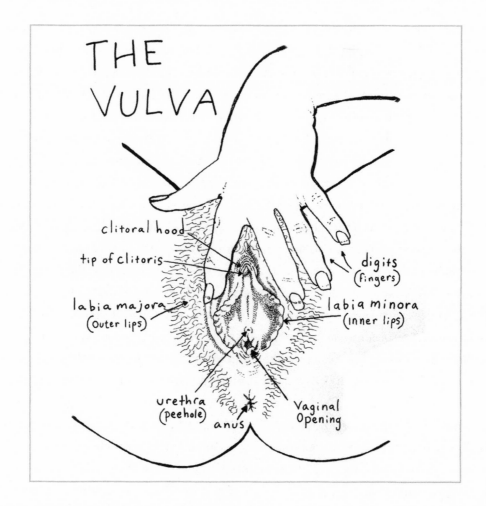

and can see them. Look at the color, texture, shapes. See the beauty of your vulva. What kind of flower would you say she looks like?

A Public Cervix Announcement

In my teens I was terribly afraid to look at my pussy: I didn't dare. But eventually I just had to look—I wanted to know. On first sight, I was quite critical. Today I can honestly say that my vulva is perhaps my most beautiful body part! And I can easily name every centimeter of her anatomy. That's a good feeling.

For five years I toured the world doing a one-woman theater performance about my life as a sexual adventurer called *Post Porn Modernist*. Toward the end of the show, I sat in a plush chair at the edge of the stage, inserted a speculum into my vagina, opened it up, and invited the audience to come and take a look inside me with a flashlight. I held a microphone down by my thigh to amplify people's comments. This part of the performance was called "A Public Cervix Announcement." I figure that about forty thousand people in sixteen different countries viewed my cervix in the context of this performance-art piece. I didn't do this to shock or excite but to share with people the mysteries of female anatomy and to demonstrate that there's no need to be ashamed of our genitals. This might sound shocking to you, but for me it was quite natural and easy. I sold speculums in the theater lobbies and gave away printed instructions so women could take them home and have a look at themselves. Many women have thanked me for this service. They looked at their own cervixes and found the experience freeing and fun. Speculum self-exam was one of the cornerstones of the seventies feminist movement, but somehow the practice got lost along the way.

You can buy a speculum at any medical-supply place and take a look inside yourself. (See Resources.) If you are uncomfortable using a speculum on yourself or having your partner (or friend) do it with you, then next time you go to your gynecologist for a pelvic exam, you can always ask for a mirror to take a look. Gynecologists are happy to show you what you look like inside and point out all your beautiful, amazing, miraculous parts (although they may not describe them that way). After all, it's *your* body.

I've seen a lot of vulvas in my time, and every single one of them was exquisitely beautiful. (If you want to see some great color photographs of vulvas, I highly recommend the book *Femalia* from Down There Press.) Every vulva is special and unique, including yours. Love, honor, and respect your vulva. Be good to her, and she'll be good to you. *Viva la Vulva!*

Reach Out and Touch Yourself

Masturbation can provide the foundation of a good sexual life. It is a wonderful way to love yourself, build your self-esteem, and get you in touch with yourself. Or selves, if you include your alter egos. So do give yourself a hand.

If anyone ever told you that masturbation was bad or dirty, they were wrong! If someone told you masturbation wasn't as good as having partner sex, they were also wrong. It's better simply to think of them as different. Any good sex therapist will tell you that masturbation is not only normal but also healthy and productive. If the word *masturbation* sounds too clinical or conjures up negative associations, then use the term *self-pleasuring* instead.

These days almost everyone has heard the good news: Even people with thoroughly satisfying sex lives enjoy masturbation. It doesn't have to take away from a relationship with a partner.

You can masturbate with a quickie to release excess sexual tension, to feel good for some moments, or to relieve some stress. A quick "getting off" is nice, but it's also sometimes wonderful to take more time to really "pleasure yourself" and "make love to yourself." You can masturbate as if you were banging on the piano, or you can do it as if you were playing Bach. Here again, there are choices. You can masturbate alone or with your partner.

Even though I'm in a wonderful relationship with plenty of great sex, I still like to masturbate on occasion, when I find myself home alone. I appreciate and need that special connection that I get with myself only through masturbation—especially if I'm having a hard day, jumbled up with emotions, or need a pick-me-up. I find that I feel very much a new person after a little session with myself. It's like coming home.

Some folks who are in a lover relationship prefer not to masturbate at all. They choose to share every single sexual experience with their partner(s). The idea is to choose what works best for YOU but not make your choices based on guilt, shame, or misinformation.

Variations on a Theme of Self-Esteem

Here is a variety of ways you can use masturbation to love yourself more and to build self-esteem:

* *Spread the love.* Touch more than just your genitals. Touch your whole body. This spreads the good feelings out from your genitals to the rest of your body, especially to your heart.

- *Medibate.* That means to masturbate and meditate at the same time. This can be very relaxing and nurturing. Empty your mind, let your whole body relax, and focus on your breathing. Keep it simple. Think Zen masturbation.

- *While you masturbate, tell yourself, "I love you. I'm here for you."* Murmur sweet nothings to yourself. "I will always love you." "I will always take care of you." That's right; whisper these words out loud to yourself! Try it! If that feels too strange, then speak silently.

- *Don't have an orgasm.* That's right, I said "don't"! Once in a while it's wonderful to masturbate just to pleasure your body and charge yourself up. Retain any turn-on to keep yourself energized throughout your day. This technique is sometimes called Karezza.

- *Explore what is going on deep inside you.* Masturbation is a natural mood elevator and a great time to get in touch with your deeper feelings and express them. I have learned that all different kinds of feelings can coexist with sexual ecstasy. For example, you can be highly sexually aroused and simultaneously feel sadness, anger, longing, confusion, guilt, or depression. Simply witness your thoughts and your feelings while in a state of arousal. You may not be really conscious of exactly how the transformation occurred, but afterward you will usually feel nothing but happy.

- *On occasion, be as creative and total as you would be if you were with a lover.* If you break a sweat you get an A-plus.

- *Be an erotic alchemist.* Imagine your sexual energy coming up from your genitals to your heart, and when it gets to your heart, transmute it into love and fill your heart with your love.

- *Be a sexual healer to yourself.* If you have a headache, for example, or menstrual cramps, masturbation is a fantastic cure. Use masturbation like medicine for whatever ails you.

- *Fantasize (visualize) that you are healthy, happy, well loved.*

- *Be grateful.* While you are masturbating, simultaneously think about all the things in your life that you are grateful for.

The Pleasure of Company

Let's say you're doing really well with the positive self-talk and affirmations. You're doing great at appreciating parts of your body with unrestrained love. Wonderful. But how can you hold on to your progress while making love with a partner? Here are a few ideas that will keep your self-esteem intact when things get hot and heavy.

- *If you become self-conscious, turn your focus toward something else.* Noticing the chip in your coral toenail polish can point to more negative self-talk. So shift your focus to something about yourself that you *do* like. Maybe you're feeling self-conscious about how the flab on your upper arms looks, but you really love your breasts or your buttocks! Distract yourself by touching the parts you love or rubbing them against your partner's body. Or move your focus to sensual sensations: touches, smells, tastes, visuals, sounds. That's called "sensate focus."
- *Refrain from telling your lover what's "wrong" with you, or soon your lover might start to believe you.* How you view and treat yourself can influence how others see and treat you.
- *If your partner has a negative attitude, talk with him or her about the importance of being more positive.* And if your lover is not being present with you, communicate your feelings. You must state the things that are important to you, because your lover probably doesn't automatically know. (The next chapter will help you do this.)
- *If your lover is treating you really badly, you might need to get help.* Physical and/ or emotional abuse are serious matters and often require support from professionals or agencies trained to help you. Reaching out for this support is an act of self-esteem.
- *Visualize or fantasize about how wonderful you are.*

Next time a love song comes on your radio as you are driving in your car, dedicate it to yourself. Have it be a self-love song. Go buy yourself a bouquet of roses or a special treat. Fill yourself up with your love. Give yourself a kiss and a hug. Here's one from me!

Learn to Speak Sex-lish

Good sex begins when your clothes are still on.
VIRGINIA JOHNSON AND WILLIAM MASTERS

*I*n fairy tale after fairy tale the prince without any instruction awakens the sleeping beauty with exactly the correct romantic kiss. But the modern beauty, unless she really is comatose, knows that her lover needs at least a bit of direction to really awaken her passion.

Having great communication skills is an essential part of having a spectacular love life. Perhaps you excel in this area and are able to communicate to your lover perfectly: your needs and concerns, as well as your love and heat. But if not, then learning some better communication skills is an important part of your love-life makeover. With a bit of practice, you'll soon be fluent in "sex-lish."

Teach Me Tonight

In the many sexuality workshops that I have led, when I ask women what they want to learn, they most often say, "I'd like to learn how to ask for what I really, deeply want." Women have all kinds of needs and desires—emotional, sexual, romantic—but too often we don't express them. Our conditioning tells us that if our partner really loves us, he or she will just know intuitively how to pleasure us. Hogwash! Our partners aren't psychic; often they need to be told and sometimes taught. The popularity of the TV show *Sex in the City* was due in large part to the fact that the characters' frank sexual discussions did our talking for us. Research shows that partners who discuss their feelings with each other report having more satisfying sex lives than those who don't, by far. Clearly, she or he who can ask clearly for what she or he wants and needs sexually—gets!

If you're afraid that your partner will think you're being too bold or aggressive when you tell him or her what you like, you're in for a pleasant surprise: Most partners really appreciate being given the straight dope. The number-one issue for women is probably self-esteem, but the number-one issue for men is performance anxiety. Men want to please. One woman I know became enlightened when a male partner asked her what she wanted, and when she was too shy to tell him, he said, "Well, how am I supposed to make you feel good if you don't tell me?" My friend decided to work on being open with sexual partners after that—and discovered that they were grateful and she was gratified.

Sex is universally interesting—everyone experiences sex on some level, and so everyone has something to contribute to the dialogue. Yet many people never talk about sex, finding it difficult or uncomfortable. Some folks believe that talking about sex will somehow take away its mystery and beauty. But in my experience, you can never take away the mystery and beauty of sex. In fact, conversation just increases the allure. Silence can be detrimental, while talking about sex honestly, openly, and explicitly will ultimately enhance our lives and relationships. It can be fun, educational, and a wonderful turn-on.

Speechless

These days I absolutely love to talk about sex, and I do so constantly, with my lover, friends, and with just about anyone appropriate. However, I wasn't always comfortable doing this. Throughout my twenties, I didn't have a clue as to how to ask a lover to please me. Oh, I could say "harder," "faster," "slower," but that was pretty much the extent of my erotic vocabulary. I think I was not unusual in this. Being a porn star certainly loosened my tongue but not in the direction of my own pleasure. I even had a lucrative phone-sex gig, making $50 for each prerecorded minute's work of fantasies and faked orgasms. But it was far different to be face-to-face with a lover, especially for something more than a fling. However, I was so busy being the world's hottest woman, I didn't notice I was frustrated.

When I turned thirty-one, I started going to a therapist, and I found that I was totally unable to discuss any real sexual issues with her. I felt ashamed and embarrassed. I also couldn't bring myself to ask my gynecologist a sex question without stuttering and turning red. In my relationships, I didn't know how to communicate my feelings or how to handle real intimacy: I would break up with a lover at the slightest irritation, because I didn't know how to process problems or the feelings that came up.

All in the Family

Eventually, I did learn. I had to; not communicating well was just too painful. I read, took classes, and gathered more life experience—and I now have the communication skills I need. What a relief! It's amazing how fast and relatively easily we can learn to communicate better.

It's normal to be a bit nervous when we start honestly communicating our needs, thoughts, and desires with each other—especially for those of us who grew up in families where we didn't discuss our feelings. Some families only express one feeling—anger—by fighting; other families are experts at ignoring or repressing feelings. Traditions like these are meant to be broken.

If your partner doesn't want to talk about it, ask in a curious tone, "Why?" Perhaps his answer will help explain. If he really refuses to talk about sex, you may need to accept that, but perhaps you can talk about sex on your end more and eventually maybe he'll come around.

Listen, Honey

Besides asking for what you want sexually, it's also important to know how to listen. We tend to make assumptions, but sometimes we can be quite wrong. I learned this when I was close to breaking up with a boyfriend I had been with for two and a half years. We took a workshop on communication for couples, during which we did an exercise where one partner would express her or his feelings to the other, and then the other would repeat back what she or he had said. I would think that I was listening, but then I couldn't actually accurately repeat back what he had said to me. I learned that I wasn't truly listening even though I thought I was. But by the end of the day, we could finally hear each other, know what we meant, and accurately repeat back what each other said. So let's start communicating! And listening.

Clarity Begins at Home

Try not to censor your thoughts, feelings, and desires from yourself. More easily said than done, I know. I don't remember ever once crying as an adult until I hit thirty-three; I was that out of touch with my feelings. If you can't feel your pain, anger, or sadness, then how will you feel pleasure? The more you feel and express the full range of your feelings, the better sex gets. Some ways in which people get in touch with their feelings are doing meditation, swimming, art, spiritual practices, church, being in nature, therapy, masturbation, deep relaxation, beating a pillow, workshops, martial arts, dancing, support groups, sports, and yoga. The more comfortable you are telling yourself what you want, the easier it will be to tell your lover.

Listen to Your Vulva Talk
(And for the Men: Listen to HER Vulva Talk)

Let me start by saying: You may think this is one of the stupidest things you've ever heard of in your life, but I've done this with hundreds of women and couples, and it really is helpful.

Here at Dr. Sprinkle's Sex Life Makeover Center, we sometimes use vulva hand puppets. They're beautifully handmade of lush velvet in a variety of colors by my friend Dorrie Lane at her Vulva University. You can purchase your own vulva hand puppet from the House O'Chicks Web site (listed in Resources). We use the puppets to help us hear what our vulvas have to say to us and then to be able to tell our partners.

Your vulva wants to tell you exactly how she feels, what she thinks and wants. And she doesn't beat around the bush. Believe me, vulvas sometimes say the darndest things! When we speak from our vulvas, we often get very different messages than when we speak from our heads or hearts. And when it comes to sex, you can't really ask for what you want until you get a clear idea of what you truly desire, and for that you'll certainly want to take what your vulva says into consideration.

Curious about what your vulva has to say? Let's find out. Use a vulva puppet, or if you prefer, you can do this without one. Just use a pen and piece of paper and follow these three simple steps.

(If you are a man you can do this too, in slightly different ways. Tune in to what your penis has to say. Or imagine what your lover's vulva would want to say to you if she could.)

1. Sit or lie down. Take some deep breaths, and relax your body.
2. Shift your attention and awareness to your vulva.
3. Using stream of consciousness, jot down whatever your vulva would say if she could speak to you. Tune in and just write freely. Absolutely do not censor her.

Try doing this again on several different days. You'll likely get different messages each time: sometimes funny, sometimes very serious, and sometimes very horny. The point, then, is to become more consciously aware of listening to your vulva more often. Maybe your vulva wants to keep her own diary!

One actual example from a workshop: "Hi. It's me, Ploochie. Thanks for your interest in me. It feels good. I am rather shy. But I would like to be more confident. Please help me. You've been working so hard at the office. I need a little more attention. I need your love and affection. I'm tired of living in the dark. Maybe you can lie in the sun and let me see the light of day… Oooh, I'd just love that. By the way, your date last week… mmm, very yummy, I definitely approve. Let's have more of that. Meow!"

What my vulva has to say to me is:

_____

_____

_____

_____

_____

How to Communicate Better with Your Lover

Here are tips you can use to enhance communication before, during, and after lovemaking. Timing is important, as is the location where you choose to do your communicating. Some things are better communicated in bed, or wherever the action is taking place. Other concerns are best taken far away from the bed. Better to sit by a stream, take a walk, sit on a park bench . . . Some people think it's not polite to talk about sex during a meal, but frankly I have found that over a meal is a fine time.

This section is in three parts. Tips for using before or after sex, for using during sex, and tips that can be used any time. I hope you will find some of these tips useful.

1. Communication Enhancement Tips to Use Before or After Sex

#1. Write lusty love letters. You can give your lover lots of hints and pointers about what you like and desire by writing explicit e-mails, cards, and love notes. Post-its are also perfect little vehicles for communicating what you want and need. Post them on pillows, mirrors, etc. Be as specific as possible. If you're worried that someone might find a note that's very explicit or incriminating, give it to your lover to read when you're together and then rip it up. Don't forget to ask your lover to write you a juicy note back.

#2. Talk seductively about the things you would like to do with your lover once you're alone together. Do this over a romantic dinner at a restaurant, driving in the car, or walking down the street. Go into detail. "I would love to _____ with you. That would feel so _____ Would you like that? Do you like it when I _____?" Tell your lover what you were thinking of doing to him/her earlier that day, or tell him/her what you like about him/her, what you find sexy, hot, romantic. Whisper the words directly into his/her ear for extra heat. This plants seeds for later and keeps a little sexual tension going. It's a form of teasing—and most people get turned on by being teased.

#3. Start up a general conversation about your sex life. If you are in an ongoing relationship, have a check-in conversation every few months to see if each of you is sexually satisfied. If one or the other isn't, talk about it, from the heart. During a walk together is a great time for this. Simply bring up the subject by asking some questions like "Do you feel that you're getting enough sex?" Or "Do you wish I initiated sex more often?" Or "Do I come on too strong sometimes?"

Other nice questions to ask are: "Would you please tell me one of your sexual fantasies?" Or "Tell me about one of your best sexual experiences." "Tell me about your worst sexual experience." Simply ask (even if you've asked before) your lover what he/she likes sexually and then listen with open curiosity.

#4. Discuss sex-related topics in the news. If personal sex issues are still too threatening to discuss, then bring up a topic from the news, such as, "What do you think about stopping people from accessing pornography on the Internet in public libraries?" Theoretical conversations can easily end up becoming personal—even if they don't, you can learn a lot about someone by finding out his/her opinions on sexual issues in general.

#5. Take a relationship class or couples' communication workshop. Many community centers have these, although such classes don't usually include much talk about sexuality, but you can later apply the same communication techniques you learn about relationships to sexuality. One group that does include sex talk is the Human Awareness Institute organization (in Resources). They offer some great weekends all around the USA, Europe, and Australia. At HAI workshops you get to practice their excellent communication techniques, and they "provide a nurturing path to understanding and improving your relationships." (Their workshops are also wonderful for singles.)

#6. Do couples' sex therapy. There is no shame in seeking out help. In times past, communities had elders, shamans, or sages who were the sex educators to impart wisdom and support. Sexuality teacher Harley Swiftdeer tells stories of his Native American tribe having a long tradition of having "phoenix fire women and men" who would be the tribe's sex experts whom you could go to to learn or if you had a problem. Today most of society has lost touch with those kinds of traditions, but we've developed a whole new group of advisors.

Warning: Most regular therapists, psychologists, and psychiatrists don't have much, if any, training to deal with sexuality and might be far more uncomfortable with sexuality than you are. If you are having issues that are specifically sex related, it's definitely best to work with a specialist. You can call the American Association of Sex Educators, Counselors and Therapists for a referral in your area. If money is an issue, look in the phone book for a nonprofit or charitable organization that can offer inexpensive or free therapy with someone who is knowledgeable about sex.

Think of your sex therapist as a wise guide rather than as a referee or someone you need to "fix" you. Couples' sex therapy can be really fun, if you get the right sex therapist. Don't settle for someone you don't like or can't relate to; shop around.

I know one couple who didn't like their sex therapist, but each partner was afraid to tell this to the other one. Finally, after a few months, one of them told her partner she felt their therapist was too simplistic, especially when she kept referring to "the river of love." To her relief, her partner confessed he didn't like her either. The two of them began making jokes about the therapist, until they were laughing hysterically. They bonded over dislike of their sex therapist, confronting her and finding a new therapist who brought them closer. Once they found the right sex therapist, they were able to deal with their concerns and got along swimmingly.

There are also some other kinds of sexual teachers and healers. Rather than talk therapy, these women and men work with people in hands-on ways. Sex surrogates (they work in collaboration with your psychotherapist), sacred prostitutes, and sacred intimates (folks on a spiritual path who embody the "divine spirit" and are conduits for others, through sensuality and sexuality), sexological body workers (sex educators who use erotic trance and pleasure as a modality for education, to teach what is erotically possible). There are also "sex coaches." I have some friends who are working this way, and they are doing fantastic work. However, these types of hands-on modalities are relatively new. My friend and a sex coach, Loraine Hutchens, Ph.D., points out, "We're still in the process of developing methodology, codes of ethics, and training standards." I'm sure that, in the future, these kinds of sexual healers and teachers will become more appreciated, understood, and widespread. If you are open to it, if you can find one of these more hands-on educator/healers, if they come personally recommended, if you've checked them out and feel comfortable with them, then you will likely learn a lot and have an amazing experience.

As with all my tips and suggestions, take what you like and leave the rest. Different strokes for different folks.

#7. Talk with other people about sex. One of my friends who is a phone-sex operator says that the minute she tells people what she does for a living, they immediately start confessing their sexual secrets. "They're starved for someone to talk about sex with," she says. I couldn't agree with her more, and the more freely you communicate about sex with others, the more comfortable you'll be with your partner. People often assume that they can't talk about sex with friends, but when someone opens that door they often find that people do want to and enjoy talking about it.

Try to cultivate at least one friend you can talk with whom you trust who knows a lot about sex and is understanding. Make an agreement that you will keep things confidential.

If you're going through something in your sexual life, sharing it with friends can be so very helpful. You may need a friend's support, and usually friends are happy to give it. Then again, you might have to go outside your circle of friends. For example, say you're becoming interested in exploring some kind of "kinky" sex. Your friends might not be open to that, but most large cities have kinky group meetings/societies. Maybe you're involved in an intergenerational relationship or coming out of some kind of closet, and you need to find support specific to that issue. Perhaps you have a pelvic-pain condition and need to connect with other women with the same thing. You might want to get into an Internet discussion group. There's a support network out there for just about everyone. You only have to reach out.

If you really want to have some fun and learn a lot, start a human sexuality study group or a Venus Circle. (Or name it whatever you like.) This can be composed of all women, or men and women together. Write up a plan for gathering once every other week for twelve weeks or so. Each week schedule a few things, such as guest speakers, a topic for discussion, share information, discuss a book about sex, etc. Then have a little tea and social time at the end. Make a little flyer/invitation and distribute it.

2. Communication Enhancement Tips to Use During Sex

#1. Risk asking for what you want. Just do it! Even if it's difficult for you, and even if you stumble on the words, or feel uncomfortable. Asking for what you want may be hard, but you simply must take that risk. It's likely that the reason you *aren't* asking is: (a) you feel you don't deserve it, (b) you are afraid your lover won't comply, or (c) you just aren't used to talking about sex. You can do it!

#2. Frame things in a positive way. Always frame things positively. Be kind. You're not on the Jerry Springer show trying to create drama. We all feel vulnerable about our sexual skills, prowess, and "performance." Always come from a place of wanting to make things better, not wanting to criticize, hurt, or blame.

Example A
Before: You might get the urge to say something like "Ouch! You're sucking my nipples way too hard. Take it easy, you brute. That hurt! You're really insensitive and rough sometimes."

Better: "Eeee. My nipples are extremely sensitive right now. I'd like you to suck them super gently. That would feel better."

Example B
Before: "Honey, I hate it when you jump out of bed after you come. You must be afraid of intimacy. You make me feel totally abandoned and unappreciated."

Better: Honey, after you come, I feel really close to you, and I really need you to hold me. When you jump out of bed, I miss you so badly. How would you feel about just staying close? (Be sure to give positive reinforcement when your partner comes through.)

Can you tell the difference between these two ways of talking? Notice the use of "I" statements in the second one; you're not forcing your partner into a defensive stance; you're saying the way you feel and the exact way you would like the behavior to change.

#3. To find out what your lover would enjoy, ask leading questions and in juicy detail, instead of generalizing.

First Attempt: Do you like that? (A good question, but it doesn't get you where you ultimately want to go.)

Better: Would you like me to do this harder or softer? Which is nicer, slower or faster? Which of these spots feels better, this one here or this one here? Tell me exactly how you'd like me to do it?

#4. Communicate nonverbally. Makers of pornography have banked on the fact that an extrawordy script pales in comparison to lots of "m and g's." Moan, groan, and sigh just as much as you please because almost any lover will tell you it's a real turn-on. Besides, communicating with moans and groans and sighs is easier than talking. If you're a very quiet lover, consider being more vocal.

Listen intently to your lover's clues. You can tell your lover you'd really like him/her to be more vocal. You may be surprised how loud your lover becomes once he/she is given permission.

I once had a lover with whom I could never tell what she liked or didn't like, because she barely responded. I couldn't even tell if and when she had an orgasm. So I asked her please to make some sounds to let me know what she liked. Because she was so quiet I was tempted to be more quiet myself, but I resisted the impulse and instead chose to become more vocal. She got used to my making lots of sex sounds, then eventually followed my lead and became much more vocal. I in turn could be a better lover to her. It was a win win.

Try to be sensitive to body language and to interpret it. Sense the slightest pressure from your partner when she/he wants to shift positions or wants you to move in a certain way. Listen for telltale changes in her/his breathing for clues.

Communicate through touch. Lovers do this automatically to some degree, but you can also do it more consciously. For example, place your lover's hand where you want it on your body or face. Squeeze your partner's body really tightly, or go limp, to make a point. Pat your lover's ass with some urgency if you want him/her to move his/her hips faster. Express what you want to say more clearly with how you move, touch, rub, hump, and smooch. As the great Olivia Newton John hit song "Let's Get Physical" says, "Let me hear your body talk."

#5. Listen to what your partner says without judging. If you are making love and you ask your lover what she/he wants you to do, never act shocked or repulsed when she/he tells you. Be curious instead of critical, angry, or shocked. Expect or request the same from your lover.

For example, your lover tells you that he/she would like to lick your anus. Maybe this kind of freaks you out. But instead of showing your alarm and exclaiming "That's disgusting!" try to maintain a neutral expression and ask him/her with curiosity what excites him/her about that. You can confess that this doesn't really appeal to you, but you're willing to try it (if you are). When saying how you feel about it, don't accuse or even imply that anything is wrong in any way with your lover because of this interest. Again, use "I" statements: "I feel a bit hesitant and shy about you licking my anus, and I'd rather not go there at this point." Or "let me go wash there, and I might feel more open to it."

#6. Talk "dirty." On special occasions talking "dirty" can be very stimulating—and can communicate a lot. You can learn to do this in steps.

1. Start by saying things like "That's good."
2. Then go to the next level and develop it to *"Mmmm,* it feels so good when you lick me down there."
3. Develop that into "Oh, *mmmm,* I get so wet and juicy when you flick your tongue around my clit and hole. That's so good; lick my pussy harder while you finger my G-spot, honey. *Mmm,* yeah . . . My pussy is drooling, baby."

On the phone while both members of the couple are masturbating is the best place to practice "dirty" talk. Professional phone-sex workers speak in the present tense, as if they're actually having sex together right this minute: *"Mmm,* yeah, I'm pushing your head down between my legs. Now I'm wrapping my thighs around your head. Stick your tongue inside me, honey, feel how wet I am—*Ooooh!* God, that feels good! I'm squeezing my pussy muscles—can you feel them with your tongue?" But really it's not what you say that matters; it's more the way you say it that's a turn-on: your tone of voice and the *mmm*s and *oooh*s in between the words. You can read a macaroni-and-cheese recipe, and it sounds sexy with the right delivery! Try it for practice.

If you are nervous or shy about talking "dirty," all the better. That nervous energy you stir up will get transmuted into electric excitement once you take the leap.

#7. **Watch your partner's facial expressions.** To have deeper intimacy and more passionate sex, open your eyes during sex. Then you can see your partner's face change from neutral to turned-on, and you'll know that whatever you're doing, it's working. Besides, it's such a joy to see your lover's face in ecstasy. Don't miss it!

#8. **Say "thank you" when your lover tells you something she/he wants or doesn't want.** For example, if your lover says, "That's too rough," answer, "Thank you." This encourages her/him to continue to speak up for herself/himself and also can take away the sting of any criticisms.

3. Communication Enhancement Tips for Any Time

#1. **Looking at some porn or erotica with your lover is a terrific way to generate conversations about sex and discover what turns you and your lover off and on.** Okay, I know, you might not like porn at all. Maybe you've seen some, and it just plain turned you off. Sure there's a lot of really bad porn out there that is offensive to many of us. But let's you and I talk about this for a moment.

If you've seen a porn movie or two or three, don't think that you've seen 'em all. There is now a much wider range of adult movies than before, some even made by women for women and for couples. We have come a long way, baby, in the porn arena. The fact is that many women (as well as men, of course) do enjoy and get turned on by sexually explicit movies. A *Ladies' Home Journal* survey in 1997 reported that 47 percent of the women surveyed used erotica and porn to heighten their sexual experiences.

Did you know that these days there's also what I call "alternative porn?" *Good Vibrations* gives detailed reviews of sex films, with detailed contents with symbols indicating what's in a film, so you are really able to find what you might prefer, and also produces some great films that feature performers that appeal more to women. There is now also "edu-porn," sexually explicit but made to be educational, on topics like oral sex, anal sex, or kissing. Candida Royalle makes wonderful "erotica for couples." Tantra.com has more spiritually oriented movies. Ex–porn actress Veronica Hart directs sex films with sexy plots and focuses on good acting. Queer pornographers Shar Redenour and Jackie Strano at S.I.R. Video make THE world's hottest real lesbian porn. There's also "amateur porn" in which you can watch other couples just having sexy fun without any pretensions. The production quality on amateur porn movies is often poor, but some viewers claim that's part of the charm. The more recent sexually explicit movies that I've produced—such as my *Annie Sprinkle's Amazing World of Orgasm*—are in the "art-porn" and "docu-porn" categories. Debbie Sundahl of Fatale Video makes moving sex films about her personal sexual discoveries, like *Tantric Journey to Female Orgasm—Unveiling the G-Spot and Female Ejaculation*. Betty Dodson's *Celebrating Orgasm* shows five individual sex coaching sessions that are excellent and inspiring.

If you really don't like porn, some alternative possibilities would be to watch some sexually oriented TV shows, like HBO's *Real Sex* (I've been featured in four of their segments). Read erotic stories out loud to each other. (There are many books with nothing but erotic short stories.) Read the erotic literature classics to each other. You could look at an erotic photography book together and critique it. Glance through a sex magazine together, or look at erotic art. Get on the computer and surf around some adult Web sites. If you don't like the porn or erotica you see, talk about what kind of porn or erotica you'd make if you were to make some. Or best of all, make some porn or erotica that you do like! That will certainly get a conversation going!

If porn really disturbs you, take a look at why. Most porn simply depicts people having sex. Interestingly I have found that the better my sex life is, the more porn seemed rather interesting and enjoyable. If I was having a difficult time in my sex life or was feeling critical of my body or my life, I felt that porn was a big turnoff. So maybe porn is pushing some of your buttons. Watch some, take a look, and think about why it freaks you out or totally turns you off. Perhaps you were told/taught that porn is simply bad and disgusting and harmful. (As most women have been told.) Make up your own mind about if and why you like it or don't.

If you are a man who enjoys watching porn and your female partner doesn't, you might just have to agree to disagree. Try not to feel guilty about it. But try to be sensitive about how and when you use it. Maybe you're a man who doesn't like porn; so be it. Okay, so pornography is not exactly highbrow intellectual entertainment. I see it as a folk art, by the people for the people. The fact is that porn and erotica CAN inspire lovers and make them really hot. It's sort of like fantasizing, but someone else does it for you.

Honestly, I don't watch porn very much at all. But on a special occasion it's kind of fun. Especially at a hotel on pay per view during a romantic trip.

#2. **Ask your lover to reveal a sexual fantasy.** What a great way to get an idea of what turns your lover on. After telling a sexual fantasy, your lover might feel vulnerable, so if anything freaks you out, save your thoughts for another time. Remember, just because your lover has a particular fantasy doesn't actually mean he/she wants to act it out. Sometimes just talking about it can be satisfying. Thank your lover for sharing those secret thoughts.

#3. **Critique your lovemaking session together after sex.** You can do this during the pillow talk part of lovemaking, or a day or two later.

Don't overprocess, but you can deconstruct parts of your lovemaking session, examine them, and marvel at them. Say what you really liked, and even what didn't quite work. Some people might find that this sounds too clinical or cold. However, done sensitively, this makes for very good conversation, and you'll learn for next time. You can start the conversation in a playful way, laughing and pointing out something positive that happened during sex. Then segue into something that perhaps didn't feel quite so good. It can be helpful to frame it as: "I like it better when you . . ."

Remember, when you give feedback you must be prepared to get it as well. After you tell your lover what you liked or didn't like, he or she will probably reciprocate; in fact, you hope she/he will, as that is the whole point of all this! Try not to get defensive, but listen with an open mind and heart. If your lover is unskilled at this kind of sex talk, he or she may not be careful to be nonjudgmental. Try to overlook this, perhaps pointing out later the way you would prefer to be talked to about your sexual performance. Remember, this is all going to lead to a more fabulous sex life, so it's all good.

Poetry in Motion

Having sex is actually an act of communication in and of itself, whether you are communicating "I love you," "You turn me on," "I need you," or "I gotta have you." Making love can communicate profound things that words—not even poetry—can't begin to describe. Deep communication is one of the beauties and benefits of making love, but the better your communication is, the more clearly and fully your important messages will get across.

Making Complaints Work for You and Not Against You

If you have an important overall complaint about your sex life, it's usually best to talk about it out of bed. The most important thing is to be extremely sensitive to your partner. Sex is one of the most intimate topics there is, and a criticism of another person's sexuality can be extremely hurtful to him/her. Never ever berate or insult your partner. This can require a great deal of self-restraint when one is upset. But you can ruin things for a long time. Even if your lover attacks you verbally, don't attack back.

Before you speak, be sure your motives are pure; that what you're aiming for is better sex and better communication. Search your heart to be sure you aren't wanting to criticize your lover out of a resentment about something else, or just to push him/her away. If you're sure that's not the case, go ahead. But if you've had a bad day and are upset or tired, wait until your energy level is more positive, when you are in harmony.

Always talk in "I" statements: "I feel such and such" rather than "You do such and such" or even "You make me feel such and such." Be specific. Don't say "I feel that you are totally inconsiderate." That's just an attack and leaves your partner no room to figure out how to change his/her behavior or the desire even to want to! Much better to say "I feel hurt when I flirt with you and don't get the positive response I desire." This has a much better chance of getting the response you want.

Be ready to hear his/her response. When someone complains about your behavior, it is natural to feel hurt or angry. Give your lover time to take in what you've said. If he/she comes back with a complaint about you, try to be open to criticism and focus on what you can do to better the situation.

When I was doing theater performances about my life in sex, I always learned more from the criticisms than from the compliments. Thanks to the criticisms, I grew, and my show got better. At first the criticism would be upsetting, and I didn't want to look at what people said, but then I would think about it, get over feeling personally attacked, and make improvements. It takes courage to offer an honest critique and shows caring as much and sometimes more than flattery.

The Flip Side

Take a moment to try to understand your partner's point of view. Maybe something in your lover's past is making him/her feel a certain way about something. Always try to empathize with your lover's feelings. You don't have to agree with his/her point of view, but you can relate to his/her emotions and try to understand where she/he is coming from.

Figure out together what solutions there can be to a problem. That way your partner won't feel that you are simply dictating changes. Recently I did a sex-life coaching session with an unhappy couple. All they wanted to do was blame each other, to tell me who did what to whom, and bicker and complain. They were like dogs chasing their tails. My job was to get them to focus on stating clearly what they wanted and on finding some ways to give each other what they wanted. I had them each make a list of their top three priorities, share the list with each other, and discuss solutions. They told me that communicating very clearly this way was so helpful for both of them.

Reluctant Romeo

Of course, sometimes your partner may not want to change or to comply with your requests. You might not always agree on everything. Sometimes you might just have to agree to disagree. Or compromise. Sometimes it's best to let something drop, for a while at least. Maybe the seeds of change have been planted and will blossom later. And some difficulties may continue to be a part of the relationship forever. You need to sort out what you can live with and what you can't. Something like asking your lover to give you foot massages because you love foot massages, but your lover doesn't like giving them and says "no" probably isn't a deal breaker. But let's say you've discussed wanting a monogamous relationship and your partner absolutely doesn't want one; something like that could ultimately mean a split.

Fill in the Blankety-Blank-Blank: A Lover's Mad Lib for Good Communication

When you and your lover have something difficult to communicate about your sex life, use this mad-lib game to help. This can make something that's difficult much easier and can clear things up beautifully. It works like a charm. I promise.

INSTRUCTIONS

Sit or lie comfortably together. Designate one person the listener, the other the talker. The talker reads through the whole paragraph below, filling in the blanks. The listener only listens, without communicating anything back, refraining from comments or strong expressions. Pause for some moments, then trade roles. The listener becomes the talker and then reads through the whole mad lib, filling in the blanks.

The air may feel clear after you have each gone through the mad lib one time. But you might need to go through it two or three times each. Keep going through it until you feel done. Fill in the blanks in the spirit of cooperation, if possible. Notice how well the "I" statements work. Always try to balance out any criticisms with praises.

(Name of person you are speaking to) _____, thanks for doing this with me. There's something I've been wanting to talk with you about. Sometimes when we make love, I feel _____. I notice that _____. I get uncomfortable when _____. I think _____. I expect _____. I am afraid that _____. I prefer when _____. I realize _____. I hope _____. I would prefer _____. I feel bad when _____. I feel good when _____. I like it when _____. My heart _____. Let's _____. Together we can _____. Thanks for listening. You really are very _____ (compliment) and _____ (another compliment).

Change happens over time. Don't expect any major shifts immediately. Eventually things will get worked out. Then, don't be surprised when a new challenge arises. It's all part of the fun. In the words of the late, great Gilda Radner, "There's always somethin'."

The "Tell Me How You Like to Be Touched" Game

This is a fun way to learn more about how to please your lover and let your lover know how to please you. It works beautifully.

1. Sit or lie comfortably with each other.
2. Lover A asks Lover B, "Tell me how you like to be touched."
3. Lover B answers in detail. For example, "I like the side of my neck nibbled. I like to breathe together in the spoon position. I usually prefer being teased first before you go near my clit. Then once you get to my clit, touch it really lightly for a while. Then once I'm aroused, press hard. I love when you touch the opening of my pussy for a while, before you enter me. When I start having an orgasm, I like you to keep going even if I squirm. . . ."
4. If Lover B slows down or stops at any point, having run out of things to say, Lover A asks the question again to coax more answers and get more details. Lover A asks again, "Tell me how you like to be touched" whenever B stops answering. Continue for about two minutes straight. (Use a timer for each round if you want.)
5. Then Lover B asks Lover A the question over and over, and A answers in detail.

Results: It's amazing what you will find out about each other simply by asking and listening. Later you can implement some of the specific things your lover said he or she likes.

The "One of the Things I Love About You Is . . ." Game

My good friend Jwala taught me this sweet and simple—yet extremely effective—lovers' game. It's absolutely wonderful to do. Trust me on this one! Don't just read about this; try it! You have to *feel* the delicious results. Besides, this game is always good for a giggle.

When to do this: This can be played in or out of bed. It's great to do any time at all, but especially good whenever you want to rekindle the love between you, make each other feel good, or to ease any raw emotions after a difficult conversation. If anyone is feeling insecure, it helps to rebuild confidence. This game will always remind you of the reasons why you are together in the first place.

1. Lover A starts by saying, "One of the things I love about you is _____." Fill in the blank. (Some examples would be "One of the things I love about you is your big nose." Or "One of the things I love about you is the way you kiss and hold me tight at night." Or "One of the things I love about you is how cute you look in those red shorts." Or "One of the things I love about you is how honest and willing you are." Or "One of the things I love about you is your love for family." Answers can go from serious to silly and back again, big things and small.)

2. Take a moment to let Lover B savor the statement of one thing Lover A loves about him/her.

3. Then it's Lover B's turn to say "One of the things I love about you is _____." Fill in the blank.

4. Go back and forth, each taking a turn to say one thing that you love about the other, continuing for about three to five minutes.

Energize to Eroticize

Ecstasy is always available just for the asking.

It's a beautiful day today here at the center, so let's do the next phase of your program out on the Lover's Lawn by the pond. Notice our two beautiful white swans and how in love they are? Isn't that sweet? Notice the sun rays shining on your body. Do you feel the energy of the sun coming into you?

Sex in its simplest form is energy. It's the heat you feel in your body when you're spooning with someone you love. It's the tingly feeling on your tongue during a special French kiss. It's what's behind the grunt you expressed during those first moments of penetration. It's the excitement in your chest when someone you're attracted to walks into the room. It's the little tremors in your body when you are basking in afterglow. All these are energy rushes. Nothing makes a woman feel more like a real live sex goddess than when this energy flows freely through her. And guys love it, too. You can learn to fire your engines anytime.

Now I'm going to lead you through some fun and pleasurable sexcercises, designed to show you how to build, move, and utilize sexual energy. But first, let me give you some basic information that might be helpful.

Back to the Future

Most sex manuals today don't even mention the conscious use of sexual energy to enhance lovemaking, something that absolutely confounds me because learning about sexual energy certainly revolutionized the way I view and experience sex. It is at the core of my pleasure program. I predict that as more people become more consciously aware of how to build and circulate sexual energy, it will become the wave of the future—literally.

In the Far East, in places like China, India, Tibet, and Japan, people are much more consciously aware of "life-force energy," which flows through our bodies and all living things. It's simply part of Eastern culture; children learn about it as they grow up. These concepts have been introduced to Westerners through practices such as acupuncture, yoga, martial arts, t'ai chi, chi kung, Reiki, and shiatsu massage.

The existence of life-force energy is a scientifically proven and biological fact. It's not a religion or hocus-pocus. It's a natural part of being human though it can be subtle, so feeling it and being aware of it don't always come easily; it needs to be taught.

I realize that for some people, the word *energy* can be a turnoff. They think it sounds either too New Age or too scientific. If you are one of those folks, here are some replacements for the word *energy: electricity, vitality, pep, steam, zip, vigor.* Or how about *juice, inner radiance, power?* In yoga they call it "prana." In martial arts they call it "chi." In some religions and spiritual traditions it's called "Spirit." In Hebrew it's "Ruach."

Some traditions recognize a particular type of life-force energy specific to sexuality. In Taoism, this sexual life-force energy is called "ching-chi." In Tantrism some people call it "kundalini." Wilhelm Reich, a visionary therapist and protégé of Freud, called it "orgone." I like to call it simply "sexual energy." Please call it whatever you wish.

Exploring Inner Space

Many years ago I had read about sexual energy in a number of esoteric "ancient sexual secrets" types of sex manuals. I read that Taoist sex masters circulated their sexual energy to stay youthful, build charisma, and gain personal powers. They could heal their body of pain and illness by mentally moving sexual energy to the troubled areas. I read about male Tantric practitioners who could have long, full-body, multiple orgasms without ejaculating. I read about techniques to "orbit" sexual energy with a lover in order to generate more love. I read about people who practiced traditional Native American techniques for mind-blowing sex that lasted for long periods of time and who knew how to have energy orgasms—even with their clothes on. I thought I knew a lot about sex, but I couldn't imagine how people actually did these things. So I set out either to disprove them or to learn how to do them myself.

Well, I learned to do them—and relatively easily, to my surprise. Since then I've met many hundreds of people who practice these kinds of techniques. Today I am extremely enthusiastic about what I call "the energetics of sex," and I want to share the basics of these super sex technologies with you.

Anyone can learn these sexcercises, designed to generate, move, and utilize sexual energy. Most sexual adults already know how to do some of these things subconsciously. The basics of these techniques are actually fairly obvious, and so right under our noses that people don't see them or use them effectively. But by becoming more conscious of and practicing these techniques, you can use them to your greater advantage.

So, let's start your sexcercise workout. Most of the sexcercises each take less than a minute to do and are very simple. They can be useful and beneficial whether you are celibate or sexually active. They all work for both women and men. During the sexcercises, I will refer to your "energy." It can help to imagine your "energy" as something you can visualize flowing through your body, such as glowing molten lava, cool blue water, warm sunlight, thick red blood, silky pink sand, white electricity, or whatever works best for you.

Generate, Move, and Use Sexual Energy with Your Mind

THE CLIT/MIND CONNECTION
(OR THE PENIS/MIND CONNECTION FOR MEN)

1. Sit comfortably in a chair with your knees apart, the bottoms of your feet touching each other, and your hands resting on your thighs, palms up. Or lie down on your back with the bottoms of your feet touching, and arms resting at your side with palms up. Take a few deep breaths and relax your body and breathing.

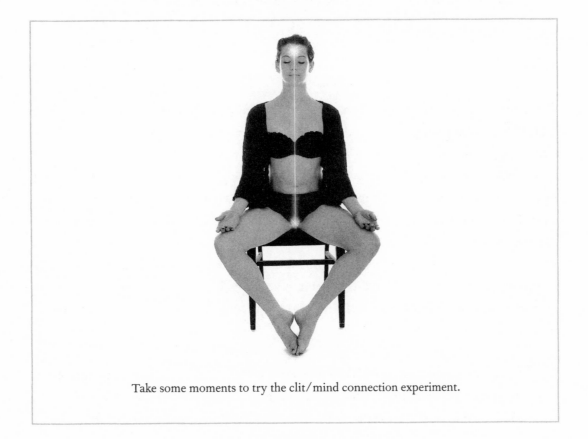

Take some moments to try the clit/mind connection experiment.

2. Do a mental check-in to notice how your body feels, or doesn't feel. Notice how your clitoris feels—or doesn't feel. (See my handy chart on page 99 if you don't know for sure where your clitoris is.)

3. Using your mind and imagination, visualize moving all the energy in your body to your lovely clitoris. Close your eyes and really give it your mental all. Continue for a good minute. Focus your mind on moving your energy from your feet, hands, top of your head, nipples, tongue, thighs to your clitoris. More, more, more. Focus. Focus. Focus. See if you can give yourself the chills. Use the power of your will. (See photo.)

4. When the time is up, notice how your clitoris (or penis) feels. Does it feel slightly different? If so, how? The difference might be extremely subtle, or it might be quite noticeable. Usually people will say things like it feels "heavier," "throbby," "more alive," "bigger," "slightly aroused," and "tingly." Sometimes it can also make your mouth water, lips tingle, and give you the chills.

HOT-WIRED

What this sexercise is designed to show you is, in short, that ENERGY FOLLOWS THOUGHT. You can generate and move energy with your mind. Your mind has power over your subtle energy, and there is a body/mind connection.

So what happened to you? If you didn't feel anything, don't worry about it: At first it can feel as though nothing is happening. But just knowing it's a possibility is already a start. In our culture, where multitasking is considered an admirable trait, concentration may be an underutilized skill. Try again. Practice this once a day or more, and eventually the feelings will become very real for you. Soon you will notice the warm flow of sexual energy to your clitoris, which radiates out into your pelvis.

So, how is knowing this useful? Here are some examples of how I have used this technique and how you can use it:

- I was having intercourse with a new lover, whom I'll call Al. The sex was hot, but it was not very heartfelt. What I really wanted in the moment was to feel closer to him emotionally. So with my mind I visualized our sexual energy coming up from our genitals and into my heart. I stimulated my nipples a bit to guide the energy upward. I imagined the energy spinning around my heart and opening it up. It was as if Cupid had shot an arrow into my heart and it burst open. Within seconds our hard-core, rather mechanical sex turned to sweet lovemaking. He didn't even know what hit him!

- My lover and I flew from San Francisco to Barcelona for a romantic vacation. We checked into our hotel seriously jet-lagged. After just a few hours' sleep, my lover surprised me with some oral sex. But I felt positively numb and unresponsive. So I focused on sending energy to my clitoris, and *voilà!* My clitoris woke up, and the romantic vacation began.

- During a hot date, with a new female lover, I set up my massage table and proceeded to give her an erotic massage. When I got to her vulva, I felt a tidal wave of insecurity. Suddenly I felt totally unskilled. I admit, I wanted to impress her. So I imagined crackling electricity flowing into my hands. This diverted my mind from further self-criticism, and soon my hands felt more sensitive and pulsed and tingled with energy. Whether she felt the shift or not, I didn't ask, but I definitely felt that my touch became sweeter and more sensitive to her body's desires.

Generate, Move, and Use Sexual Energy with Kegels

Dr. Kegel, I Presume

In 1952, gynecologist Dr. Arnold Kegel invented an exercise to help women who had urinary incontinence, and he named it after himself: Kegels. (Of course, squeezing vaginal muscles, a.k.a. pelvic-floor muscles, is actually an ancient sex technique practiced by clever women for centuries.) Kegels will indeed help women with incontinence, but let's focus on the very sexy side effects.

Kegels are also helpful and useful for a man. They can help him increase arousal, make his erection more erect, withhold his ejaculation if he wants to, and have better orgasms.

He can do them by squeezing the same muscles he would use to make his penis jump, or stop the flow of urine if he's peeing.

KEGEL-CIZE

1. Sit or lie down. Relax and take a few deep breaths. Mentally scan your body. Notice how you feel, or don't feel.
2. Find your pelvic-floor muscles by squeezing them. They're the ones you would use to cut off your flow of urine if you were peeing.
3. Squeeze and release the muscles a few times. Squeeze, release, squeeze, release . . . and keep going for thirty seconds to a minute.
4. Try doing Kegels at different speeds: slow and then fast and fluttery. Take it easy. You're not at the gym. Let it be gentle, and most of all make it feel erotic. I think of my Kegels as little gentle pussy kisses!
5. Imagine that you can charge up your sex battery with Kegels. Try to give yourself the chills a few times. Continue for about a minute.
6. When time is up, check in with your body. What do you feel? Do you feel different than when you started? It can be very subtle or very noticeable. Usually people will say things like "I feel more clear headed," or "sexier," "makes me want to kiss my lover," "mildly aroused," . . . etc.

So how is this useful? Here are some ways I've used Kegels:

- Once when I was masturbating, I had my favorite dildo inside me. I was holding my vibrator with one hand on my clitoris, and wanted to stimulate my nipples with the other hand. My hands were quite full, so I couldn't move the dildo around. So I started to Kegel, squeezing my muscles around the dildo, which felt wonderful. When I started to have a very intense clitoral orgasm, I kept Kegeling, which extended the orgasm into a huge long series of multiple orgasms.
- I like to do Kegels when I'm in line at the bank, so that when I make a monetary deposit into my checking account, I'm also making a sexual-energy deposit into

my body. This puts a bounce into my step while doing the rest of my errands. Kegels actually can stimulate the clitoris from the inside.

- If I wanted to make a male lover's penis more erect while inside me or give my lover added pleasurable sensations, I would do Kegels. I've been told it's a good turn-on. This sort of milking technique is poetically and popularly called "pompoir" and has been practiced by skilled women over the centuries, especially in Asia. Although to get really good at it takes a lot more practice than most of us gals care to commit to.

Generate, Move, and Use Sexual Energy with Movement

SHAKE AND BAKE

1. Stand with your feet shoulder width apart and soften your knees so they're slightly bent.
2. Take a few deep breaths. Check in, notice how your body feels, or doesn't feel. What is your level of arousal? Unless you just had sex, it's probably somewhat low.
3. Close your eyes.
4. Shake your hips rigorously for thirty seconds to a minute. Let the rest of your body go, too, along with your hips, and shake it too.
5. When done, take a big, deep breath.
6. Compare the way you felt before with how you feel after shaking your hips. Do you feel a difference? Usually people say they feel things like "energized," "tingly," "awakened," "high," and "electric." If you don't feel a difference, you may not be shaking rigorously or long enough, or you may need to pay closer attention because the feelings can be subtle.

So how is this useful? If you want to have a more ecstatic, energized, and spectacular sex life, MOVE! If you are a pillow queen—one of those women (or men) who just lies back and doesn't move much when having sex (whether partnered or alone), you might want to consider moving and undulating those hips more to increase your energy, power, and thrills.

Dancing is also a great way for lovers to get their mojo rising. Playful wrestling can also be thoroughly invigorating. If you want to have great sex, stage a wrestling match first. Put a mattress on the floor, don some short shorts and a sexy bra, have a timer to time the rounds, and go at it. After your match, great sex is virtually guaranteed, so there are no losers.

Recently a woman named Dalia came to me for advice. She had worked as a stripper for over fifteen years. She wanted to go on to some other line of work because she was sick of working in bars, but every time she tried to do something else she invariably found herself returning to the strip joints. She was very frustrated at her inability to change her career. For months she couldn't seem to quit "the biz" even though she desperately wanted to and even had other job options. So we had a long talk, and we discovered that she was basically addicted to the good feelings generated in her body from dancing erotically, gyrating her hips for eight hours day after day. The dancing released endorphins, which kept her in a mild state of arousal. Once we figured this out, she was finally able to energize her body in other ways and kick the habit of dancing in bars. She went on to become a very successful public-relations person who did a lot of aerobics classes.

Generate, Move, and Use Sexual Energy with Your Sounds

Seventeen years ago, I had a brief affair with a wonderful woman, who then became one of my best friends, and a cofacilitator of many workshops, Barbara Carrellas. One night, as our affair was winding down, we were too tired and lazy to make love, so we got into the bathtub together. We relaxed and closed our eyes. I let out a long sigh. Then she made a long sigh. Then I made a bigger sigh, she made a bigger sigh. Then I made an *"mmmmm . . . ,"* and she responded with one herself. We then took off and created a symphony of all kinds of sex sounds. If you were to have heard us, you'd have thought we were really going at it physically, but we weren't moving a muscle. After a while, we were so turned-on that we really *were* making love, but using only our moans and groans. Eventually we reached a simultaneous crescendo where our energies burst out of the tops of our heads. It was a delightful experience and one we will always cherish. That night we discovered we could generate and move a lot of juicy sexual energy and make love just with sex sounds. You can read her side of the story in her wonderful book, *Urban Tantra*.

SOUND OFF!

1. Lie down somewhere comfortable, alone or with a partner.
2. Relax your body. Close your eyes.
3. Scan your body to see how it feels or doesn't feel.
4. Begin to make some very low-pitched sighs and moans from the gut and from the genitals. Start slowly. Continue for about one minute. Try using various *oooohhh, oooohhh, oooohhh*–type sounds. (I did research into which sounds stimulate which parts of the body, and *oooohhh* works on the lower body.)
5. Next, bring your awareness up to your heart, go up about two octaves, and make higher-pitched *aaaaahhhh, aaaahhh, ahhh*–type sounds. (*Ahhh* sounds stimulate the heart area.) Continue for about one minute, going somewhat faster. Don't force the sounds; let them come naturally through you with your willingness.
6. Finally, bring your awareness up to your third eye (or "mind's eye"—the area between your eyes) and make some very high screechy sounds, the way teenage girls scream at a rock concert. Use *eeeeeeeeeeee, eeeee, eee*–type sounds. Increase your speed. Keep going for about one minute. Let your sounds be loud and realistic! Fake it 'til you feel it!
7. Feel free to giggle if you want to. After all, this can be very funny.
8. Keep going, bringing the sounds to an *energetic climax*. Give it your all!
9. When you feel you are done, then relax. Keep your eyes closed and bask in the afterglow.
10. Scan your body and notice how you feel. Do you feel a shift in your body? In your consciousness? How do you feel? Usually people say things like they feel "more open," "energized," "lighter," "happier," "like I just had sex," and "clearer."

Try a sound-gasm and feel your sexual energy flow up your body.

If you didn't feel anything, try it again another time, longer and louder. Perhaps this seems really weird to you. You're right! It is really weird. Lots of sex acts are really weird! But hey, I promise that practice makes you purr.

SPIN CYCLE

So, how is this useful? Here is an example of how I have used the sound-energy connection:

When I lived in a midtown Manhattan apartment, for several months I had a horrible, thuglike neighbor. He played loud music constantly at all hours and was rude, inconsiderate, and a thief. One day, when I went down the hall to do my laundry, I found that the nasty neighbor had broken the washing machine and left a huge mess. I was really angry and frustrated and thought I was going to explode. So I went back to my apartment and lay down on the couch with my vibrator. I proceeded to masturbate, letting myself make lots of sounds to vent my anger, starting with low sounds and going higher and higher until I got some anger out. I made the sounds again and again until I exploded in a humongous orgasm with an ear-piercing scream. I learned I could use the energy of my anger to my benefit. Making the sounds helped me express my frustration. Then I calmly called the superintendent to fix the washing machine. I am woman; hear me roar!

After a full day of writing this book, I was making love one night and was still too much in my head, thinking too much. So I consciously made lower-pitched sounds to bring my sexual energy and awareness down to my pelvic area, where I wanted it. Then as I approached orgasm, I made higher-pitched sounds, so my orgasm would shoot all the way up my body and out the top of my head.

Generate, Move, and Use Sexual Energy with Your Breath

If a person were to playfully mimic someone having sex, she/he would probably begin by panting and exaggerating the standard breathing pattern. Anyone who has received (or made) an "obscene" phone call or who has engaged in phone sex knows the routine. During the human sexual response cycle normal breathing speeds up and builds to a rapid pace; the breath is held for a few moments before/during a climax; after the climax there is a long exhale, and then the breath slows down and gradually returns to normal. Breathing during sex is something people are aware of but are not usually taught to use consciously.

Deep, conscious, rhythmic breathing creates pathways for ecstasy energy to travel throughout your whole body, providing a more full-bodied sexual experience and amplifying sensations. In a nutshell, ECSTASY TRAVELS ON THE BREATH. Lovers can speed up their breathing to increase excitement or slow it down to prolong enjoyment.

It doesn't take a sex manual for lovers to discover the bliss to be had from spooning when combined with synchronized breathing, or alternate breathing. (One breathes in while the other breathes out, and back and forth.) Some lovers enjoy the intimate act of breathing in and out of each other's mouths, which I consider a form of EnergySex intercourse—"penetration" of the lungs with the breath. It's a delightful way to have your lover inside you.

There are many different techniques that work well to enhance sexual feelings. Ecstasy Breathing is my absolute all-time favorite, which is the next sexsercise I invite you to try. It's an advanced technique. Some folks resonate with it and get it right away; others can take a long time to learn it. But first let me tell you about how I learned it.

Through the grapevine, I'd heard stories about an incredibly knowledgeable Native American shaman and spiritual teacher, who presented some very intense and brave sexuality workshops. His name was Harley Reagan Swiftdeer. I was intrigued, so I pitched doing a story about one of his "Quodoshka" workshops to my editor at *Penthouse Forum* magazine. Next thing I knew I was in a small suburb in snowy Michigan, in a big house with about forty other workshopees. We spent several days learning many interesting things, trying various techniques and sharing our experiences. But it was at the end of the workshop that I learned about the most valuable lesson for me, the "fire-breath orgasm."

The "fire breath" (not to be confused with the "breath of fire" in yoga) is an ancient breathing technique where you lie down and breathe into ecstasy, and sometimes into a full-bodied "energy orgasm." Harley's wife and assistants first demonstrated for us. They lay on the floor with their clothes still on, heads all pointed together in the shape of a wagon wheel, started breathing rhythmically, and a few minutes later they writhed in absolute ecstasy. It may sound impossible—but seeing was believing. They looked as if they were being made love to by an invisible being. Their ecstasy and energy orgasms kept going and going for a long time. I had to learn!

It took me almost a year to really get the hang of the fire-breath orgasm, but once I really got it I came to love it and have used it often, including while making love.

Years later now, I have modified and simplified the fire-breath-orgasm technique to teach it in my own way, to what I now call "ecstasy breathing." It's based on the fire-breath orgasm but is somewhat different. I have taught ecstasy breathing to many people. For years I have hosted an ecstasy-breathing evening session and class once a month here at the center so people can come together and do this in a group. It's much more exciting to do it in a group, as there's much more energy and a coach to keep you breathing ecstatically. (We usually breathe for about forty-five minutes.) It's a wonderful way to spend an evening, believe me.

The best way to learn this technique is to have someone demonstrate it for you live first and then teach it to you. Many people now practice and teach ecstasy breathing and the fire-breath orgasm over North America, Europe, and Australia. If you're interested, and you look around, you can probably find someone to teach you. Or watch it on video or DVD using one of the two films I list in the Resources.

How to Do Ecstasy Breathing

(See photos on page 141 to make these nine steps more clear.)

You'll need to breathe for about fifteen to forty-five minutes to really experience this fully. Put some nice rhythmic music on your stereo. Turn down any lights. Unplug the phone.

Lie down on a flat, firm surface, such as a hard bed, a carpet, mat, or a soft lawn. Don't use a pillow because it works best with your neck and head flat. Bend your knees, putting your feet flat on the ground. Take some moments to empty your mind, relax your body.

1. Begin to take deep, rhythmic breaths. Inhale through your nose and fill your belly and lungs with your breath, so that they fill up like a balloon. Then exhale through your mouth as if you are blowing out birthday candles. Make the breathing completely circular, continuous, with no pauses between the inhalations and exhalations. Get into a nice, slow rhythm. Then add a pelvic rock, arching your lower back on the inhale, flattening it on the exhale. Undulate your pelvis, as if you are having intercourse. Add some gentle Kegels on some of your exhales. These squeezes help make it more erotic and pump up your sexual energy.

2. *Light the fire in your genitals.* Keep breathing rhythmically. Think of it as an erotic dance and let your body do what it naturally wants to do. Just don't stop. Keep breathing. Undulate your spine from top to bottom. Let your head and neck roll around loosely.

3. *Genitals to belly.* Use your mind and imagination to pull energy in between your legs from the atmosphere into your genital area. Breathe it upward to your belly. Fill your belly with your sexual energy. Go back down between your legs and gather in more. Circle that energy around from the genital area to the belly and back and forth.

4. *Belly to heart.* When the areas below your waist are charged up, and the fire is burning, go to the next level, to your heart. Circulate energy from belly to heart. Spend several minutes breathing at each level.

5. *Heart to throat.* Now bring your energy up to your throat. Let some moans and groans emerge. Remember, sounds build energy. Make lots of sounds. High-pitched sounds. Bring it up your body, breathing faster now.

6. *Throat to third eye.* Next bring your energy up to the third-eye area (the area between your eyebrows), from the heart to the third eye and back again. Remember, to get the full effect, you'll need to breathe from fifteen minutes to an hour so spend at least a few minutes at each level.

7. *Third eye to out of the top of your head.* Speed the breathing up to high gear as if you are in the heat of passion. Then pull the energy up and out of the top of your head. At this point pull the energy up through your legs into your body and out of the top of your head in one whole body stream. Make high-pitched sounds. Roll your eyes up into the back of your head to help pull the energy farther up. Have fun with it. See how much pleasure and ecstasy you can generate from breathing your sexual energy up into and through your body.

8. *Advanced ecstasy breathing:* Keep breathing heavily, and see if you can take yourself into an "energy orgasm," or an orgasmic state. I will tell you all about these in Step 13. I promise.

9. When you feel complete, just relax and bask in the afterglow. Take plenty of time to enjoy it.

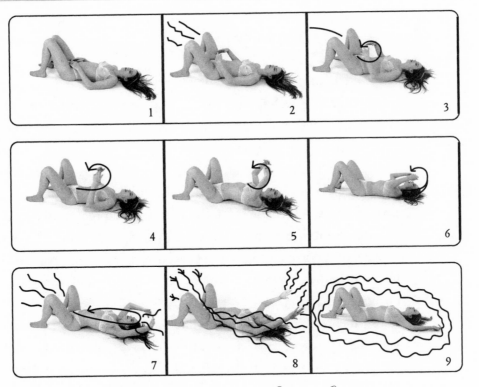

Ecstasy Breathing and Energy Orgasm

Of any sex technique I have every learned, Ecstasy Breathing has been the most powerful, and helpful. I recommend it to everyone. It's also a key to experiencing more of your orgasm opportunities, such as energy orgasms (see Step 13).

1. Relax.
2. Light the "furnace" in your genitals.
3. Breathe the "fire" from your genitals to belly, and back around again and again.
4. Breathe from the belly to heart and keep circulating the ball of energy. Let your heart open.
5. Breathe from heart to throat. Make sounds.
6. Breathe from throat to your third-eye area.
7. Breathe up out the top of your head, and enjoy.
8. Open up to let orgasmic energy pass through your whole body.
9. Bask in the afterglow. Isn't it great to be alive?

A Message to Consumers

- At first, learning this technique might feel mechanical, just like when you're learning techniques for playing tennis or the violin. But with some practice, your body will eventually be able to do it quite effortlessly.

- It's very helpful to use your hands and arms to coax and direct the energy. Circle them over the areas you are breathing from and to.

- Energy levels will rise and fall like mercury in a thermometer. You might have moments when you suddenly feel that you have lost your connection with your energy, then you can always go back down between your legs and gather more sexual energy and bring it back up again, at any time.

- If you are breathing deeply for a while and your body is not used to it, you might experience what is called "tetany." Your hands and/or mouth area may feel funny, frozen, and tingly. That is when the energy hits blocks in your body. Don't worry; these feelings will go away once you slow down your breaths or breath less deeply. This will likely only happen the first few times you practice ecstasy breathing.

- Sometimes while you are breathing, and in an erotic state, you may also want to cry, cough, or gag, or you might feel old painful memories surfacing. Don't be afraid of this: Moving energy up your body can be like having a wonderful psychic enema. It's a cleansing, and it's good for you. As you keep breathing, have a cry, or pound your fists by your side, or growl. Let your feelings out and bathe them in ecstasy. These "blocks" will pass through, and then there will be more room for more ecstasy to come into your body.

- If you feel too light-headed or too dizzy, slow down the breathing a bit. Be sure you are putting the accent on the exhale only. Relax the inhale, then forcefully exhale with blowing-out-candles sounds.

- Your experience will vary depending on how you feel in the moment and on a particular day. If you feel tired, you might have a very quiet experience. If you have a lot of feelings to express, it might be very emotional. If you are excited, it can feel super erotic. Ecstasy breathing will intensify whatever feelings are inside you. And the more you breathe, the more you feel. It's your life. Why not live it to its fullest?

For me, learning this technique ultimately made partner sex much more ecstatic and fulfilling, because it taught me how to feel, generate, and move sexual energy in a very clear and physical way. It's also a natural high, a great substitute for harmful addictions. It helped me to quit smoking. I have used it many times when I need some healing. It's sexual healing, so it actually feels good. For example, when my heart was broken, ecstasy breathing helped me move the pain and sadness out of my body. I've used ecstasy breathing to gain insight into a question, as it helps me access inner wisdom. For example, when I needed to move to a new city, I asked the question where I should move, did the breathing, and got a clear answer. So it can be used as a sort of shamanic journey. I've also had some of the most amazing full-body energy orgasms to where it felt as if I were being breathed by the forces of creation, and so electric it was as if my body were plugged into an electrical outlet. Ecstasy breathing can be a wonderful, profound, and deep experience, giving one the feeling of making love to the universe. I highly recommend it!

Again, don't be discouraged if you don't experience the benefits of ecstasy breathing right away. It might take some practice. However, just learning that such a thing as this is possible is a seed that has been planted in you. One day that seed might just sprout into something . . . spectacular.

Your Energy Assessment

What times of the day do you generally feel the most sexual energy?

_____

(continued)

What times of the day do you generally feel the least sexual energy?

_____

You might want to try to make love during those times when your energy level is highest.
What seems to drain your sexual energy?

1. _____

2. _____

3. _____

4. _____

5. _____

Of these things, what can you change, and what can't you change?
What are some ways you can build up your sexual-energy levels?

1. _____

2. _____

3. _____

4. _____

5. _____

What is one thing you can do to support yourself in having more experience in ecstatic
breathing?

1. _____

Step Seven

Prop Yourself Up

All the world's a live-sex-show stage and its men and women and trannies merely players.

Up until now, your makeover program has focused within. Now let's leave the center grounds and return to your very own home and take a good look at your erotic environment. We'll peruse the contents of your closet and your body-jewelry box to see how we can fashion your passion. Clothes, body décor, props, and a well-prepared and sensuous boudoir can really help set the stage for spectacular sex.

Have you ever been in a mood that is totally nonerotic, when the opportunity for sex suddenly came along and you couldn't pass it up? Well, I have. I was once sitting at home, snuggled in a very nonsexy long flannel nightgown, reading a great nonsexy magazine on a rainy night, perfectly content with where I was and whom I was with (myself); I got an unexpected phone call from a workaholic lover who'd suddenly found himself free and in the mood for lust at 8 P.M. on a weeknight. I thought I wasn't in the mood, and my first impulse was to turn him down and just go back to my *National Enquirer*. But something funny happened on the way to saying no: I remembered that I have rarely, if ever, regretted saying "yes" to sex with a great lover. When you say "no," you get just that—no sex with no body. When you say "yes," though you may not know exactly what will happen, you've opened the door to real possibilities.

Harem in a Hurry

Saying "yes" in my flannel nightgown meant performing some makeover magic in just the time I hung up the phone until my eager lover arrived a scant hour later. Rapidly I assessed the bedroom, where chaos and debris told the sordid tale of my morning: a half-filled teacup, several blouses I'd tried on and discarded, a pair of sneakers from an early run. I whisked through the space, and within ten minutes I'd changed the bedsheets from wrinkled plaid flannel to soft, smooth pink Egyptian cotton, lit some strategically placed candles, straightened up the bedside shelf, put away my books, and put out my sex toys, condoms, and lube. I put three discs into the CD player. I only had time to ensure that my musical selections were sultry without being intrusive. Next I jumped into the shower, did a once-over on my legs with a razor, then creamed and scented my skin and donned a pink negligee and a purple kimono. I brushed some color onto my cheeks and banded my damp hair up high, leaving a few wispy curls to dangle. I looked in the mirror at my flushed and happy face: In just forty-five minutes I'd primed myself and my space for lovemaking. And—*abracadabra!*—I found myself sexually turned on.

If you think about it, nothing in this routine is unfamiliar or terribly unusual. I'd venture to guess there is not a woman alive who hasn't at one time or another had to change her physical presentation in a short space of time. And every woman knows that by changing your appearance, you almost always change your mood. Which is just what happened when I removed my flannel nightie, rearranged my bedroom, and primped myself for a lover; by the time I was finished, I was miles away from my drowsy tabloid-reading self, my primed body softly humming with an anticipatory erotic charge.

It's not a big leap to imagine performing this same kind of artistry intentionally—that is, not only because you have to do a quick change but because you want to set the mood for lovemaking and, even more specifically, for extra-special lovemaking. If you've ever seen *Queer Eye for the Straight Guy*, then you know that this same kind of makeover magic works for men, too.

Clothes Minded

Sex is the arena in which grown-ups get to play and spend quality time together. Having sex can be, among other things, a kind of theater in which plays are staged and we get to act out various parts of ourselves. One thing this has meant for me is that costumes and other forms of adornment to delight the senses are among my specialties and great pleasures. In this chapter I will share with you some ways to improve your "theater of the bedroom" by actively directing and starring in your own hit show.

I can already hear some critics objecting that this kind of play is phony, that it reminds them of old-fashioned sex advisors telling women to dress up in Saran wrap and play games to keep their husbands interested and happy. Well, the difference is that I'm not telling you to dress up in order to please your *partner*. **I'm telling you to do it for yourself.** Dressing up in sexy costumes can expose the many facets of your erotic and sensual self as well as that of your lover.

If you think sexual theatricality is strictly for the radical or kinky, consider this: The most wholesome woman in American films, none other than Donna Reed, staged a complete honeymoon fantasy for Jimmy Stewart in the movie *It's a Wonderful Life*. While Stewart is saving his loan agency by giving all their honeymoon money to his customers, Reed creates a Hawaiian dreamscape in the abandoned house they'd played in as teenagers. She roasts chicken on a spit, dresses herself in a lei and flowered skirt, and plays ukulele music on the old phonograph. A stunned Stewart stumbles into his bride's arms, and of course, the camera looks politely away. This was, after all, the 1940s, but everyone then knew these two were gonna have more rip-roarin' sex in that drafty old house than they would have had in any hotel's honeymoon suite.

But, my still-resistant critic is saying, that is so much work. Well, it doesn't have to be; preparing for sex can take as much or as little work and time as you want to put into it. I'm going to break down these preparations and show you that they can be wild and extreme or, if it feels like a burden to you, how to K.I.S.S.—Keep It Short and Simple.

The three aspects of this part of your sex-life makeover program are (1) your erotic environment (usually the bedroom); (2) your body (beyond everyday hygienic and beauty care); and (3) props and costumes (from simple scarves to elaborate leather).

Your Erotic Environment

It's hot to have sex in a variety of places: in the shower, in the backyard, in the kitchen, in the car in the garage—just about anywhere. However, most people have sex most often in their bedrooms. So let's see how we can make your bedroom more sexy. Do note that you can apply these same principles to any spot in your house, or outside your house as well. We'll begin with an exercise.

Exercise:
Discover Your Ideal Erotic Environment

Step 1. Sit back, close your eyes, relax, and take a deep breath. In your mind's eye visualize an imaginary place in which you'd most want to make love. Is it on a tropical beach? An ancient erotic temple? Is it on a cloud? In a leathery dungeon? Is there a canopy bed, or are you lying in soft green moss? Do bright colors predominate, or is it mostly black, or white, or are there muted tones and soft pastels? What is the light like? Bright and sunny, or dark and mysterious? Note the temperature. If there is bedding, is it femme-y chintz or L.L. Bean flannel? Let your imagination go and daydream it. Whatever comes to mind as the imaginary place you'd like to be in when making love, that is your Ideal Erotic Environment.

Step 2. Take a very critical look at your actual bedroom, as it exists. Is it truly a place where you can easily be sensual with someone? Or are there newspapers on the bureau, overflowing ashtrays lining the floor, kids' toys strewn around the bed? Maybe your space is neat and clean but simply not sexy, or it has no real personality or self-expression, or it's dominated by a television set. What are your bedroom's lighting, temperature, textures, and colors like?

Step 3. Make a list of ten things you can do to make your bedroom more like your ideal erotic environment. What can you physically do to make it more enticing?

1. _____
2. _____
3. _____
4. _____
5. _____
6. _____
7. _____
8. _____
9. _____
10. _____

Step 4. DO the things on your list, or at least some of them.

Feather Your Love Nest

I hope that making your list was easy. But if not, here are some ideas. If you imagined a tropical beach as your ideal lovemaking environment, you could add a few exotic plants, seashell decorations, a beaded curtain, and some ocean-themed artwork. If you imagined a dungeon, you might want to get rid of your cute stuffed animals and add a few black leather pillows, paint your bed frame black, put a red lightbulb in your lamp, and get some chrome nightstands. If you imagined making love while floating on a puffy white cloud during a hot and sunny day, why not paint some clouds on your ceiling, add some angel art, put on some extrasoft white sheets, fill a vase with white plumes, and put the heater on high? The idea is not just to redecorate your bedroom but to sensualize it so that it matches your erotic impulses and fantasies.

I understand that there are perhaps some limiting considerations to creating a sexier boudoir. If you have guests and you show them your bedroom, they might be shocked at how sexy it is. But so what if they think you enjoy sex and they get mildly titillated? Enjoy their reactions. Maybe you'll inspire them to sensualize their own bedrooms.

If your budget is limited, that's absolutely no excuse. Changing your space doesn't have to be expensive. There's always Target or thrift shops. Candles and peacock feathers are cheap. Creativity and an inexpensive glue gun raise the caliber of your erotic space.

On the other hand, if you have lots of money and want to hire an interior decorator, be sure you find one who you sense is sex-positive, one with whom you can feel comfortable discussing your design needs. (And by all means, if you do have a lot of money, spend a chunk on your boudoir! It's an investment that will pay many rewards.) According to most practitioners of feng shui, the Chinese art and philosophy of home decoration and place-ment that recommends arranging furniture and objects in such a way as to maximize one's highest potential, the bedroom is the most important room in the house.

While creating an erotic environment is a highly personal and individual matter, some changes are simple common sense, and some are even mandatory. Here are some common problems and important must-dos for creating a sexier bedroom:

Closet the TV

Before: You've got a big television in your bedroom, and it always seems to be the center of attention. I enjoy a good TV show as much as the next person, but nothing distracts from intimacy so much as the drone of the tube. Even the very presence of a TV in the room, though it is turned off, can be psychologically distracting.

After: The best thing is to either take the television out of the bedroom, or you might think about hiding it inside a cabinet. At the very least, cover it with some pretty fabric, and put a vase of flowers or a (safe) candle on top. If you are deter-mined to keep it near the bed, you could at least play some decent erotic movies on it once in a while. Or come up with some good sex games connected to what's on, like *Jeopardy* for lovers.

Before: Your bedroom feels "flat" and "boring" to be in, or you think it is too small to spend so much waking time there.

After: Add a big mirror or two. It's no accident that every good brothel and strip club is full of mirrors. Watching yourself and your lover having sex can be tremendously erotic. (If you have serious body-image issues, this one may not be for you—or maybe it is.)

Toys "R" Plus

Before: You've heard mention of sex toys, and you really don't know much about them or why you need some. Or you feel your bedroom is ill equipped. You own just one old vibrator that's dead and gathering dust.

After: Shopping for sex toys can be a wonderful erotic adventure, in and of itself. Many shops today are women owned and stocked not just with a plethora of femme-friendly items but a knowledgeable, hip staff. When they aren't in use, your toys should be wrapped in fabric or plastic bags. Dildos, emotion lotions and lubes, cock rings, handcuffs, leather gear, latex stockings, Tiger Balm, and on and on. The list of toys is endless, and more are invented each week. You can also find things around your home that can be converted for use as sex toys/tools: a piece of fur for sensual sensations, a Ping-Pong paddle for butt "massage," clothespins for nipple stimulators, an old electric toothbrush for tickling, a feather duster for teasing the skin, a carrot for a dildo, etc. In my community, these are called "pervertables."

They don't call sex toys "novelty items" for nothing. They can certainly add novel sensations and variety to your sex life.

Before: You have "convenience issues." Your sex toys, lube, and safe-sex supplies are hidden away in a variety of places around the room. Your massage oil is stored in the bathroom.

After: Create an easily accessible place near the bed with all your lovemaking supplies together, even if this means buying or building a new nightstand. Either organize all your clean toys in a nightstand drawer, or get some wicker baskets or elegant-looking storage boxes and keep them under your bed. If you want to be open and unashamed of your sex life (which is my recommendation—if you don't have kids), keep your toys displayed on their own special shelves by the bed. You certainly won't always want to use sex toys every time you make love—but it's nice to have them close at hand when you want them.

Before: You have much more serious "convenience issues." You own an excellent electric vibrator, as everyone should—but it is tucked away in a drawer, with its cord wound tightly around it, and the cord isn't long enough for the vibrator to reach you anywhere on the bed.

After: Keep an extension cord on your vibrator and keep it plugged in and stored near your pillow at all times. If you're going for a Western theme, you might hang a holster from your bedpost and keep your vibrator hanging in it.

By the way, do be sure you do have an excellent vibrator. If you have tried one or two types, you haven't tried them all. Some vibrators are pretty useless. Most of the women I know love the Hitachi Magic Wand, the Rabbit Pearl, and the Wahl Coil the best. There was a serious outcry a few years ago from clit-conscious consumers when it was thought that Hitachi had stopped production of its Magic Wands. The Hitachi is the Rolls-Royce of vibrators. If it's too strong at first, you can put a soft cloth between you and it while you are getting used to it.

A good vibrator and some dildos are a must for a man to have, too—for using with his woman as well as on himself. Besides using a vibrator for sexual pleasure, you can also massage tense shoulders. Very important.

Sheri came from an extremely conservative family that taught her that sex was "dirty" and "sinful" unless she was married and procreating. Having not yet married or procreated, she had lived a pretty sexless life. She came to me because she was "fed up with being pent up" and was ready to date and have some sexy fun. However, she still felt strongly that she didn't want to have intercourse until she was married.

After

We began by looking at what party poopers might be raining on Sheri's parade (Step 3). As it turned out, there were several, and we confronted and kicked out all of them. Next, we expanded her idea of what "sex" was, exploring EnergySex so that she could start enjoying erotic pleasures right away and without intercourse (Step 1). Finally, she selected some attractive possibilities from the "spa relationship menu" (Step 8) and got up the courage to go on some dates. Some of these dates were actually quite erotic and sexy, and all without intercourse. Sheri soon found her man and told me she was having spectacular sex beyond her wildest dreams. I couldn't help but notice that she was positively glowing.

Before

Sandra, a physical trainer, was very physical but not very sexual. She'd had some horrible sexual experiences in the past, and whenever she attempted to have sex, it wasn't pleasurable, but mostly emotionally painful and scary. Sandra had shut down her sexuality completely. She had processed her sexual traumas in talk therapy for years, and was ready to move on. She came to me because she wanted to find a lover and to learn to be able to have orgasms.

After

First, we talked about how Sandra might make over her mind (Step 1) so that she might see all that had happened to her as an opportunity to learn and grow. Then it was time for her to begin to reawaken her sexual self. I sent her shopping online for a good-quality vibrator and a few appealing sex toys, which I encouraged her to play with on a regular and steady basis. I also gave her a book full of erotic fantasies by way of example and encouraged her to explore her own fantasies freely while masturbating (Step 2). Finally, I gave her more information about what orgasm actually is (Step 12) and then explored with her all the various kinds of orgasms there are (Step 13). After just a few weeks, she told me that she was having many great orgasms and had asked herself "to go steady." She was also feeling less desperate, and much closer to finding a lover.

Before

Lilly came to my Sluts and Goddesses workshop, which her friend had taken and recommended enthusiastically. Lilly wanted to learn about ecstasy breathing (Step 6) and energy orgasms (Step 13). She also mentioned that sex with her boyfriend wasn't all she knew it could be.

After

Lilly found that creating sexy alter egos was very liberating (Step 2). Pictured here are Lilly's slut persona, "Tammy Tornado," and her goddess persona, "Lady Lilith."

She discovered that she absolutely loved utilizing erotic costumes and props to enhance lovemaking, which she had never really dared do before. She even gave her bedroom a makeover, designing it to be more erotic and conducive to sensual and sexy fun (Step 7). Needless to say, Lilly's boyfriend responded to all her changes enthusiastically.

Before

Karla, a legal secretary, was miserable when I met her. She had a very sexual side and thoroughly enjoyed sex, but her live-in boyfriend constantly put her down, continually telling her to lose weight. He would rarely have sex with her, let alone make love to her. She came to me to learn how to "ask for what I want and need sexually" (Step 5).

After

It turns out that what Karla really needed was a lot more than good communication skills (Step 5). What she needed was to finally see that her boyfriend was an abusive, freeloading lout and that she needed to dump him—which she did. That done, we immediately started working on rebuilding her self-esteem and creating a better body image (Step 4). I suggested that she seek out a lover who preferred and enjoyed having sex with a large, curvy woman, and she did. Bob worshiped every inch of her . . . often. Plus, he encouraged her to experiment. She discovered her inner dominatrix alter ego, "Ilsa," and had a blast with her (Step 2). Last, I encouraged her to dump the dorky hairdo and get some hair extensions, which made her "feel ultra sexy and glamorous." Bob further contributed by gleefully giving her a new pubic hairdo (Step 7). Karla now had the spectacular sex life she desired and she was thrilled . . . as was her new boyfriend.

Before

Craig and Jo Anne were down to once a month or less for sex and feared they were "drifting apart." With a one-year-old baby and full-time jobs they had very little spare time. But they were still very much in love, and wanted help in reigniting their passion.

After

First I suggested my Prescription to Reincarnate from Bed Death, which they tried, and it definitely got the ball rolling (Step 9). One thing they realized was that if Jo Anne gave up a bit of her reading time and Craig his TV time, they'd have plenty of time for love. Craig and Jo Anne were also interested in spirituality, so I suggested they try taking a Tantra workshop together. They signed up for a Tantra for Couples weekend in sensuous Hawaii, and the workshop opened up whole new erotic worlds for them. For one thing, they discovered that Jo Anne had a desire to be sensuous with another woman. Craig was not just supportive but titillated by the idea. They decided to become an "adventurous monogamous couple" (Step 8). Their home fires are burning quite nicely again.

Ron and Ruth were stockbrokers and very career focused. Ruth felt that Ron didn't pay enough attention to her or listen to her. Ron felt that she was constantly nagging him and being needy. This was putting a damper on their sex life. "We need a sex-life makeover!" they told me.

After

We spent several sessions working on Ron and Ruth's communication skills. They found the Lover's Mad Lib quite helpful for resolving conflicts and processing hurt feelings, and they particularly loved the "One of the Things I Love About You Is . . ." game, (both in Step 5). I filled Ron in on how important positive emotional interactions are in terms of making a relationship work and Ruth learned how to love herself up more, so she wouldn't be so dependent on Ron for all her emotional needs (Step 9). The benefit: Spectacular Sex!

Before

When Joy came to one of my workshops, she had the idea in her head that she had to learn to look like a centerfold model in a men's magazine to become more sexually attractive to her boyfriend. But she felt absolutely silly and ridiculous when she tried (see her here in her classic slut lingerie). Joy was trying to act like someone she really wasn't.

After

Instead of teaching Joy the ins and outs of garter belts, stockings, and centerfold poses, we worked on finding her own inner truth (Step 1). Creating a sexpot profile helped her on her way (Step 2). Very soon, Joy began to develop a sexual identity and style which was uniquely her own. She felt empowered and sexier than ever. Now she's happy with herself, and it has really rubbed off on her boyfriend, so to speak.

Before

When Nora came to me she was an introverted twenty-three-year-old student. She was absolutely gorgeous and sexy but always hid it behind baggy clothing and behind her computer screen, hanging out in chat rooms. Nora needed some money fast to finish college and, having often fantasized about becoming an erotic dancer in a gentlemen's club, she had applied for a job and gotten it. But she was terrified to start and wanted some "moral support."

After

We began by creating a slut alter ego named Juicy Lucy to help free Nora up (Step 2). We then took a look at the rich history of erotic dance and watched some erotic dancers at work. I taught her how to circulate her sexual energy to energize her body (Step 6). Last, we practiced some communication skills so that she could learn to say "no" when necessary (Step 5). Off to work she went. Over the next four months Nora had a good time on the job and made even more money than she needed, but quickly tired of working in a bar and quit her job. Yet through the pole dancing she had discovered that she absolutely loved performing, and that she had a talent for acrobatics. So after she graduated from college she became a trapeze artist and joined a small circus. Today she's ecstatically happy, and doesn't even miss having a computer.

Before

Mr. and Mrs. Elton had very serious professional white-collar jobs. They had sex occasionally, but mostly out of a sense of duty. Basically, they took sex far too seriously to have any fun.

After

Clearly the Eltons needed to learn how to play and lighten up. They came to me for fourteen sessions, and each week I took them through one of the Spectacular Sex steps. In addition, I gave them some fun "home-work." For the first few weeks I found that they were taking their homework just a little too seriously, so I finally resorted to lending them my game of Twister. I asked them to play it for half an hour every day for the next week. They ended up having lots of silly sexy fun that week, which led to some big breakthroughs. In the end, the Eltons realized that sex could be the equivalent of adult play. At our last session, they told me some of their friends had been commenting on how young they were looking. Someone even asked if they'd both had plastic surgery!

Before

Julie had enjoyed sex with her husband over many years. But a radical hysterectomy had led to the loss of much of her pleasurable physical sensation and she really didn't enjoy intercourse that much anymore. She was also having a problem with vaginal dryness. Her husband was complaining. He "missed making love" to her and was, as he put it, "not a happy camper."

After

Julie and I looked at various desire discrepancy solutions (Step 9) and I also suggested she practice the clit/mind connection exercise and ecstasy breathing so that she could explore getting turned on using just her mind and her breath (Step 6). I taught Julie and her husband sexual massage, which they took to fabulously, and which became their new primary sexual activity (Step 11). I also introduced her to some of the excellent lubricants available today, which she had never tried before. Peace was restored and camping was fun again.

The Naked and the Bed

Before: Your bedding isn't conducive to lovemaking. Your sheets aren't sexy, and your bedspread is synthetic and scratchy to lie on.

After: True, there can be a certain sleazy charm to stained, ripped old sheets. But do you really want to invite someone to make love on them on a regular basis? Maybe you need new sheets. If you have a scratchy polyester bedspread, seriously consider getting a soft, inviting spread, which feels nice to lie naked on.

Before: Your bedroom is no place for "family drama." But you have photos of your mom and dad in your bedroom.

After: Parents are absolutely wonderful, but do you really want them watching over you while you are having sex? Probably not! Keep family photos in the den or on the piano, and in your bedroom hang erotic or romantic art, such as a Georgia O'Keeffe flower print, or any art that hints of the phallic or vaginal, or that speaks of love and romance.

Dim the Lights, Fan the Flames

Before: You're no lighting designer, and your bedroom has one overhead light with an on/off switch and a bright lamp for reading next to the bed.

After: Sexy lighting is essential for creating a sensual atmosphere. At the very least, put a dimmer switch on your overhead and add another, smaller lamp with a pinkish bulb—pink light is flattering to most skin tones. You can't go wrong with some white Christmas lights. Better yet, if you can afford it, consider hiring a professional lighting designer to really create drama and mood.

Tantra teacher Jwala is a master at creating a sensuous bedroom, and she takes it to the nth degree. Just walking into her bedroom, one feels aroused. It's like a fancy harem, filled with erotic statues and art. If you lie down on her bed and look up at her ceiling, you see a huge *yoni* (that's Sanskrit for "vulva") fashioned out of velvety fabrics, with a mirrored ball as the clitoris. She has beautiful, exotic handmade silk sheets and pillows. Not everyone has the talent, desire, or money to create such an elaborate boudoir, but we can at least improve on what we have. Simply aim to transform your bedroom into a space that's more seductive, sensual, and supportive of lovemaking. I guarantee you'll be glad you did.

Body, Baubles, and Beads

Making love is an art, and your body is your primary canvas. Its curves, hills, and valleys offer a multitude of opportunities to be playful, expressive, and provocative. I'm going to leave the basics of simple hygiene and skin care to you and move on to some of the more exotic aspects of body décor.

The first thing to understand is that tastes and styles of body adornment and display change with the times. In the hit show *Chicago* there's a line in one of the songs that reads, "I'm gonna rouge my knees." During the time of the show's action, the 1930s, women's legs were a major emblem of their sexuality and, not surprisingly, also considered an especially erotic zone by many. Knees had only recently been bared by raised hemlines. So accentuating them was considered daringly risqué. Although legs will probably never cease to be alluring, today it is women's breasts that are more eroticized. So, while attention to your breasts is perhaps the most obvious place to begin thinking about eroticizing and displaying your body, I want you to think much more broadly.

A Bosom's Buddies

Maybe you're among the millions of women who've delved into the arena of body piercing and tattooing, which many people find very sexy. If not, you can have fun with temporary tattoos and nipple jewelry that doesn't require piercing. Such nonpiercing jewelry and temporary tattoos are widely available in stores and on the Internet. Madonna and Gwen Stefani have popularized the bindi, those Indian beauty stick-ons that go on the forehead between and slightly above the eyes, so now you can easily find them in glittery designs online or in shops. Use a few to decorate your belly button, eyes, nipples, or cleavage. Another gift from India, henna paste, isn't just for hands. Use it anywhere—on the feet, calves, belly, breasts. Prior to a Hindu wedding, the bride has her hands and feet artistically and elaborately hennaed by the women in her bridal party and other women to whom she's close. It's a ritual that has the heavy erotic undertones of the handmaidens preparing the virgin (whether she really is or not) for the man who will relieve her of her virginity. For groups of women, or for a loving couple, henna-pasting each other can be an extremely erotic activity, ideally done outside on a hot summer day. Body jewelry is another delightful option. Waist chains, ankle bracelets, and toe rings beautify, highlight, and celebrate your luscious body.

Long hair extensions are fabulous fun, too, and can really make a woman feel sexy. My hairdresser (hair artist actually), Deena Davenport, does hair extensions for lots of erotic dancers. The dancers tell her that their tips actually triple after getting the extensions! Guess it's that hyperfemininity thing. (Of course, hyperfemininity isn't what a lot of women are about. I'm all for the natural look, the butch look, the sporty look, the Amazon-woman look, the androgynous look, the whatever look. It's just that those are not my specialties. These are simply suggestions, but, please, develop your own style and enjoy your own fashion truth.)

Of course, there's no reason why you shouldn't adorn your breasts, too. For example, you might rouge your nipples with lipstick, and for extra sparkle, sprinkle on some very fine glitter. Nipple adornment with pasties is a blast and can be a real turn-on. The most beautiful, best-quality pasties in the world are made by twirlygirl.net, and come with or without tassels. Their high-tech, handcrafted pasties are relatively easy to learn to tassel-twirl. Their fluffy marabou pasties are my favorites. If you don't want to mess with spirit gum on your nipples, you can use gentler eyelash glue, or for extra-easy removal, simply use a circle of tape.

Again I can hear the critic protesting: "Isn't my naked body beautiful and sexy enough as it is? Why do I need to adorn it?" And that person is right, too. You and I are magnificent when we are naked, but a steady diet of even the most delicious treat can be kept more interesting by variations in spicing and preparation. Sex goddesses have been adorning their bodies for centuries, because it looks and feels sexy, it's attractive, and perhaps most important, it communicates that you're in the mood for love.

Fluff Your Muff

Many women today experiment with pubic hairstyles. Instead of thinking of trimming your pubic hair as a "solution" to the "problem" of maintaining your bikini line, think of it as a chance to express your sexuality in a variety of new ways. Making over your muff can be hot for your lover, but it's even more luxurious and exciting for you. First do some experimentation with a pair of small, sharp scissors. An easy way to trim your pubic hair is to spread your legs over the toilet and stretch out strands of hair with one hand and clip them off with the other. Some women say that, after trimming, they feel like they've given their vulvas some breathing space for the first time in their lives, and they enjoy new, pleasurable sensations. Once you become tuned in to the appearance and feel of your newly denuded self, you will realize it's a living, breathing thing that enjoys space, air, freedom—and attention.

While a monthly trim is probably enough for most women, being clean shaven can be an even greater turn-on. You feel more naked under your clothes. You're more aware of your genitalia, and naturally that makes you feel sexier. For a partner, the unobstructed

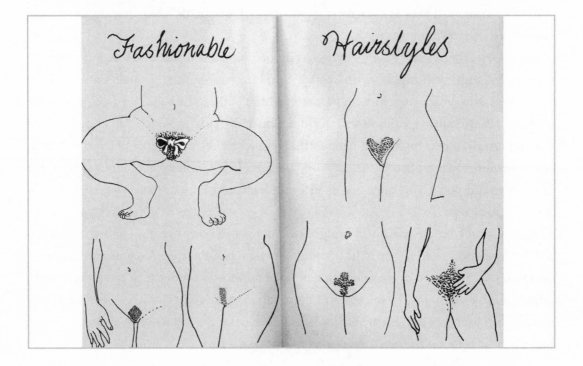

view and the prospect of not having to deal with hair in the teeth makes the pubis more lickable and the clitoris easier to find. So, if you want to go bald, here are some tips:

- Before shaving, first use scissors or clippers to trim as much pubic hair off as possible.
- Always use a brand-new, high-quality razor to avoid razor bumps.
- Take a hot bath first to soften the skin and pubic hairs.
- Rinse the razor frequently.
- Soap or olive oil sometimes works better than shaving cream.
- Be creative! You can style your pubic hair into heart shapes, diamonds, or "landing strips."
- Try the "half and half," in which you leave the top of your mons lush and bushy while shaving all around the labia.
- Experiment. Don't worry; if you aren't happy with your creation, it will grow over relatively quickly.
- Trimming and shaving *each other* is fantastic foreplay. Men enjoy a trim, too. This doubles as a good trust-building exercise or can feed into a hot dominant/submissive fantasy scenario.
- After you're shaved, powder helps soothe any bald skin and prevent red bumps. Finely ground cornstarch works well—it doesn't contain potentially irritating chemicals and perfumes, it's readily available in supermarkets, it does double duty for sensual massage, and it costs next to nothing. Some women prefer a good lotion or oil instead of powder.
- When your pubic hair is growing back out, it can get kind of itchy. Aim to eroticize the itching; let it remind you of your genitals, and let that be a turn-on.
- Some women swear by hot waxing or even plucking instead of shaving. While the effects of those techniques do last longer, this is not for the pain averse.

And if you've trimmed or shaved your bush for years, try something radically different. Let all your pubic hair grow out. I did this once, after decades of trimming, and it was a real adventure! Lots of pubic hair can be terribly exotic, especially if you're not used to it. Remember that the point of your sex-life makeover is to try something new, not necessarily to do whatever is trendy.

Each woman must learn what works best for her through a process of trial and error. For a man a trim or going bald can also feel really good and the results can be visually pleasing. But do be careful with that razor!

Dressing for Pleasure

It is a great adventure to explore the full range of erotic personas inside you. Costuming brings them out and creates the possibilities for pure magic. One of my mottoes is "Accessorize to eroticize!" The power of costumes and lingerie really hit home to me when I began teaching my Sluts and Goddesses workshops and I saw women go to amazing inner places simply by donning erotic costumes (as I described in Step 2).

Sure, being totally naked when you make love is wonderful. No doubt about it. Nude bodies are beautiful and feel divine up against each other. Costumes are in a sense superficial, just pieces of cloth. A garter belt is just a piece of fabric . . . but it conjures up associations that can make nudity seem even hotter. Think of a portrait inside a frame. Some frames are elaborate and gilded and show off the portrait in a certain way. Others are simple; still others might be whimsical. Inside the frame, the portrait remains essentially the same, but a different frame will give the entire package a different flavor. Think of costumes as frames, and the portrait in this case is your nude body. If you don't like the frame, you can always change it or take it off completely. The essential portrait, however, is always the same.

Ready-to-Wear and Dare

Let's take a critical look in your closet. How big or small is your collection of lovemaking attire? What shape is it in? How much sexy stuff do you have to wear? If you think at first that you haven't got much, you should probably think again: every woman has at least a dozen characters sitting right in her closet, personas that can be formed from what's already hanging on the racks. Consciously or not, you've accumulated the items in your wardrobe to reflect various sides of your personality. With the right kind of focus, you can create lots of sexy new outfits from the ones you have.

If you have a walk-in closet, lucky lady, just step inside. What catches your eye? What sexual activity comes to mind from an article of clothing? Which fabrics do you want to touch? Reach out and touch the first thing that draws your attention. Is it a cashmere sweater? A lacy, swirly skirt? Whatever it is, take it out. How can this piece of clothing be used? Forget preconceived notions of wearing a scarf around your neck (it can be a bra), or a skirt falling from waist to knee (it can be a strapless minidress). Make up your own uses! In this way, you will discover that most articles of clothing have many uses other than the ones for which they were intended. Spread out on your bed anything and everything that you think is sexy or has sexy potential. Begin to put together an outfit. Let a character emerge from the clothing. How does she wear the clothing you've chosen for her? How does she walk? Talk? Feel?

Ragtime

While I'd rather you discover these costumes and personas for yourself, if you're stumped I'll give you some hints: Almost any piece of fabric can be turned, with a rearranging of folds, into a toga or sari. A leotard and fringed shawl make you a Spanish dancer. Animal prints launch you into a jungle persona; flower prints take you into the Hawaiian zone. Move yourself into different historical periods by making adjustments to belts and hemlines. Go into his closet and borrow his boxer shorts. Take an old bra that's ready for the Salvation Army and cut out the cups, and—*voilà*, an entirely new look. Just one sarong can be made into at least eight different sexy outfits. (See the photos on page 160.)

The Delicious Dozen

Let's see if you can put together twelve different costumes for some different sexy personas. Here are twelve sexy archetypes and some of their sample characters. A man can

Schemata Magic

With a little of my guidance and your creativity, you can find a whole new erotic wardrobe right in your very own closet. Feel how the outfits inspire the various sexual archetypes within you. Look how just a simple sarong can make you into a slut, goddess, virgin, ancient Egyptian Queen, island girl, and sexy genie.

certainly also enjoy donning a variety of sexy costumes and personas as well, so some suggestions for men in parentheses.

1. THE ROYAL—princess, queen, C.E.O. (king)
2. THE SLUT—whore, nymphomaniac, horny housewife (stud)
3. THE MYSTIC—goddess, gypsy, tantric priestess (tantric)
4. THE HEALER—doctor, naughty nurse, psychiatrist (naughty nurse)
5. THE GENDER BENDER—butch lesbian, sailor, construction worker (male geisha)
6. THE INNOCENT—virgin, cheerleader, shy librarian (virgin)
7. THE NURTURER—breast-feeding mother, Earth mother, massage therapist (big daddy)
8. THE ANIMAL—slinky cat, dirty dog, jungle Jane (dirty dog)
9. THE DANCER—Spanish dancer, belly dancer, lap dancer (male stripper)
10. THE SENSUALIST—mermaid, movie star in a white satin negligee and fur coat, chef with delicious aphrodisiacs (nature boy)
11. THE SUBMISSIVE—French maid, sex slave, sweet biker girl (sex slave)
12. THE DOMINANT—dominatrix, wicked witch, prison matron (pimp or policeman)

For each category, choose an outfit and a character. I suggest you write them down and make notes with each one.

For example:

My Royal archetype is _____. Her/his name is _____.
She/he wears _____. She/he likes _____.
She/he feels _____. She/he _____.

Heart on Your Sleeve

Now try on some of those outfits. When you dress up in a costume, don't just don the accoutrements and remain unchanged. At least temporarily, step into the role the costume inspires—feeling, walking, talking, and acting like a barmaid, a nurse, or a dancer. Give that persona a fitting name. As you respond to your getup, imagine your character, yourself, in a sexual situation. Does she/you do anything differently from what your everyday self does? Are her/your partners different? Are there any new positions you/she wants to try out? Let your mind wander where it will; take yourself fully into the fantasy. Imagine acting it out with a lover. If you get excited, that's an excellent sign.

Embodying these personas doesn't have to feel phony or contrived. You can do it subtly and very naturally. Even without the costume. Simply be yourselves. Or, if you feel like it, take it over the top by exaggerating the archetype into a stereotype.

With a little imagination, creativity, and willingness you'll find that you will step out of your everyday reality and go somewhere very special. Growing up sexually can be child's play. Enjoy your costumes and toys.

Three Affirmations for a Prosperous Sex Life

It's worthwhile to spend money on my erotic pleasure and sexy fun.
Money spent on my sex life is a great investment in myself and in my future.
I get value from the money I spend on my sex life.

Invest in Your Sex-Life Portfolio

True, the best things in life are free. However, what you spend money on shows what you care about. How much money do you spend on your love life per month? (Maybe more money will come to you as you become more sexually satisfied and happy.)

Women especially are not taught that it's "okay to spend money on sexual pleasure." See if you can at least double what you spend on sex. It's a great investment, so then you can retire. To the bedroom, that is.

$ex-$Life $pread $heet

	WHAT I USUALLY SPEND	FUTURE SPENDING
Sex toys		
Sexy lovemaking attire		
Erotic entertainment		
Condoms		
Lubricant		
Pornography/erotica		
Gifts for my lover		
Miscellaneous sensual items		
Bath supplies		
Perfumes		
Lotions		
Books about sex		
Boudoir décor		
Beauty products		
Other		

Step Eight

Feast from the Makeover Center's Relationship Menu

Life is a banquet and most poor suckers are starving to death.
AUNTIE MAME

Woman doth not live on bread alone—not even on chocolate. Nor doth man. We do, however get much of our true nourishment from our relationships with friends, family, and lovers. What's been your nutritional state as of late? A steady diet of the love/sex combination plate or the daily blues plate not-so-special. Have you gotten your just desserts? Has your appetite been satisfied? Don't be content with scraps from the table without perhaps sampling the full menu. You are what, and whom, you eat.

Let's go to our lovely dining room back at the Sprinkle Center by the sea. Here's a menu, consisting of various types of lover relationships. Perhaps you've tried some of them before or are enjoying one of them now; perhaps there are new "recipes" you've never even dreamed of, or you want to try something new. What I suggest is that you simply read the menu and put all the information in your pot and let it stew. Then pick and choose from the menu as you like. Or stick with what's on your plate. Will you be a party of one, a party of two, or more?

One Egg Over Easy

Perfect for the party of one. You are single and content and prefer not to have a steady lover.

You may be up against tremendous social pressure and perhaps family expectations to pair up, but be strong! Don't let other people tell you how to live. Be single and proud.

When the gynecologist asks my friend Laura if she's sexually active, she says, "Yes, with myself." When you're on your own, you can get to know and enjoy yourself sexually in wonderful ways.

Being single means you can read the paper while you eat. Maybe you don't want to spend your time and energy in a full-on relationship. "Will she call?" "Does he feel the same way I do?" You might need the time to recover from a divorce, or from the death of a partner, or you prefer to work on other personal issues, such as building your financial security, or spiritual growth.

You can be single and celibate, single and looking for a lover, or single with sex on the side. You're certainly not the only single person out there. According to the census, approximately one-quarter of all adult households are single-person households.

The Celibacy Juice Fast

I've talked with so many women who go through times in their lives when they find that they've unintentionally become celibate for a year or two or five or more. It's much more common than most people realize. Rather than thinking of it as a time of "not having any sex," I like to think of it as a sort of "afterglow phase," a time of integration, of rest. Celibacy can be a phase in which you turn your focus within. For some it's a very important phase, a personal vision quest of sorts, a time for reassessing one's life.

There are several styles of celibacy. Some include masturbation; others don't. Some include flirting, and some don't. Some celibates include intimacy, sensual touch, and sleeping in bed with another person; some don't. Some people will make a conscious decision— "I'm going to be celibate until a year from today." Some just go day by day, month by month, or year by year.

There's a lot of social pressure to be sexually active, and we often put most of that pressure on ourselves. Well, *I* certainly won't put more of that pressure on you. As long as you are happy and content being celibate and you are taking good care of yourself, then go for it! Or should I say, don't go for it?

Single-Egg Omelet with Sausage or Tomato

You're single and hungry for a mate. Waiting for a lover to come along when you really want one can be agony. Use this fertile single time to prepare yourself for the lover you desire. Put your attention on improving your self-image. Fill yourself up with your own love. There's nothing wrong with devoting a whole evening, day, or weekend to your own pleasure. Think of some things you would like your lover to do and then do them for yourself. Buy yourself love gifts. Pamper yourself. Give yourself everything you need. Use the nice sheets and the fancy dishes. Wear your favorite lingerie. Build a fire and sit by it just as you might do with a lover. Take yourself walking in places you'd ideally like to walk with your lover. Masturbate regularly, with prolonged masturbation sessions every so often. You won't be pining away, wishing you had a lover so you could do these things. Relax and remember it's not wise to shop for groceries when you are starving.

If you keep yourself happy, by the time you find the right person, you won't be needy— you'll be irresistible.

Where to Shop for Ingredients— Some Ways to Fill Your Plate

1. Take time to figure out and get clear about what kind of partner you want. Here again, use the role-model idea. Watch your friends and acquaintances to see whose relationship you admire. I recommend reading Harville Hendrix's book, *Keeping the Love You Find: A Personal Guide to Creating a Lasting Relationship.* It's excellent.

2. Look through your address book and see if there's someone right in your own backyard you'd like to spend time with, and phone for a date. That's how I found my life partner—right in my very own address book.

3. Try a reputable on-line dating service. It works fantastically for many people; it can be free or cost as little as $25. I can't tell you how many happy couples I know who've met and fallen in love via the Internet. It's a fantastic place to find people who are into similar kinds of relationships and sex. (For your first dates, be sure you meet in public places to be extra safe.)

4. If you want a sexually adventurous and sex-positive partner, I highly recommend you enroll in some sexuality classes or workshops. If there is a woman-run sexuality boutique in your town, they frequently host workshops on everything from The Art of Kissing to Japanese Bondage. You might have to travel outside your town to find these, but there is a really high success rate here. Or, for your next vacation, take a tantra workshop in Hawaii. I've seen many singles fall in love at these and end up living happily ever after.

5. Use positive affirmations, such as "I am a magnet for the lover of my dreams." "I deserve a wonderful lover." "I am ready for my perfect lover." By saying these affirmations to yourself or out loud, you put the message out into the universe, which helps manifest your dream.

6. Have a party and invite all your single friends, telling them to bring some of their single friends. I've heard of parties where each single woman has to bring one nice single man, and vice versa, in order to get in.

7. Ask your friends and family to introduce you to eligible partners. Friends and family often know best; if they know you well enough, they might know who would be right for you. Think of all the cultures in which arranged marriage is common. We in the West tend to look down on this as some kind of enforced bondage, but, in fact, arranged marriages often work very nicely and have an extremely high rate of long-term success.

8. Go to in-store book signings for books that are sex related. Usually there's a Q-and-A session with the author. This is a good time to check out who is there. If there's someone who interests you, introduce yourself, and then the two of you can continue the Q-and-A discussion afterward over coffee.

9. Make the process of looking for a lover into some type of an art project. Write about it, take photos, or make a series of drawings. Write a poem or short story about each blind date. A little documentary video about yourself looking for a lover could be fabulous fun. This helps you take more initiative. This approach can also make a sometimes uncomfortable process more fun. Art skills are not necessary. You can keep your final product private or share it publicly, which could increase your chances of finding your mate.

10. Consider some kind of therapy to explore your issues and to help you learn what might be holding you back from a successful relationship. Build more self-esteem. It's when we're feeling confidant about who we are that we attract other people to ourselves and begin a healthy relationship. But who knows? You may discover you really aren't as ready for a lover yet as you thought you were.

11. Keep your sexual energy flowing. Masturbate regularly. Keep it juicy! This will help attract a mate on an energetic level.

Your sweetie could be anywhere at any time. Stay open to all possibilities, and maintain your positive attitude at all costs.

Just the Appetizers, Please

You are single and you enjoy a bit of "casual sex" until a good relationship partner comes along. You may want to keep your sex life "casual" indefinitely. The stress of a heavy meal can give you ulcers, and you may want to eat lite and avoid an upset tummy. Some treats are just too rich or too messy to be eaten on a steady basis. For others, we need time to build up a taste. Be sure to be clear about this up front with your partners, and let them know that you want to order lite, so no one will be stuck with a big check. Too often we get involved with someone who is a great sex partner but wrong in every other way. Madeline, a friend of mine, says that now, as a mature woman, good sex comes easily for her—it's negotiating everyday living with another person that she finds difficult. She's opted to stay single but have casual sex partners. But, she says, "a casual relationship doesn't have to be superficial. Just because you're not sharing *everything* with someone doesn't mean you share *nothing*." Sex and the emotions it raises bring people close no matter what the parameters of the relationship—so a casual sexual relationship can turn into a deep friendship.

Sometimes a casual sexual relationship can go on for years, deepening, without being exclusive or committed. Throughout my twenties and thirties, there was a handsome policeman in my life. I would call Officer Ray to come and make love with me. Or he would call me after a day's tour of duty. We were "fuck buddies," intimately connected by fantastic sex, and we cared about each other. But it was mutually agreed that we weren't going to have any kind of more serious relationship, let alone even go to the movies or out to dinner. Sometimes he wouldn't hear from me for a year or two or three when I was in a more committed relationship. But then when we reunited, we could pick up right where we left off. It was a very nice arrangement, which ended when I moved cross-country and said good-bye to my man in blue.

Partner Pot Roast, Home-Style Meat and Potatoes

This dish requires a party of two. It's the classic totally monogamous couple. There are many advantages to this relationship model. It serves a lot of people and is very popular at traditional celebrations such as weddings, birthdays, holiday events, and anniversary parties. Traditional monogamy is comforting and romantic. When one focuses all of one's erotic and sexual energy on one person, love and intimacy can deepen enormously in ways that only a monogamous relationship can. Some women might have desires outside of this traditional framework, but they know that emotionally they couldn't handle "a walk on the wild side." It's good to know that.

Monogamy can be restricting for some and absolute liberating for others. Boring for some, incredibly exciting for others. It's a tall order that two people can handle deliciously.

My pal Nancy recently got divorced. She had sex with just one man, her husband, for thirty-one years. Many of those years were extremely happy, and she was sexually content for a long time. However, today she is enjoying being with several different men, and monogamy is the last thing she wants. My story is just the opposite. I was wildly promiscuous for years, tasting every kind of sexual dish imaginable. Today I'm in a committed monogamous relationship and find it superexciting. When ordering such a dish, timing and what you're truly in the mood for is everything.

Steak-and-Potato Kebabs

The experimental "monogamous" couple takes the basic traditional dish but cooks it up slightly differently by adding spice and extra veggies for a more exotic result. Many women answer their call of the wild with enthusiasm and a pioneering spirit. You and your partner can agree to be monogamous and still have erotic adventures with others as a couple. For example, invite someone else, or another couple, into your bed for a sensual massage or to snuggle with you both. Or the two of you go to a sex party together and just watch. Or agree to flirt with, kiss, and touch others but not have any genital sex. Some couples consider themselves monogamous as long as genital sex is reserved for each other. When experimenting in this way, it's important that you go only as far as each of you is comfortable going. This can be tricky, since someone may *think* she/he will be comfortable with something, only to break into a sweat when the spice gets too hot. To be experimental a couple needs to have excellent communication and trust and to allow each other room to make mistakes and learn from them. The classic book *The Ethical Slut,* by wise and experienced writers Dossie Easton and Catharine Liszt, will answer all questions and prepare you for such adventures.

A high rate of "nontraditional" activity goes on in small towns and big cities, but much of it remains underground because of strong social pressures. If you want to go beyond traditional monogamy, consider what kind of support you have in your life. Do you have friends you could talk with about your experiences? Have you found an Internet community where your questions and experiences can be shared? Some couples find another couple to be "buddies" with and share support for their experimentation.

Whipped Sweet Potatoes and Fruit

Many S/M- and tantra-style activities can be nongenital, so folks feel they can consume them and still be "monogamous." I know of one couple that has been together eight years. The man loves S/M and getting his naked body flogged, while his partner is more interested in spiritual styles of sex and sensuality such as tantra. They found a conference/retreat, the annual Dark Odyssey gathering, which "brings together sexuality, spirituality, education, and play in a fun, supportive, nonjudgmental, diverse environment." They went there, agreeing that they would not have genital sex with anyone but each other but could get their desires met with other people in any other ways. So over the weekend, he got flogged by several different people, while she got to chant *om*, get fed fruit, and have some ecstatic tantric breathing sessions. Both fulfilled their desires, but without any genital sex beyond the two of them together. After the weekend, they were more in love with each other than ever.

Hot Open-Face Sandwich

This is the nonmonogamous sexually active couple with an "open relationship." This can take the form of one or the other or both partners having a mistress or stud on the side. (Interestingly, there's really no male equivalent of "mistress" in the English language.) This is where everything is out in the open and approved of by all involved.

All-You-Can-Eat Buffet

The owner of Plato's Retreat, the famed New York swing club, boasted jokingly that his club was as famous for its buffet of hors d'oeuvres as for its smorgasbord of sexual treats. It was true. People enjoy "all you can eat."

If you and your mate choose to be a nonmonogamous couple, then you have an "open relationship," each of you being free to have sex with other people. Some couples agree to have sex with others only separately from each other. Other couples agree to have sex with others only when they are together in the same room. Some couples agree to do both.

You may feel inclined to join the "Lifestyles" community, which is a huge, well-organized group of people who engage in what in decades past used to be called "swinging" or "wife swapping." The Lifestyles community holds conventions around the country and local parties in many small towns. Contrary to popular misconceptions, group sex is rarely a free-for-all where everyone consents to everything.

So what really goes on at swingers' events? Some couples switch partners, but a couple can also simply hang out and watch other couples. This is also a good place for a woman who is interested in sex with women to have that experience. The men frequently watch the women together. In this community the men are rarely, if ever, sexual with one another. A couple can maintain their relationship as their primary relationship and be "swinging" on the side. These events are frequently as social as they are sexual, with people meeting for brunch or going on sea cruises together. You can be a single woman and join in Lifestyles events—but generally not a single man.

If you're interested in swinging, you might want to attend the annual Lifestyles convention in Las Vegas. They take over an entire huge hotel, and people from all over the world come together for several days. You'll meet all types of people from a variety of groups, and it's quite interesting. You can just go and mingle with your clothes on, or you can participate in a wide array of sex parties and events.

In most big cities these days you can find sex events where there's more variety and different kinds of folks than at the Lifestyles events. There might be men with men, people practicing S/M, women-only parties, as well as groups with dancing, singing or chanting, drumming, piercing—you name it, it's out there. There are some groups that have masturbation-only parties, such as at the annual Masturbatathon, which raises money for charity. Willing participants get financially sponsored by their friends to go to the event and masturbate. What has now become a nationwide event was started by cultural sexologists Dr. Carol Queen and her partner, Dr. Robert Lawrence, and they've raised many thousands of dollars for worthy causes, and also helped to destigmatize masturbation.

Carol and Robert also host the well-known Queen of Heaven evenings in San Francisco. Their sex parties start off with a simple pagan ceremony, everyone holding hands and forming a circle. As a group they make agreements as to conduct, such as making it clear that safe sex is not an "optional" individual choice; it's a unifying point for building community and saving lives. They create a warm, inviting atmosphere that is playful and positive. Even artsy. Participants consider these sex parties a form of goddess worship; they practice the credo "All acts of love and pleasure are worship to the goddess"

There are also some wonderful hands-on sexuality workshops such as those presented by the Body Electric School of Massage, which leads guided, group erotic massage rituals throughout the USA and Europe. These events are excellent for adventurous couples as well as for singles.

Again, if you are going to have any kind of open relationship or group sex, it's of utmost importance to be really honest with each other, and clear, and keep any promises you make to each other. Make sure that both partners are getting their emotional needs met.

Polyamorous Paella

This dish has a delicious mixture of ingredients all held firmly together. In my local newspaper I read an interview with the leader of a polyamorous group who explained his polyamory this way: "Polyamory is not an alternative to monogamy. It's an alternative to cheating. For some of us monogamy doesn't work, and cheating was just abhorrent to me." Polyamory is not the same as an "open marriage." It is the philosophy and practice of loving or relating intimately to two, three, four, or a network of people all at the same time with honesty and integrity.

There are many variations of polyamorous relationships. Some require a lot of stretching, compromise, and negotiating to feel safe and to work for all involved. The key is that everyone involved know that this is the nature of the relationship and agree to it. They are in the mix together. I know one heterosexual couple that negotiated that the wife could have lover relationships only with other women, not with other men. The woman's lovers knew she was married to a man, and usually met and befriended the husband.

Some polyamorous partners make an agreement to have sex with other people only when they're out of town, because they don't want people where they live to know they have relationships with others. Some couples agree to have sex with others only when both partners are present. For some couples intercourse is only to be shared with each other, while kissing, flirting, and oral sex with others are fine. Other couples commit to their relationship being primary, while allowing each other secondary relationships; if the primary relationship gets threatened in any way, they agree to end the secondary relationship. Some polyamorous groups have worked out detailed protocols and formulas for creating successful polyamorous lifestyles. If you are interested in polyamory, I suggest learning about these protocols.

There's actually a lot of crossover between polyamory and swinging. It's not as though they are two opposed groups. Polyamory is not necessarily about group marriages, triads, or multiple relationships only. It's more about being open and honest and preferring emotional connection with sex and having agreements and negotiations be aboveboard and consensual for all involved. Whereas some swingers are basically into recreational sex, "polys" have recreational emotional intimacy and then sometimes take it to sex as well.

Poisonous Mushrooms

Some meals are less nourishing than others. This one is downright dangerous, and for a cheater it is haute cuisine. The "shrooms" are gathered in dark hidden places, and the sneaking around continues in their consumption. Although these "shrooms" can even be deadly, a whole lot of people dare to eat them. There is a nonconsensual aspect to cheating that can wreck a good relationship and tear a family apart. People can get horribly hurt. Often cheating occurs when a person is feeling trapped in a relationship or looking for adventure. Cheating can happen when a person wants a radical sex-life makeover but doesn't know how to get it another way.

A kinder, gentler form of cheating is when there's an unspoken, or a spoken, agreement to "don't ask and don't tell." The couple assumes they are monogamous but knows something could happen outside the relationship with one or the other partner, and neither would want to know about it.

Some people cheat and "accidentally" get caught, which can add drama, shake things up, and raise passion levels in the relationship. Cheating can also be used for revenge. Occasionally cheating can ultimately help a relationship get the attention it needs to improve—but there are much better ways to accomplish this.

I can't imagine having a sexual affair on the side if I have promised to be monogamous. I'd die of the stress and guilt, and I'm such a lousy liar that I'd certainly get caught. If I wanted sex with more than just my partner, then arranging for an open relationship right off the bat seems so much less messy and easier to me. But my friend Barbie defends her cheating. She tells me she loves the drama and excitement and swears that it's the best kind of sex, that the sneaking around and doing something "forbidden" make sex much hotter for her. I'll leave the ethics up to you.

Hot Tart

You can also be the "other woman" or the "other man." My friend Dolores French loves the relationship she's had with a married man. "It is very dangerous and safe at the same time.

There's the element of getting caught and then what would happen? I've developed a real liking for this kind of relationship, although I didn't plan it. It's lasted for years, and I know it wouldn't last if I became the main partner. We would probably both get bored with each other. I find it easy to be in love with another woman's husband, because you don't have all the other mundane responsibilities and daily stuff." Again, I leave the ethics up to you.

Purely Platonic Pasta

This can be a very filling dish. Some folks might consider "platonic lovers" to be an oxymoron. But it's possible to have a good, long, romantic, affectionate, satisfying lover relationship with everything that entails, including marriage and living together, but without any sex. Some people might have an extremely low libido or simply not have any interest in sex, or really not like sex, or one partner has a serious illness and sexual relations have come to an end. Or the couple may just be done with the sexual part of their relationship and simply not have any desire for that type of intimacy.

If both partners are indeed happy with such an arrangement, then, this can work out fine. Who says a couple *has to* have sex? But if one or the other is having difficulties with the arrangement, then this is not a very good option and adjustments need to be made, perhaps a little sauce puttanesca. Provided in the form of a professional sex worker or erotic masseur for one or the other partner.

Usually it is men who have sex with prostitutes, and many are married men. In most cases, their wives have no idea their husbands use such services. But in some relationships, the husband is perfectly up front, and it's fine with the wife. Women who know their husbands have sexual tastes or needs that they don't share may be relieved that they're getting their needs met by professionals. Since their husbands are buying a service, they may not consider this "cheating." They know that sex workers usually have their own relationships and rarely get romantically involved with clients. Wives, too, can take advantage of such services. Believe it or not, these days there are some wonderful men and women who service women's sexual needs and do a fine job, with great integrity. Such a couple could say they were "emotionally monogamous," since the sexual aspect of their relationship isn't as important to them.

Platonic Pasta Arrabiata

This is the nonsexual primary relationship with hot sex on the side. This is another kind of nonsexual lover relationship, where a couple that was at one time sexual now feels fine about letting go of their not-so-hot sexual relationship in order to stay life partners, to co-parent, or to be in a romantic friendship. They don't want to split up, but they don't have sex together. However, if one partner really desires sex and the other partner isn't interested or available, then it's probably best to let the lover know and perhaps he/she would consider your having another lover—while keeping the relationship intact (or vice versa). There's no way to find out if you don't have the courage to ask and discuss it.

I know a married couple who've been together for over twenty-five years. During that time they started and built up a magazine; raised two children; ran a horse ranch; and, at different times, engaged in being experimental, being open, and being totally monogamous. They explored all kinds of sexual permutations, including threesomes, swinging with other couples, and S/M. Throughout it all they remained madly in love and lust with each other.

But as they entered middle age and she went through menopause and he through manopause, they both began to lose interest in sex—with each other. They found that they could occasionally get turned-on to other people for one-night stands or casual relationships that lasted a few months. After holding a second wedding ceremony in which they renewed their commitment to stay together, they allowed each other to have these kinds of independent affairs. Because they were so secure in each other's love and commitment, they have been able to maintain this arrangement for many years now. They're best friends and are now grandparents who share all kinds of interests and activities. Every once in a while they watch porn videos and masturbate together—but otherwise their sexual activity occurs outside the marriage.

Cherry Jell-O

This choice is favored by people involved in a friendship that has erotic undertones. Friendship. It's sweet, but if you let it get too hot it melts. The erotic friendship occurs when sexual energy and erotic love exist between the two people but, for one reason or another, having actual physical sex is not a good idea. This kind of relationship is grounded in EnergySex, as mentioned in Step 1.

For example, when I was in college I had a huge crush on one of my teachers. Though he was single, it would have been inappropriate for us to be lovers. Besides the fact that he was my teacher, he was a strict Catholic and didn't believe in sex outside of marriage. However, there was no denying that we wanted to spend time together, and there was definitely a very warm, romantic, and erotic element to our connection. So, after the semester was over, I suggested that we enjoy an "erotic platonic relationship." He agreed. So, we would go out on romantic dates, hold hands, flirt, tease, but not kiss or go any further. And it was just perfect! Very delicious.

Another example was how my friend Veronica, a sultry brunette, and her friend Craig, a handsome blond, were very drawn to each other, though he was gay. On a visit to Jamaica, they rose early each morning to watch the sunrise as Craig "the Golden Dolphin" carried Veronica on his back across the pool. People of different sexual orientations can make great erotic friends.

Sometimes this is a good arrangement when you have an enormous crush on a co-worker, or your doctor. You can agree, verbally or implicitly, to spend time together as erotic platonic lovers.

Virtual Cookies

This is the latest in nouveau cuisine. These kinds of lovers are found all over the Internet.

I know a woman who has had nothing but virtual relationships, in a serial monogamous fashion. She never meets the men in person but goes through the dating process, sex (cyber sex), and the breakup—all online. She claims she truly enjoys this kind of love affair. I also know of a couple that consider themselves monogamous but enjoy cybersex together with other couples.

Another form of virtual lover could be someone who carries on a lover relationship totally on the phone and never meets the object of his/her affection.

One of the major drawbacks of a virtual lover is that there is no body-to-body contact. When it comes to sex, a body is a nice plus. In fact, some people might think that bodyless sex is another oxymoron. But as somebody pointed out, a lot of great sex takes place "between the ears." For some people sex is more of a mental, than physical, activity; for those people, virtual sex works very nicely.

Are You Ready to Order?

These are just some of the offerings on the relationship menu. The important thing to realize is that you can always whip up a recipe that suits your individual tastes, needs, desires, circumstances, and personality. You have choices, and every choice has its advantages and disadvantages. Just know that you don't have to potluck.

Step Nine

Resolve Any Troubles in Paradise

Sex is emotion in motion.
MAE WEST

Come into my office. Here, lie down on this nice leather couch and relax. Yes, love is grand, but sometimes things come up that can push your love off track. Let's take a look and see if you have any issues or concerns that are getting in the way of having a spectacular sexual relationship. Tell me what your issues are, and I'll suggest some ways to manage or resolve them.

Is your lover right for you, and are you right for your lover? If you and your lover are in a really bad, mismatched relationship, no amount of sexual skill will help make it better unless you get to the roots of your problems. But if you are basically well matched, boredom can transform into excitement, frustration can change to lubrication, and dry spells can become big wet spots.

The Couple That Plays Together . . .

The most successful lover relationships I've seen are when a couple shares the same enthusiasm for a particular kind of sex or sexual lifestyle. Lover relationships can also work very well when one of the duo has a strong sexual desire of some kind and the other is supportive because she/he wants the other partner to be happy and satisfied. For example, if your husband wears your dress.

My dear friend Veronica Vera, dean of Miss Vera's Finishing School for Boys Who Want to Be Girls, believes that "for every woman who burned her bra, there is a man eager to wear one." Some studies say one in ten men cross-dresses. Perhaps your partner is part of this very big sorority: men who feel a strong need and take great pleasure in wearing women's clothes. The first thing to understand is that this is part of your man's sexual makeup; it's most likely been with him since childhood and is not likely to disappear. If you are at least supportive and nonjudgmental of your transvestite man, chances are you can work things out. The very best way you can be supportive of your mate is to be very clear as to your own needs, particularly your sexual needs. It's much easier to be kind and loving when you are feeling fulfilled.

You could really benefit from encouraging your husband to enjoy this sexual interest when he is with you. Often husbands "bribe" their brides into allowing them to dress, by doing a lot of the housework and cooking, leaving you much more time to indulge in more luxurious activities. But if you really don't want to do that, you can also encourage him to join a support group/social club, like those found in many major cities. Most have groups for wives, and great friendships can develop. Wives are always invited to accompany their husbands to Miss Vera's Finishing School. When Lauren sent her husband, Dee, to the school, she told him it helped her feel more free herself to evolve sexually within their relationship. She was allowing herself a makeover by being understanding of his.

Uptight or Tight Waist?

A prime example of resolvable differences is the story of my friend Antoinette. Early in her marriage, she was totally put off by her husband's strong interest in seeing women dressed up in lace-up corsets and high-heeled boots. He wanted her to wear corsets and boots as much as possible. At first she resisted, but eventually she began to dress up to please him. She soon found that it really turned HER on. She was reminded of her childhood and the many happy hours she spent dressing her dolls in sexy clothes of her own design. A few years later she started her own fetish fashion business, Versatile Fashions, and fetish clothing became her passion and life's work. She made many wonderful lifelong friends in the fetish-fashion world, and her business became hugely successful. Her corsets are now sold in Nordstrom's and Victoria's Secret and worn by celebrities like Madonna, Nicole Kidman, and Donna Summer.

Runaround Sue

You need to decide if your different sexual interests are deal breakers or not. Some definitely are. For example, if your partner has a strong desire to go out and explore sex with other people when you want a totally monogamous relationship, it might be best if *both* of you find more like-minded partners—unless there are some very compelling reasons to work things out, such as having had children together. If you are the partner wanting to be with others, be sure you examine your motivations. It may be that you simply need some time away from your partner or an ego boost. There might be ways to satisfy your needs without getting sexually involved with other people and ending an otherwise good relationship. But if you can't work things out, you must stand up for yourself and your needs and have no shame about your interests.

Most people in monogamous relationships are sexually attracted to other people from time to time, but they don't act on that attraction because they enjoy monogamy, choose to honor that trust, and don't want to risk complicating or losing their primary relationship.

They forgo hot and quick sexual gratification for the benefits of a long-term commitment. Only you know what's negotiable for you and what isn't.

Voyage to the Bottom of the Sea (of Love)

Having a good sex life doesn't necessarily mean that there aren't challenges and adjustments to make. This is normal. You can have a fantastic relationship and still get hung up on some sexual thing or other. Perhaps you are changing, and what worked for you and your partner before doesn't work anymore. A sexual relationship goes through phases, and sometimes it has to get worse or may even "hit bottom" before it can get better. Consider this: A 1999 article in the *Journal of the American Medical Association* reported that a third of the men and almost half of the women surveyed (ages eighteen to fifty-nine) said they had a sexual problem ("dysfunction") within the last year. Sometimes you can feel that your sexual problems are the end of the world, but they're probably not. Perfectly functional couples have difficulties from time to time.

Work with Me, Baby

Sexuality is fertile ground for gathering self-knowledge, and it's the bumps in the road that remind us there's something here worth examining. So remember to try to welcome sexual issues as opportunities to learn, grow, and build trust.

Compromise is sometimes a perfect strategy for working out differences. Once I was in a monogamous relationship living with a woman for three years who'd had sexual trauma in her past: Her stepfather had sexually and emotionally abused her. We had a great erotic connection, but she couldn't handle it when things got too hot and heavy and I displayed my intense sexual energy, wild abandon, and total surrender. It scared her. However, she was a champion snuggler and very affectionate. So when we made love I stuffed my sexual power and energy in order to make her feel safe. I didn't know if my patience would ever pay off. The good news was that, by putting the brakes on some aspects of my sexuality, I developed others: I became much more sensitive and developed a more intuitive gentle touch. In time I, too, became a champion sensitive snuggler. As trust developed between us, eventually she became comfortable with more intense sexual energy, including her own. It was a win-win situation in the long run, sex became really good, and we eventually became quite well matched. (When we split up it was for other reasons.)

You might have to compromise in some way, either temporarily, as I did, or permanently. In cases like these, you need to ask yourself if the compromise is worth it. Often it is, but when it's not, people are likely mismatched and both people ultimately end up happier with someone else.

Wandering Eyes

It's completely normal to be jealous at some time or another in a relationship. It's all right to ask your partner for reassurance: "Honey, seeing you talking with that cute blond checkout girl made me a little jealous. I'm still the one who floats your boat, right?" Maybe you're not in a good place in your life to be able to let your partner flirt with other women. It's perfectly okay to say "I need you not to flirt with other women right now. It hurts me."

If you go crazy when your partner shows interest in other women/men, consider that sometimes just looking is enough. Your partner may be telling the truth when she/he says she/he's "just looking."

Green Eyed and Going for It

Some jealousy can be a turn-on. Try this out: When your lover flirts with the checkout girl, don't say a word. Later on, when you're in bed, include her in your hot talk: "You really get turned-on by that sexy blond checker, don't you? I saw you looking down her blouse. . . ." If your lover gets turned-on and you feel those jealous sensations, incorporate them into the sex. Express your feelings with your body (and I don't mean by hitting him/

her over the head!). Chances are, when you think of your lover wanting, or even having, someone else, the jealousy will intensify your passion.

Of course, this might not work for you. You might find jealousy a complete turnoff, or be too upset by it even to think about having sex. If so, you won't want to even attempt to use jealousy in an erotic way.

I happen to love it when my partner gets a little bit "jelly" if someone flirts with me. It makes me feel desired and extra sexy. We play with the eroticism of jealousy. I honestly enjoy it when my partner looks lustfully at others. But then I'm very secure in my current relationship, and I trust my partner wholeheartedly and want my partner to be happy. I've also been in situations where a partner's jealousy was not just uncomfortable but threatening and scary. There's no doubt that jealousy can be destructive and painful in some situations.

Steamed and Steamy

For some people, it's fine and natural to express and even work out feelings—for instance, anger—they're having toward one another during sex. Some people can manage to have "angry sex"—and I don't mean beating up your partner; I mean just feeling the anger in the way you move, in your touches and facial expressions, maybe even verbally. Anger generates energy. For some people, though, the idea of allowing anger into the sexual arena is anathema. If you and your partner are okay with the idea of expressing such emotions with your lovemaking, then you need to give yourself permission, to know that it is okay.

Jealousy can also be an incredible teacher. We can learn a lot about our insecurities, our fears, our passion, and ourselves by witnessing our jealousies. Ever notice how you can be a single person and be jealous of couples? Or be a couple and be jealous of single people?

If jealousy is a big issue for you or your lover, it's well worth making the effort to learn more about it and how to manage it. There are some very effective techniques available for managing jealousy. Seek these out and use them.

Is It Bed Death or Is It Just Life?

Have you been in a long-term relationship? If so, then you probably know how you inevitably go through periods of low attraction or even complete disinterest in sex with your partner, falling in and out of lust with each other. At times you'll wonder if it's all over, if you should have an affair or end the relationship. Other times you are actually so happy, content, and in your hearts that it's hard to get back down into your genitals. Being madly in love doesn't necessarily make for hot sex either. Or libidos can simply be low.

It's perfectly okay and often very helpful, particularly in long-term relationships, to take some breaks from sex. It's the judgments about the breaks that are troublesome. So try not to judge, but be compassionate about whatever is going on at the time. A successful relationship is one in which both partners understand that levels of sexual attraction rise and fall, so that during a lull they don't panic but tell themselves—and each other—that this, too, shall pass. It's good to acknowledge and talk about the fact that there's a lull and set a time when you might try to restart your engines.

If you both share the idea that sex in a relationship is an important family value, then you can do what you need to do to "keep it up." When there's a will, there are plenty of ways.

Better and Better

The good news is that, despite the lulls, some couples tell me that they have better sex the longer they stay together, even after thirty, forty, or fifty years. This is one area where I don't have personal experience; however, it is my current goal. Some couples who do stay together tell me that when the infatuation aspect of the courtship period died down, the sexual relationship developed more intimacy, depth, and comfort. Clearly it is possible that sex in very long-term monogamous relationships can be magnificent. The eroticism of being with someone for so long, someone with whom you've built a lifetime of trust, someone who knows every inch of your body and how to make it sizzle, over and over . . . ah, it excites me just to think about it. How about you?

Ways to Turn a Dry Spell into a Wet Spot

Has sex in your relationship become too much effort, too mechanical, too predictable, too goal driven? Here are some things you can try:

- *Unwind to Wind Up.* Get completely relaxed and more connected with each other before delving into sexual activities. Sometimes it's from this very relaxed connection that eroticism emerges. Try a longer than usual period of just lying side by side, kissing, looking lovingly into each other's eyes, and hugging—for half an hour, at least.
- *Quickies.* Add lots more brief sensual and sexual moments throughout your day and night, playfully grab your lover's butt, pull up his or her shirt and suck a nipple, feed a grape, lick an armpit, scratch a neck and shoulders, flash a private body part . . . These sparks add up to igniting more passion.
- *Jazz It Up.* Are you both simply being lazy? Put more effort into it. Wake up! What you put into it is what you get out of it. Just do it, and give it your best.
- *Take In a Matinee.* Try new things. New things add excitement, curiosity, and energy. Draw upon some of your creativity.
- *Change Your Clock.* Most people think of having sex at night, when they are the most tired. If possible, why not have sex in the middle of the day.
- *Deep Throat.* Perhaps you need to communicate more about your sex life in deeper and more honest ways. Maybe you are hiding something from each other, or from yourself, and it needs to be revealed. Review Step 5 if you need to.
- *Dramatic Flair.* Create some sparks of excitement. Sex therapist and visionary Jack Morin, Ph.D., did a study of what people's most exciting

peak sexual experiences were. And in most cases there was some obstacle that created great excitement: like longing, anticipation, violating prohibitions, searching for power.

- *Sleep Around.* Change your environment. Rent a hotel room, take a little road trip, find a hot-tub place with private rooms by the hour. Do it in the bathtub or shower. A deserted beach or remote place in the woods almost always guarantees great lovemaking.

- *Pump It Up.* Try out a CTD (clitoral therapy device), a.k.a. "clit pump," which is a little suction cup that you or your lover puts on your clitoris, then you suction out the air, and your clitoris gets "sucked" and gets very erect and throbby. The CTD is prescribed by a medical doctor, used for "female sexual dysfunction," and costs hundreds of dollars. But you can get a similar and equally good version that does the exact same thing for around forty bucks at a decent sex-toy shop or online. Although not that widely used, some women swear by them, saying they are very arousing and increase sensation and lubrication.

- *Easy Does It.* If you've gotten into goal-oriented sex, both always pushing for orgasm, then decide simply to pleasure each other without orgasm for several sessions. Build up the charge. It sounds really simple, but it's quite effective.

- *Take Some Space.* David Schnarch is a marriage counselor and sex therapist. In his book *Passionate Marriage* he talks about how couples can creatively use space and individuation (NOT more merging) to rekindle the spark in their sex lives.

Desire Discrepancy Solutions

About how often do you ideally like to have sex? How often does your lover ideally like to have sex? (If you really don't know, ask.) Are your answers both the same or quite different? Usually, especially in long-term relationships, one partner desires more or less sex than the other. (Interestingly, the person who wants sex the least often is actually the one in control of the couple's sex life.) This difference can spark frustration, resentment, rejection, anger, and even a breakup.

Good to the Last Drop

One California couple I know has some kind of sex every single morning for at least an hour before they get out of bed, and has done so for years. It's like their morning cup of coffee—just part of their routine. They do seem to be quite happy. But then again, their kids are all grown up and out of the nest, and the couple is independently wealthy, so they don't have to work for a living.

Some of us can't imagine having sex every single day. It's too much of a good thing, like eating an entire box of chocolates every day—or it's a luxury we simply can't afford.

A friend told me the following story: In ancient times, some sects of tantric practitioners wouldn't have sex for an entire year. Then they'd spend a month preparing for one big long group sex ritual. The sex ritual would last for ten days and ten nights, and they would practice very advanced sexual yoga and lovemaking techniques. The intensity of the ritual was so powerful that the participants would all become "enlightened." They would be so satisfied and blissed out at the end of the ten days that they didn't need sex for another whole year. Whether or not this is true, it's a nice story, and I like what it conveys. So one thing you might want to try if you're not being deeply satisfied is to devote more time to a long, thorough session, instead of several short sessions. Personally, I'd rather have one longer lovemaking session than several little quickies. But that's just me at this time in my life. Perhaps you feel differently.

Yes and No

So, what happens when one partner wants to get it on and the other doesn't? Desire discrepancy is extremely common. It can be very frustrating and painful—but it doesn't have to be. There are a couple of schools of thought about this. One suggests that whenever one partner wants sex, the other should try never to say "no," that it's better for the relationship always to go for it, and to make sex available to each other at all times. Another school of thought says that the couple should only make love when both partners really want to, that it's better for no one to have sex when one person really isn't in the mood. My own thinking is sort of a combination of the best of both schools.

Some people feel that if they are horny they need to get that itch scratched. They believe that when you are an adult you shouldn't have to masturbate and that partner sex is better than masturbation. No one's partner wants to feel like a masturbation device.

Rub-a-Dub

A newlywed couple came to me for some sex-life coaching. They were very concerned because the groom was quite horny and frustrated because the bride frequently didn't want to have sex. As we talked, we realized that she actually wanted to have sex but was simply too tired, because she had a very demanding job and didn't always have energy left for sex. I suggested that he use his energy to give his wife a body massage, not just with his hands but also with his body, rubbing his penis against her to orgasm. She could just relax, get an energizing massage, and not feel pressured to have to do anything. At the same time, he could have his pleasure and outlet. It worked beautifully for both of them, once she learned to totally receive without feeling guilty. When she wasn't tired, their energy levels were very well matched, and they enjoyed a variety of other styles of lovemaking.

Perfect Posture

At one time I had a lover who was an airbrush artist. He would sit the whole day slumped in a chair airbrushing. At night his back hurt terribly, and he was often in no mood for sex, but I sometimes was. So I came up with a solution. He would lie in bed on his belly and relax, while I rubbed my vulva vigorously on his tailbone until I felt done. In this way he got his lower back massaged, and I had my fun. He claimed that my vulva treatments helped more than his cortisone treatments.

Proactive

If ever your lover does reject you sexually, you need to take care of yourself and give yourself whatever it is you desire. If you need to be held, hold yourself. If you need an orgasm, give yourself an orgasm. If you need attention, give yourself some attention. Be your own best lover to yourself.

Here's what you can do if your lover isn't in the mood and you are:

1. Make some private time. Turn off the phone.
2. Go into your bedroom and put on some music that touches you deeply.
3. Get a vibrator and a big, fat dildo or some other toys you enjoy.
4. Make yourself feel sexy. Vibrate your head, heart, feet, etc. Stimulate yourself sexually until you are aroused. Use a dildo rigorously if desired.
5. While in a state of arousal, feel your feelings, including sadness, longing, and frustration. Go deeper into your feelings. Maybe have a good cry. Put your hand on your heart. Open up your body to the love that's available in the universe just for the asking.
6. Have orgasm(s) if desired.
7. Make yourself feel well loved by heaping your own love onto yourself. Give yourself a hug and tell yourself, "I love you." Maybe stroke your forehead tenderly.

8. If you still are unhappy, then have an out-of-bed talk with your lover about what's bothering you.

Here are some things you can do when you want to say "Not tonight. I have a headache." You're not in the mood and your lover is:

1. Invite and encourage your lover to go masturbate in the other room.

2. Offer to hold your lover while he or she masturbates and whisper sexy things in his/her ear.

3. Be as polite as you possibly can about why you aren't in the mood. Load your lover up with compliments. "It's so nice to be desired. You are so sexy, and sweet, but I'm sorry, I . . ." Then give a definite "no." A mixed message is frustrating, so be clear.

4. Choose to go ahead and have sex, and accept and eroticize the fact that you don't really want to. Just be okay with not being that into it. Sometimes having sex when you don't really want to can be cathartic, interesting, and a relief in a strange way. Or you might end up actually getting into and enjoying the sex, which can often happen.

5. Sometimes you may not want to have sex with your lover, not because you are tired or uninterested or upset with him/her, but because *you have been feeling very close to him/her,* and any more intimacy can be scary and feel over the top. Sometimes you may just want to spend some time alone, and that's fair. As the Kahlil Gibran poem says, "Let there be spaces in our togetherness." Or you can be very brave and push past your fears of even more intimacy.

6. Perhaps you just need more time to warm up to sex than your lover does. You may need to teach him/her how to better entice you with a slow seduction, lots of loving touching, extended kissing, no-pressure cuddling, and eye gazing.

7. Offer to give or receive a therapeutic nonerotic body massage. Sometimes this can be nice and intimate and bring you close without "sex." But be sure to honor the nonerotic boundary without going over it when you say this.

What Makes or Breaks a Relationship?

Psychologist John Gottman conducted studies with thousands of couples to determine what made marriage a success or a failure. He noted that "it is the balance between positive and negative emotional interactions in a marriage that determines its well-being—whether the good moments of mutual pleasure, passion, humor, support, kindness, and generosity outweigh the bad moments of complaining, criticism, anger, disgust, contempt, defensiveness, and coldness." Married couples who said they were satisfied reported a ratio of about five positive interactions to one negative one.

It's clear that it's very important to get and give lots of positive reinforcement, to amass enough of those sweet little moments to outweigh the bumps in the road. After all, life is just a collection of moments, and good moments don't always last. It's perfectly normal to go from satisfied to dissatisfied at the drop of a hat, or pajama. The good news is that bad moments don't last long either. Sexual satisfaction as a constant experience is for most of us an unrealistic fantasy. Our sex lives are more like a kaleidoscope effect, different at every twist and turn.

Duly Noted

When attempting to change a relationship that's become stuck, try using lots of positive reinforcement. Everyone loves presents, compliments, and loving attentions. Find the things you honestly like about your partner and compliment him/her lots. Say "I love your body!" "You kiss so nicely." "I love the way you touch me." "Your eyes are so beautiful." If you want more affection, try giving more affection. If you want more kissing, give more kisses. If you want longer lovemaking sessions, make them longer.

A nice middle-aged woman who worked as a stockbroker took one of my Sex Life Make Over workshops. At the end of the workshop she proclaimed in front of everyone present that she was committed and determined to fix her broken sex life with her husband of twenty-two years. It had been less than satisfactory and almost nonexistent for way too long. About a year later, I ran into her in the swimsuit department at Macy's. She told me that she indeed succeeded in her goal. (No wonder she looked radiant.) I asked her how she did it. She said that she started to buy him lots of sexy little gifts, she left sexy notes all over the house (sometimes hidden in his drawers or briefcase to find), and started to pay him a lot more compliments and give him lots more attention. She also worked at being more present in the relationship and made more effort to initiate lovemaking. Suddenly he started following suit—he put more into the relationship as well. She was so happy and proud. She said that their sex life became better than it ever had been before. They were about to embark on a romantic round-the-world cruise—thus the new Macy's swimsuit.

100 Ways to Leave Your Lover— Breaking Up

Perhaps you know that you need to end your current lover relationship. If this is what you have decided, then do it.

Unfortunately there is no one-size-fits-all best way to break up. After having been through my fair share of breakups, I've finally come to learn that most people would prefer a good clear ending, rather than going back and forth forever or getting mixed messages. Be as clear and to the point as you can. Breaking up is almost always hard to do, no matter what, but doing it as lovingly and compassionately as possible is always the best policy for everyone involved. Try your damnedest to put as much energy, love, and attention into the end of a relationship as you did into the beginning of it, and generally that's a pretty good way to go.

Happy Ending

As my mentor and friend sex educator Betty Dodson said to me once when I was breaking up, "In our society, when someone ends a relationship, it's considered a failure. But often endings are natural and healthy. Sometimes the relationship is simply complete. If we could teach people how to end things better, and not be so negative about endings, we would all be better off."

Many people believe one of the cosmic reasons for relationships is to help teach important lessons about ourselves and about life. Learning involves making "mistakes," and we may have to hook up with that abusive lout more than once before we learn enough to move on. I have witnessed myself and my friends make better choices, with a new relationship much better than the last. If you learn something from that last relationship that is useful for the one you have now, or the next one, then you've come out ahead.

I've seen many women and men separate from a partner because they have a lousy sex life, then end up having an explosive sexual reawakening and a far bigger love with someone new. I have also seen long-term relationships transform and thrive. If you look deeply at your inner truth, you will find the answers as to what is right for you. Perhaps make a list of questions for yourself about your relationship, then answer them, as you did in What's Your Current Truth? (Step 1).

Johnny Tightwad

What if sexual dissatisfaction is only the tip of the iceberg when you think about your relationship? What if other problems are far more pressing right now? Unsatisfying sex is often a symptom of other problems that need to be addressed. Do your sexual problems mirror other problems you're having with your mate?

For example, maybe you feel that your partner is cheap, doesn't spend money on you, and complains even when it's your own money you spend. In bed, he/she puts limits on how much he/she will "give" and seems to measure out the giving and receiving, making sure he gets his fair share.

Bedroom distress can alert you to something else you need to address. If problems like these are undermining your sex life, you and your partner must get in there and dig deeper. While sex can relieve pressure, it won't necessarily nip it at its source. That could require quite a different action.

Boneheads: Some Tips About Erections

Many men and woman are focused on men having very firm erections, which makes the drug companies really happy and everyone else go cockeyed. With all today's TV commercials discussing "erectile dysfunction," a lot more men now think they have it. It's wonderful that there are prescription medicines to aid gentleman in getting it up. But as Sweets, a pimp I once interviewed, opined when I asked how he kept his six ladies so satisfied, "It's not the size of the battleship, it's the motion of the ocean." Viagra and other such medicines are a great aid for many people, but sometimes not without a downside. My friend Cosi Fabian, who works as a fancy call girl, complained that the pills take away her proud sense of accomplishment. Besides, she added, when her clients take Viagra, "it's like they put a speedboat motor in their rowboat." Such easy Internet availability and inappropriate use of Viagra mean that we are in danger of creating a whole generation of men who use it recreationally rather than because they need to, and they will never know what natural erections feel like! Part of a man having an erection, to me, is the wonder and suspense and unprectability of it.

At the beauty parlor I happened to strike up an interesting conversation with a woman about her husband's erection. "He thinks he can only have sex when he has an erection, and he can only keep it up with Viagra. So he's totally in charge of when we will have sex, which I really resent." I suggested that perhaps she's bought into his thinking and is giving away her power. She's forgetting about her ability to communicate her needs, and she could teach and encourage him to have great sex without having a firm erection. A soft-on is often quite sufficient. Making love certainly doesn't need to be totally centered on intercourse. A man can always use his hands, tongue, and whole body. Think of what is traditionally called "foreplay" as *the* play.

Sure, erections are lovely, but we can't let men think they are *the* most important thing. Let them know they aren't. Don't let the state of his erection rule your world and let him off the performance-anxiety hook.

Also, you must know that if your partner doesn't get a strong erection it's most likely not your fault. Your partner might be dealing with his own body shame and aging, and might blame you. Keep your self-esteem strong. Many "erection difficulties" can be cured by not drinking, smoking, and sitting around constantly watching too much TV, but by leading a more healthy lifestyle. Lowering stress and anxiety.

Men are quite capable of giving and receiving pleasure when their penises are semi-erect. They can also learn how to withhold their ejaculations until after you are fully satisfied. They can learn to be better lovers all the way around if they want to. Your man might only need some loving encouragement and support from you.

To Be Together or Not to Be

My cousin Bill is a divorce lawyer. He believes the main reason couples get divorced is largely because they just want that new sex life. Hey, there's no more extreme sex life makeover than a divorce and a new lover. But he's also seen how sometimes the former couple ends up having the exact same sexual issues in their next relationship. So if you've made a commitment and invested in a relationship, by all means, don't throw all you've got down the drain. Try to make it a success. If you can't, you can't, then have a loving split up. But in any case, when there's trouble in paradise, you have got to deal with it, in one way or another. Find what might work best for you, face it, and take care of it. You'll ultimately be glad you did.

Dr. Sprinkle's Prescription to Reincarnate from "Bed Death"

A SEVEN-DAY TREATMENT PLAN

Symptoms: You and your lover haven't had sex in ages. You want to get sex going again, but you're not sure how to break the ice.

Instructions: Make an agreement with your partner to use the following prescription. The best Rx for no sex is SEX.

Caution: Before you begin, agree that you're not going to have any genital orgasms until day seven, which takes away any pressure or goals and will help you build up a charge. Each day you will do a little something sexy. By doing something that is not goal oriented every day for seven days, you build your energy and melt all ice. But if you end up really wanting to jump ahead to day seven at any point, then, hey, no problem; the cure simply worked faster.

Day One—Verbal Appreciation Day. Throughout the day and night make love just with your words as much as possible. Tell each other what you love about each other, compliment each other, clear up any stuff you need to clear up by talking with each other. Talk about how you'd like to feel the closeness of making love. Build up some anticipation by talking about what you'll be doing the next six days. Make some plans. Book the time. Have fun with it.

Day Two—Snuggle, Pet, and Smooch Day. Get in bed and kiss, hug, and touch erotically but keep whatever you are wearing on. Keep it nongenital.

Day Three—Sensual Touch Day. Both get naked and sensually touch each other. You can caress the genitals, but no sexually stimulating the genitals or oral or genital sex of any kind! Have no goals, except to enjoy the experience of touching each other.

Day Four—Mutual Masturbation Day. Either turn yourselves on, masturbating side by side with each other, or manually stimulate each other. Remember, no genital orgasms! Just build up some energy, circulate it, and enjoy it.

Day Five—Play Around Day. You decide what to do on this day, depending on what you are in the mood for and what you enjoy. Just no oral or genital sex! You can choose to repeat doing what you did on one of the previous days. Even if you repeat something you did already, at different days and times it will be different.

Day Six—Oral Sex Day. Give each other at least ten minutes or so of oral sex apiece. (If you don't like oral sex, then manually stimulate each other instead.) Don't come! Save and circulate the energy.

Day Seven—Give-It-Your-All Day. By now you should have plenty of volts of sexual energy built up between you. Set aside a time when you can finally get together to make love all the way. Get a baby-sitter if you have to and go to a hotel. Start early! Don't wait until late at night. Allow yourselves plenty of time. Feel free to have genital orgasms. Give it your all, and then be sure to take time to bask in the afterglow.

Continued use: Aim to keep the good feelings and your sex life going by making love once a week, **without fail.** As the commercial says, "Just do it!" Even if it feels like a chore at first, or takes some effort, in the end you usually are glad you did.

Alternative cures: An alternative to this treatment to restart your sex life would be to do the Super Sex Massage in Step 11. It works splendidly.

A Visit to Our Sex Spa

Sex is part of nature. I go along with nature.
MARILYN MONROE

Welcome to the Garden of Lovers' Delights

A highlight of your makeover program is your visit to our very own Garden of Lovers' Delights, the spa portion of our center. To find the spa, walk through the elegant gates on the north end of our property and follow the path of pink rose petals. Soon you will reach a clearing that opens to an idyllic scene with a blue-green calm clear pond to one side, and on the other, a tropical sandy beach hugged by gentle ocean waves. All around are magnificent gardens with colorful birds, butterflies, and flowers. Here beauty and sensuality reign supreme. There are various nooks for lovemaking: a veranda with a canopy of grape vines, a bamboo lovers' hut with a round bed in the center overlooking the ocean, a patio with a hammock for two. The warm sun and soft breezes caress your body.

Here I am, wearing a pink luminescent diaphanous gown. My mane of long brunette curls cascades down my back. Welcome. I hope you have a lovely time while you are here and leave feeling inspired and renewed. I'm going to take you through a tour of the garden and offer you a variety of "spa treatments": exercises, teachings, techniques, sex tips, and more. Choose the ones that interest you and leave the rest. Everyone enjoys different things. All these sexy spa treatments are designed for lovers to do together and can work wonders whether you are in a budding relationship, one in full bloom, or one that has withered on the vine.

Your Spa Mate

Now I have a very special surprise for you. In order for you to get the most out of this visit, the best bang for your buck, so to speak, I have flown in your lover! (If you don't have a lover at this time, we can fly in your "future lover." After all, this is a mythical journey.) Here your lover comes now, eyes sparkling and eager. Your lover takes your hand as the three of us move forward. You can remain here together as long as you like.

Here our aims are to nurture your body, mind, and spirit, as well as your relationship with your lover. If you follow along and try a few things, I believe you will really enjoy them. These techniques are healthy, 100 percent natural, and relatively easy to do. Come; follow me into the Garden of Lovers' Delights. I want your stay here to be nothing short of blissful. Are you ready?

Detoxification Treatment

Before you is the rich, warm bath of bliss, our detoxification hot tub. How can pleasure come into our bodies if we are all clogged up with gunk and yuck? Go ahead; stick your toes in the water. You'll notice that it is heated to the perfect temperature.

Before you begin to make love, it's sometimes a good idea to do something to decompress and detoxify: clear away stress, unwanted emotions, and physical toxins. I highly recommend some similar kind of water purification whenever you can prior to lovemaking: a hot bath with Epsom salts or a shower with scented soap. Let your body stretch, feel the wet heat in every crevice as you float. The two of you will take turns scrubbing each other with your exfoliation mitts. Notice how much more sensitive your skin feels after you exfoliate? In this way you can actually create pathways for pleasure to travel all over your bodies.

Revitalizing Treatment—Exercise

Now that your muscles are loose and your limbs limber we are going to put them to use. You and your lover can wrestle all over our green velvet lawn, rolling, tumbling, playing together—body to body, skin to skin, heart to heart. The best aphrodisiac (besides falling in love) is any kind of physical exercise. Tone those muscles, work those lungs, stimulate that circulation. Anything you can do to get more *in* your body will benefit your sex life. Dance, swim, play sports, or simply get off that computer for a while and go for a nice walk.

Nutritional Counseling

Uh-oh, did you or your lover get a bit winded? Aim to get rid of any habits that are unhealthy or in which you are overindulging. I had a two-pack-a-day cigarette smoking habit for twenty years. When I heard that quitting smoking would increase my sexual energy, it gave me the extra incentive I needed to quit and stay quit. It was absolutely true. I felt sexier, looked sexier, and my sex drive increased. Plus I probably added years to my life in which to enjoy more spectacular sex!

Overdoing junk foods can trash your sex life. A heavy drug and/or alcohol addiction can zap your zip. Try to eat well, take vitamins, and have healthful habits. You're worth it. Do it for love.

Rise, Snuggle, and Shine

You and your lover take a little nap. The earth is your pillow. You awaken in a happy daze. Rouse each other with a long kiss and hug, feeling erotic, sensual, and sexy.

While you are here, and each morning thereafter, I recommend that you start your day with an erotic glance, a lick in the ear, some sensual caressing. Rather than jumping up from your cocoon of the night, luxuriate together lying naked in the softness—if just for a couple minutes. Magnify these good feelings by focusing on them more intentionally. Undulate your pelvis against your lover, straddle your lover's thigh, squeeze your lover's butt, squeeze your lover's genitals. Ah yes, do this every morning and every night, even if just for a few minutes. Begin every day in a happy daze.

Raisin' Consciousness

Sit quietly and snuggle up while I share with you a very important sex tip. It's sort of a meditation as taught to me by a wise older couple I met long ago when I took a class called Ancient Sexual Secrets. They passed one raisin out to each student in our class and instructed us to put it into our mouths and see how much pleasure we could derive from that one raisin.

Some of the students ate their raisin quickly and didn't get much out of it. But others of us started to giggle with delight, because when we really followed the instruction to derive as much pleasure as we could from the raisin, that raisin became the most delicious thing we'd ever tasted. That moment taught me the importance of being present, and mindful.

Here, take a raisin for you and one for your lover. Hold that little sweet black pearl in your mouth, explore it with your tongue and teeth, roll it against your palate. Notice its flavor and how the texture changes as it interacts with your saliva. Merge with the raisin. Be fully present with the raisin. (If you don't have a raisin at home, you can use any other sweet fresh or dried fruit.) This concept of being present can be carried over to absolutely any sensual or sexual act.

Presence is simply concentration, being aware, focusing more of your attention on whatever it is you are doing. When it comes to making love, this is so important. I learned a similar lesson from a wonderful German man and teacher named Dieter Jarzombec. At one time he had been the director of a large mental institution, but he gave up his high-powered job so he could better help people in more nontraditional ways. He invited me to teach sexuality workshops with him, and fortunately I accepted.

We taught several weeklong "Wings of Joy" workshops in the Canary Islands, Switzerland, and Italy. Some people are simply born "erotically gifted" (as my friend Joseph Kramer calls it), and Dieter is certainly erotically gifted. One day Dieter did a little demonstration of how a person could make love to his/her lover's nipples, either male or female. So a woman came up to the front of the class, and Dieter began to demonstrate. He went to work on her nipples. After some time the woman getting her nipples done virtually levitated from the table, she was so highly aroused and ecstatic. Screaming in ecstasy. What was his secret? He was totally focused, present; he used great concentration. Watching him that day changed me forever.

Perhaps you are erotically gifted. How fortunate. But if not, we can learn to be much better lovers, simply by becoming much more present and total. By giving lovemaking more of our *all*.

Try it now! Please face each other and loosen your gowns. Let your lover lick, suck, and touch your nipples, twisting and diddling them gently. Each of you becomes 100 percent fully focused on your nipples, your lover on giving pleasure, you on receiving. You both feel that your nipples are the source of an energy current that you are both plugged into, you feel the charge, and the energy orbits through your bodies.

Good. Now that I've got your attention, bring your mindfulness with you as we proceed through the rest of the spa.

Fabulous Facials

Our faces hold abundant erotic possibilities, as they contain lots of nerves and are the home of our hearing, tasting, and smelling senses. You can have entire lovemaking sessions just focusing on your faces. Try it.

Hold each other's faces in your hands. Caress and rub your cheeks. Put some saliva on your third eyes (the area in the center of your forehead) and press them together and share a "third-eye kiss." Gently stroke foreheads and temples, lick eyelids, suck earlobes, let your eyelashes flutter against each other. Blow into and lick your lover's ears, suck earlobes, bite noses . . . Let your imaginations run wild as you make love just with your faces. Do you feel your face lift?

Lip-Oh-Suction

The key to really great kissing is to dance between mindful presence and total surrender. Focus, let go, focus, let go, cha cha cha. Kiss like there's no tomorrow. Feel those kisses on your lips, on your cheeks, in your hair, on your neck. Suck each other's lips, share some nectar mouth to mouth. Lick each other like kittens.

This facial is so good for your complexion. It makes your skin glow from within.

The Goddess Spot and the Fountain of You

Every spa and garden has its fountains, and here in this special garden that fountain is you. First, let's find your G-spot (I like to call it your "goddess spot"), the source of the fountain.

About fifteen years ago, when I started teaching women's sexuality workshops, I asked a group of women how many of them knew where their G-spots were. Just two out of thirty-five women raised their hands. Fifteen years later, at a workshop at the same place, I asked the same question, and all but one or two said they knew. More and more women have become aware of this pleasurable spot, and the whole concept has become very much a part of female sexual consciousness.

When the best-selling book *The G Spot,* written by Beverly Whipple, Alice Ladis, and John D. Perry, first came out in 1982, I was of course very interested in what it had to say. The authors told of great pleasures derived from stimulating a certain spot inside the

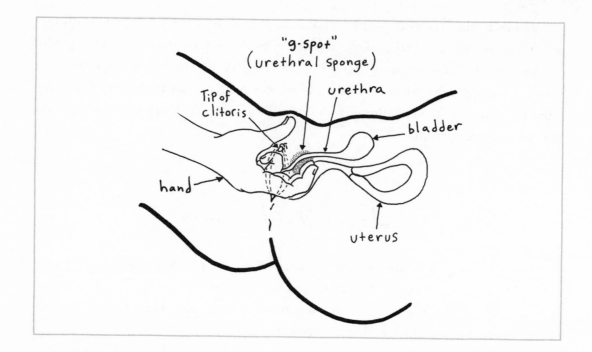

vagina, of "new" kinds of orgasms, of "female ejaculation" (unheard of at the time), and of a major "new" erogenous zone that they called the "G-spot." The book made quite a splash.

Just as I was reading the book, one of its coauthors called me out of the blue. Dr. John D. Perry was an ordained minister, psychologist, and sexologist. He'd heard that I had done some movies in which I might be "female ejaculating," and he wanted to use some clips in his lectures. I told him that I didn't know if I was "ejaculating" or not. Indeed I had been leaving big wet spots on the bed on occasion, and it didn't feel like I was peeing, but I'd never heard it called "ejaculating." So I invited him to my apartment for lunch, to teach me and some of my best girlfriends more about the G-spot and female ejaculation. My friends and I were very curious to see what this was all about.

Dr. Perry generously shared his knowledge. I asked him if he could show me where my own G-spot was as I still wasn't sure, even after reading his book. I lay back on my bed with my gal pals gathered around, Dr. Perry inserted his finger inside me and pressed up toward my pelvic bone several times. My first thought was "Oh, I know that spot very well." It was a totally familiar feeling. My second thought was "Is that all there is? What's the big deal?"

But over time I really "came" to appreciate the delights that my G-spot had to offer. Eventually I learned to go deeper into the feelings of electric pleasure that my G-spot gave when it was pressed on or stimulated. These days, G-spot stimulation is an integral part of my sexual enjoyment.

Let's find *your* G-spot, if you haven't already. Lie down on your back in the lush grass while you lover kneels before you. Spread your beautiful thighs, and let your lover slip a finger inside you. Your lover is pressing up toward your navel, hooking his/her finger in a come-here motion. Your lover is finding your urethral sponge, because it's got a rougher texture than the vaginal walls. Press up behind your pubic bone. Feel the pleasure as your lover wriggles that finger, pressing on that spongy tissue. Some women can at first find pressure on their G-spots rather uncomfortable, if they're not used to it. But with some practice you can move beyond any discomfort and uncover the pleasures. Relax, breathe. Look into your lover's eyes, breathe, relax, and surrender.

Tips for Finding Your G-Spot

If you want to find your G-spot, here are some things you can do:

1. *Talk with other women about their G-spots.*
2. *Find someone who knows about G-spots and if you aren't too shy, ask her/him to show you.* For educational purposes only.
3. *Ask your gynecologist.* Hopefully she/he will know and can point you in the right direction. Although don't be surprised if he/she says no.
4. *Know that it's actually very obvious.* Don't expect to have the same feelings and sensations as when touching your clitoris. Pressing the G-spot creates quite different sensations—more electric, similar to feeling as though you have to pee but pleasurable.
5. *Look at diagrams of G-spots in several books or on the Internet.* Some diagrams might speak to you more than others. Do take a look at my diagram.
6. *Ask your lover to help you find your G-spot, by having him/her press on various different spots.* Communicate about this as you go. Let it be rather clinical. Have fun looking.

7. *Try pressing firmly on various spots yourself, when you are alone.* This will help you better distinguish your G-spot from other spots. Some women can reach with their fingers. But for most of us it's better to get a special G-spotter type of sex toy/tool, available from any good women-oriented sex-toy shop.

8. *Feel for the area that is more textured.*

9. *Look for your urethral sponge with a mirror.* Your urethral sponge protects your urethral tube—where your urine comes through from your bladder. You can sometimes see part of the sponge from the outside. Hold a mirror between your legs and bear down on your vagina: the opposite of a Kegel, which is squeezing in. Push out. Can you see the spongy, bumpy area? The G-spot is simply more up inside. For some women the whole urethral sponge area is eroticized, and for other women it's one particular spot.

The Sensual Shower — Female Ejaculation

As you may or may not have heard, "female ejaculation" is all the rage. The latest thing is for women to ejaculate and men not to! Female ejaculation can be enjoyable for some women and their partners—if you like your sex wet.

When women ask me if it's worth learning how to ejaculate, I say that I think it is. But expect to do more loads of laundry.

Here are some pointers for learning female ejaculation:

1. *First you need to believe that it's possible.* Seeing is believing. Watch a woman do it. There are two great instructional DVDs you can watch. Carol Queen's *G-Marks the Spot* and Debbie Sundahl's *Female Ejaculation for Couples.* (See Resources.) Debbie created the lovely term "feminine fountain."

2. *Reverse all potty training.* Our mommies taught us not to wet the bed. Now we have to unlearn that. This is the biggest hurdle for most women. You have to be willing to "make a mess." Go to the toilet and pee first, before you try female ejaculation. Then you will feel more certain that you are ejaculating and not peeing. Peeing and ejaculating can look and feel very similar, but in time they can

become distinguishable. (Note: Peeing during sex can be very enjoyable to some lovers as well. And there are in fact traces of urine in female ejaculate.)

3. *Put pressure on your G-spot.* Either do it yourself with a finger, or use a sex tool. Or have your lover do it. Some women ejaculate without pressure on their G-spots. But generally putting pressure on your G-spot helps build and push out the watery fluid. The best way is usually with a hooked finger pressing hard on the G-spot.

4. *When you feel full and ready then push out. Bear down.* Let yourself gush. Visualize it happening at first.

5. *Realize that female ejaculating and orgasming don't necessarily go hand in hand.* They don't necessarily occur at the same time. You can have the release of fluid without having orgasm.

6. *Don't expect your ejaculate to look like a man's ejaculate.* Women's ejaculate is a clear or slightly milky liquid, like nonfat milk.

The Male G-Spot

Men have a "G-spot," too. It's in their prostate. If you put a finger into a man's anus, and press up on it, you can stimulate it. Men tell me it can really enhance their pleasure and their orgasm. (Believe me, I also know from firsthand experience.) Plus there's evidence male G-spot massage can help prevent prostate cancer. How wonderful that we are still discovering a lot about men's hidden capacities for pleasure as well as women's.

A Holistic Approach

A skilled and enthusiastic lover makes love to his/her lover's *whole* body. You can spread your lover's sexual energy from his/her genitals all over the rest of his/her body using your lips, hands, feet, arms. During intercourse or oral sex, you can simultaneously squeeze feet, tickle behind the knees, suck armpits, stimulate the heart area, rub the anus, press the perineum. These "add-ons" make for a more full-bodied sexual experience. Take the "roads" less traveled, making love in less obvious ways. Be creative. See if you can find your lover's most sensitive nonobvious erogenous zone—not so much for your lover's sake but for your own fun and curiosity.

The Body Wrap

Now, would you and your lover like to engage in what sexologist Wilhelm Reich referred to so poetically as "the genital embrace"? Enjoy the sensations that come from wrapping your vagina around your lover's penis (flesh and blood, or silicone) with intercourse. Lie back in this lush bed, and I will coach you into even more pleasure. Enjoy the merging, the melting, the release, the connection, the pleasure . . . the explosion!

1. *Try adding more "tummy tucks."* Undulate your pelvis and spine more, as this will activate more of your sexual energy and your cerebral spinal fluid, which equals more ecstasy. Imagine the length of your spine waving and undulating as a dolphin's spine does when it swims. Go easy, be relaxed, and move slowly. Then build up to a faster pace, give it more energy and enthusiasm. Back and forth.

2. *Add Kegels. Relax and then contract your vaginal muscles.* Kegel, Kegel, Kegel, some soft and some strong. This not only can pleasure your lover; it also can stimulate your clitoris from the inside.

3. *Go ahead, stimulate your clitoris with your fingers, too.* Many women long to have a clitoral orgasm during intercourse but can't because their clitoris isn't being sufficiently stimulated. Feel absolutely free to stimulate your own clitoris during intercourse with your fingers or your favorite vibrator. It's perfectly legal. And the hotter you get, the hotter your lover gets.

4. *Play with more breathing.* Fast shallow breaths, or deep slow breaths. Notice how when you play with your breathing patterns you can affect the flow of your energy and the levels of excitement and enjoyment.

5. *Surrender. Don't hold back.* See what happens when you fully get into any sexual feelings and magnify them. Take it all the way!

Balancing Treatments

Is something in your sex life out of whack? Sometimes it's easy to fall into patterns, where sex becomes predictable every time, and it can feel difficult to get out of the routines. Allow yourself the freedom to go from one extreme to the other—the freedom to create balance. Here are some "balancing treatments" to consider:

Balance Spontaneous Sex with Planned Sex. The thrill of a surprise complements a well-laid plan. Sex when it's least expected gives the thrill of being caught off guard. There's the excitement of knowing that sex can happen spontaneously at any time. But it's also important, on occasion, to have a lovemaking session that's well planned, where you've set up a time to in advance, so you can prepare your space, don special sensual attire, select your music, and create an atmosphere.

   If you always are spontaneous, you will miss out on the gourmet lovemaking sessions. If you always plan ahead, you will miss out on the surprises. Aim to create a balance of some of both.

Balance Giving with Receiving. Are you and your partner both having ample opportunity to give and receive fully? Or have you gotten stuck in one role or the other? If you are always the one doing most of the giving or almost all the receiving, it can get to be a drag or frustrating. Find a balance.

Balance the Slow Stew with the Hot Wire. My friend sexologist Joseph Kramer, Ph.D., calls sex that gets ignited by going right for the crotch and stimulating the genitals "hot wiring," similar to when you start a car without turning on the ignition with the key. When you hot-wire sex, you stimulate the genitals first, which then gets the rest of you or your lover in the mood. It's also lovely to cook up what I call "a slow stew," where you tease and play until you can't take it anymore, and then finally add genital stimulation toward the end. Balance slow builds with the quick starts.

Balance Intensity with Subtlety. You can go for very intense, demonstrative, rough, fast, and hard styles of sex, and balance these with extremely gentle, quiet, slow, and softer styles of sex. Lovers often end up hanging out somewhere in the middle ranges. They can miss out on the full spectrum.

To increase the intensity, move faster, breathe faster, undulate your hips more, pinch, squeeze, bite, take personal risks, kiss harder, make more noise. To explore depth and subtlety slow down your breathing, use an extremely gentle touch, or hold absolutely still. There is an old saying that if you want to be a great lover, "use three strokes for thirty." Meaning, slow way down. But sometimes it's also nice to speed way up, too. I highly recommend both, from one extreme to the other.

Balance Raunchy with Refined. Once a beautiful young couple came to me for a sex-life coaching session. They were madly in love, but after being together only two years, they were having sex just once every few months. Both clearly had the skills to be excellent lovers, were sexually open-minded, and there wasn't a thing wrong with them. They said they practiced a lot of martial arts, yoga, and were on a "spiritual path."

As we talked, I could see that they somehow thought that sex had to be "spiritual" and "transcendental" every single time. Because sex wasn't always up to their high expectations, they got frustrated and shied away from it. So I suggested they have some raunchy, fast-food type of sex. Let it be okay to have "lousy" sex. Find the spectacularness in the more mundane kinds of sex or raunchy sex. Hey, sex can't always be a "cosmic and enlightening" experience every single time.

They reported back to me several months later that this worked like a charm. Accepting more of whatever happened, and having this balance, was in fact ultimately much more "spiritual."

Nature's Delight

Are you enjoying your visit to the garden? Nature provides such magnificent erotic inspiration. Travel agencies capitalize on this fact with their romantic advertisements showing tan young couples hugging in clear turquoise water. Sex and love in a natural environment are popular in Hollywood films, like *South Pacific, Blue Lagoon,* and the Tarzan movies.

I highly recommend that you make the effort to make love outdoors at least once a year. I know it's not always easy for people to manage to get to a secluded place, so you can at least do this: One day when you are in a park, notice and marvel that sex is occurring everywhere all the time, in the lives of plants, animals, trees, fish, and bugs. Savor it. Don't just stop and smell the roses; lick them, touch them, check out their sex organs. Behold the sex and sensuality that is happening everywhere around you, and feel the energy of it.

When I taught sexuality workshops at a secluded retreat center in the country, I sent participants out into the woods for a couple of hours and suggested they have a sexual experience with something in nature, as if it were totally alive and feeling. It sounded like a crazy assignment, but when people returned two hours later and shared their experiences with the group the stories were always incredible. One by one people described how they had the most amazing experience making love with a rushing waterfall, or with a boulder with veins of quartz, or with the furry roots of a fallen redwood tree. One woman drifted off to sleep after making love with a bed of moss and woke up with butterflies all over her body. Some people claimed that this Sex with Nature assignment inspired one of the most beautiful erotic experiences they'd ever had in their entire lives (and some of the folks didn't even take off their clothes).

Life in the Garden of Lovers' Delights

Now I will leave you lovebirds alone for a while. Carry on and do whatever it is you'd like to do. The possibilities are endless. We live in a magnificent world filled with opportunities for spectacular sensual and sexual adventures, and yet so many people don't partake of this abundance. It's kind of like living near one of the most beautiful nature parks in the world and rarely taking the time or making the effort to go there. If we want more wonderful sex in our lives, we need only give ourselves permission, a gentle push, to enter the "garden gates" and follow the path.

The Eye Lift

Time: 10 minutes.

What you will need: A timer with a gentle alarm.

Setting: In bed, or anywhere comfortable and romantic. Music is optional.

When to do this: Anytime. But at the very beginning of a lovemaking session or during the afterglow is especially nice.

1. Invite your partner to try this experiment with you.
2. Set the timer for ten minutes.
3. Lie facing each other, pelvis to pelvis. Clothed works well, but naked is even better. Leave approximately one foot of space between your faces.
4. Take some deep breaths and simply relax. Then look into each other's eyes. Don't do anything but lie still and gaze. Try to stay present and breathe naturally. If you are not used to prolonged eye gazing, this can be a real challenge. You may feel very uncomfortable at first. I know I did when I first tried this. One thing that can happen is that facial features shift and change; at times you may even feel as if you were looking into a fun-house mirror or were on some kind of drug. This can be frightening, but if you just accept it as natural and let the changes shift and flow, you will eventually come to enjoy it. You may want to laugh nervously. Or you may feel some initial fear that you don't really know this person. For the first time you notice things like wrinkles or pores, and you may feel insecure that your lover will notice your imperfections. Do not analyze these thoughts and feelings; just let them pass through you—and they will pass.
5. Allow yourself to experience whatever is there, or not there, and the changes that occur. Hang in there. It's well worth learning to do this.
6. When the timer goes off, complete the eye-gazing session with a long, passionate kiss or a long hug.

Results: Although this sounds simple, maybe even boring, you might discover that this is some of the best "lovemaking" you've ever had together. You might feel your bodies and souls merging. Eye gazing can get you both highly aroused and make you feel really high. It can open your hearts so that sex is much more connected, intimate, and loving, and will add a new dimension to ordinary eye contact you make later on with your lover. One couple I know makes eye gazing a primary part of their foreplay, and of their relationship.

This "eye lift" is practice in the art of being authentic and present, and can help you learn to accept whatever is or isn't happening sexually. You can also do this with yourself, in a mirror.

If ten minutes seems too long, start with two or three minutes. Then eventually work your way up to ten minutes. Or go longer!

Step Eleven

Experience the Spectacular Sex Massage

Massage is a dance of love.
KENNETH RAY STUBBS, PH.D.

Let's reunite on the veranda, where there's a massage table set up for you. I have more treats in store. I'm going to share with you the specialty of all our sex spa treatments.

So what will it be? Swedish? Shiatsu? Reiki? Deep tissue? Actually a sex-life makeover requires a very potent form of massage—one that satisfies you mentally, emotionally, spiritually . . . and sexually. So come with me and learn more of the exquisite pleasures of the flesh. Bring your lover along. The Spectacular Sex Massage is definitely an experience to share.

The Spectacular Sex Massage?

It starts with a brief basic relaxing massage, slowly moves into a sensuous erotic massage, and then explodes into a highly sexual massage with intense and thorough genital stimulation. Often the Spectacular Sex Massage leads to oral sex and intercourse, which can become all the more amazing and profound after this massage.

Why do it? Giving each part of the body loving, sensual attention creates an ecstatic reverberation throughout the body. You will radiate from your core and be open to connect with your partner in ways that are deep, electric, and unforgettable. This form of lovemaking can create a high-frequency erotic vibratory state. Many people are even able to get into a highly pleasurable trance, which is relaxing and yet exciting. The goal of all the individual massage strokes is to wake up and excite all parts of the genitals. Almost all of us usually neglect being thorough.

Perhaps the best part is that you and your lover each get to fully give and fully receive—and not at the same time; a great experience to add to your pleasure palate. It's a perfect way to go when you don't feel particularly hot but want to make some kind of love or have some kind of sex. Spectacular Sex Massage starts slow, and easy, and doesn't demand that you be aroused. Sexual energy builds gradually. So if you haven't had sex in a while, it's a great way to get back into the swing. Over time, it can radically transform a couple's sex life, for the better.

Don't worry; you don't need to have any kind of massage training to do this. (Although it can help.) You're not doing this kind of massage for the traditional therapeutic fix-it reasons. You're doing it as a great way to make love.

In the mid-eighties I first learned the basics of this type of massage when I discovered some instructional audiotapes called *Ecstatic Sex, Healthy Sex,* by Joseph Kramer. Joseph was the director of a successful massage school named The Body Electric School of Massage, in Oakland, California. When AIDS hit, he wanted to help people cope and give them a wonderful way to have safe sex, so he developed a special erotic massage. He called it Taoist Erotic Massage, and he recommended that men withhold their ejaculations while receiving it to better experience a beyond-the-genitals sense of full-body orgasmic state that most men seldom know. When he taught his Taoist Erotic Massage to other people, he got a lot more than he bargained for: People not only had safe sex; they also had some profound, extremely ecstatic, cathartic, mind-blowing, healing, deeply satisfying, loving, sexual experiences.

After listening to Joseph Kramer's tapes, I contacted him and asked him to give me one of his massages. He happened to be coming to New York City, where I lived at the time, so I invited him to my home. We had tea and chatted and really hit it off. He set up a massage table in my dining room and went to work. At the end of two hours my body felt so alive, and loved. I had intense full-body pleasure that streamed through me seemingly forever. I'd had a lot of incredible sexual experiences over the years, but none quite like this. I don't think I had ever fully allowed myself to just receive pleasure, the way I did during Joseph's massage. He moved energy to my every cell, pore, extremity. I screamed, I cried, I melted, I relaxed, I came, I floated, I felt totally done, baked, cooked, and garnished. It was so great that Joe and I got engaged soon after! (Later we decided not to marry but remain close friends and collaborators to this day.)

Meanwhile we developed Joe's techniques more and taught them together in workshops all over the USA, in Europe and Australia. Today Joseph Kramer teaches a variety of erotic massage techniques in depth on DVD. I moved toward teaching my own version of the massage, which I have named Spectacular Sex Massage.

In my sex life today, my beloved and I enjoy a wide variety of types of sex. But our most amazing lovemaking experiences revolve around this super sex massage. If we have not had much time together and we want to really connect deeply, we make a sex-massage date. When the time comes, we set up the massage table in our roomy kitchen. (Which also makes for nice thoughts later when I'm doing the dishes.) We prepare the space and gather the items we will need. Then we take turns giving and receiving. Usually we end up having some kind of oral sex and intercourse. Doing this magical massage first always makes the oral sex and intercourse extraordinary.

However, this massage is not just foreplay for intercourse. It can be. But really it's about bringing the receiver's full sexual arousal to satisfaction. It's a very intense kind of lovemaking in and of itself.

It's difficult for me to explain the way this massage can make a person feel. You have to spend some time doing it and experience it stroke by stroke. Men are encouraged not to ejaculate until the end of the massage but to let their sexual energy build up in their bodies. Women can have orgasms whenever they feel like it, but don't let your orgasm signal the end of the massage. Keep on going.

Warning: Doing this massage while driving a vehicle or operating farm equipment can be very dangerous. So don't. Even driving after this massage can be dangerous. Be sure that you take time after the massage to get grounded before driving.

Different Strokes— *How to Use This Information*

Invite your lover to share this massage with you and set up a time to do it—ideally for at least two hours, if you are going to both give and receive it. If you don't have that much time, you can certainly do it with less. Or just massage one person and do the other the next time.

You can do this in two ways:

1. You can simply read through the description of the massage and get a feel for it. Then try to do some of it from memory and from improvising.
2. Or much better yet, make a photocopy of these pages (with the lists of strokes) and do the massage step-by-step with the papers at your side. (Photocopies are good to use so that you don't get your sticky fingers all over your precious book.) Before you start, read through the list of strokes together and cross out any that don't appeal to you. Every person likes and dislikes different sensations. Modify the massage to fit your tastes.

At first learning and doing these techniques might seem a little awkward, like learning new dance steps. You might have to go through them a couple of times in a mechanical way. But then, after you've practiced and learned the strokes, you can throw away the papers and improvise.

There are various styles of this massage. For example, you can do it very gently and sensually or quite firmly and even roughly. You can do it with a tantric flavor (i.e., with ritual and prayer) or with a hard-edged BDSM twist (i.e., with flogging and scratching). You can do it very meditatively to New Age sounds or do it with very boisterous energy to an Afro-Cuban beat. Relaxed or rigorously. Or combine all the above during one session. You can also, of course, add oral sex and intercourse or keep it "hands-on" sex only. If you like, you can also do the Spectacular Sex Massage in threesomes, foursomes, or groups.

Try not to fall into old sexual patterns and routines—like becoming goal oriented toward orgasm and forgetting all about the strokes. Although if you do end up jumping ahead, then let that be okay.

The Well-Equipped Massage Parlor— What You Will Need

A private heated room or place outdoors. Turn off the phone(s).

Some kind of massage table. It's definitely best to do this on a massage table, either professional or homemade (you can use a long, strong table covered with blankets or padding). If you don't have a table, try making something comfortable on the floor. Although in a pinch, in your bed will do. Part of why this massage works so well is that when the giver is standing, he/she has more flexibility, comfort, physical control, and stamina.

A sheet. Cover the table with a sheet.

Towels. Trust me, you'll need them.

Music. Music is optional, although highly recommended. Something with a beat that is erotic to you. Have it match your mood. Classical, rock, or New Age could all work well. I like "world beat" music best, like Brazilian, Indian, or African music.

Mood lighting. Always a good idea for any lovemaking encounter. Candlelight is the most beautiful light to use, but take safety precautions. You can get very high from this massage and space out. Once my bed caught on fire from a candle, and we had to call the fire department at the height of lovemaking. Talk about a surreal experience.

A variety of sensuous props. Incense, grapes, ostrich or peacock feathers, silk scarves, scents, chocolate-covered strawberries, etc., are optional but very fun to play with.

Massage oil, lotion, or powder. A powder massage can be very evocative. Any baby powder works, or finely ground cornstarch you buy at the grocery store is excellent and very inexpensive. If you don't have some massage oil, cooking oil will do.

Lubricant. Have plenty of it on hand. In a pump bottle is best because you can use one hand to get more, leaving the other hand to touch your lover's body. Use lubricant beyond generously.

Latex or vinyl gloves for safe sex, when needed. Use if there are cuts on the hands, or your fingernails are lethal talons, and to limit the spread of body fluids. Remember oil disintegrates latex, so use a nonoily lubricant with latex gloves.

A vibrator, but better yet, two vibrators. Have them set up with long extension cords, or use battery operated. (You can use condoms on them if you plan to share them and want to have safer sex.)

What to do if you are the person giving the massage:

Breathe deep breaths along with your partner.

Give total focus to your partner, by staying present.

Tap into your sensitivity.

Pay attention to your lover's responses. Tune in and notice what your lover likes or doesn't like.

If you get insecure, say positive affirmations to yourself like "I'm a great masseuse" or "My consciousness is in my hands, and I know just what to do with them."

Be creative and make giving fun for YOURSELF.

Get into enjoying looking at and touching your lover's body.

Ask your lover for feedback as you go. Then say thank you whenever you get it.

Move slowly as a general rule, except when your lover asks for something faster.

Limit chitchat.

If you are using just one hand on the genital area, always try to work the other hand on other parts of the body, to help spread energy to them. This will move the sexual energy from the genitals to the rest of the body.

What to do if you are the person receiving this massage:

Totally receive 100 percent. Don't try to give anything back while you receive. Simply lie back and enjoy it. Enjoy it in your own way, however you are drawn to.

Breathe deeply. The more you breathe, the more fully you will feel.

Give feedback. It's your body and your massage, so say what you want, or don't want.

Let yourself go. Surrender to whatever you are feeling.

Share your feelings verbally if you want to. But again, limit chitchat.

Don't worry about erections. Men find that being semierect is a fine way to enjoy this sexual massage. The goal is not to have an erection or ejaculation but to experience full-body aliveness, intense full-body pleasure, and to explore other kinds of orgasms (as covered later in Step 13).

Tell your partner whenever you need something. Ask him/her to use more lubrication, or oil, or give you a sip of water when needed.

Spectacular Sex Massage for Men and Women— A Touch of Venus and Penis

Both men and women can begin with these same strokes.

Basic Body Worship

Connection—Begin by connecting to your partner with a nice kiss, hug, and eye gaze. Share some deep breaths.

Laying On of hands—With the receiver lying on her/his back to start, ceremoniously place your hands on your lover. Here the goal is to be aware of the first touch and make that first touch a signal for all that is going to happen afterward. This laying on of hands is about connecting, and letting your hands melt into your partner.

The Flesh Caress—Caress, stroke, and sensually massage your lover's whole body with oil or powder. Put your consciousness (attention) into your hands.

Through the quality of your touch let your lover know that there is nowhere you'd rather be and no one you'd rather be with. Do about five or ten minutes of basic, nurturing, oil massage of the backside, legs, and arms, giving special attention to the buttocks. Then have the receiver turn over.

In a Pinch—Get energy flowing to all her/his extremities by pinching each of her/his fingertips and toes.

The Brush Rush—Brush the skin lightly with your fingertips.

The Cat Scratch—Gently scratch the skin.

Pubic Hair Tug (where applicable)—This can be delightfully invigorating!

Sensorium (optional)—Use any kind of feathers, silk scarves, furs, or whatever you have available to pleasure the skin. Feed your lover grapes or chocolate-covered strawberries. Have him/her sniff a lovely scent. The idea is to awaken all her/his senses. I sometimes call this the bells-and-whistles phase.

FOR WOMEN

Wake Up the Neighborhood

The Breast Stroke—Stroke and massage her breasts in gentle circles, clockwise and counterclockwise. Be sure to massage her nipples thoroughly. Spend at least a couple of minutes just on the nipples alone.

Over Eggs Easy—Rub your palms together to generate heat in your hands. Then circle your palms over her ovary area in an honoring way. Warming this area will ignite her subtle sexual energy furnace. (It works even if her ovaries have been removed.)

The Womb Warmer. Circle palms over her uterus area, just above her pubic hairline. (Works nicely even if she has no uterus.)

Knocking on Heaven's Back Door—Press and dig fingers into her belly/bladder area, just above the pubic hairline. You can stimulate her G-spot through pressing on her belly this way. Most women love this. Be gentle if she's having her period, but otherwise dig in fingertips quite firmly.

Vulva Massage

Vibrate That Vulva—Rest your entire hand on her mons and then vibrate. Trust me, she will love this one! Open her heart by placing your other hand between her breasts. Vibrate with both your hands. One of the goals of this massage is connecting the heart and the genitals.

Pussy Petting—Time to lubricate your hands and her vulva. Pet her pussy with long slow strokes, alternating hands with each pet.

The Outer Labia Acupress—Place your thumbs in the centers of her outer labia, press into her and release. Repeat numerous times.

Labia Lip Massage—Pinch the labia lips between your thumb and fingertips and lovingly massage them very thoroughly, as you might massage an earlobe.

Tour de France—Orbit your forefinger around between her inner and outer labia from perineum to just above the clitoris, up and down and around.

Womb Drumming—Tap and slap her inner thighs and vulva with your fingers and palms, as if you are playing a drum. Some gals prefer gentle taps, and some prefer very hard. A combination can be fun.

The Breath of Bliss—Gently peel open her labia and blow your breath just outside and around her royal pinkness. Repeat several times.

Clitoral Massage

A Gentle Touch and Tickle—Tickle her clitoris with your fingertip as lightly as you possibly can. Be sure your finger is moist with lube.

Rock Around the Clit Clock—Imagine the numbers of a clock around her clitoris. With your forefinger make tiny circles stopping at 12:00, 3:00, 6:00, and 9:00. Go around for days. Many women seem to like 2:00 or 3:00 the best.

Gentle Pinch and Pull—With thumb and forefinger, go behind the clitoral shaft and gently pinch and pull out on it. She will likely wriggle in delight.

Intervaginal Massage

The Big Tease—With your fingers, gently tease around the opening to her vagina. Make her hungry for you to come inside.

Before you enter your partner, it's always nice to ask permission. She might just prefer an external massage on occasion. But if she says "Yes please, please, please, yes," then proceed with the following strokes, being sure to use abundant lubrication.

The Crescent Moon—Slowly insert your thumb inside her vagina, and curl your fingers up around her pubic bone (fingertips pointing to navel) so that the curve of the hand can rub against the clitoris. Then wriggle and jiggle your hand. Rest your free hand on her heart area. Watch her glow. While securely holding your partner you can press on both her G-spot with your thumb and her clitoris with the curve of the hand, at the same time, or you can alternate between the two.

The One-Finger Glide—Slowly and gently insert your forefinger, then gently tease around the inside of her vagina. Use your other hand on the rest of her body.

The Two-Finger Glide—Add your index finger.

The Four Directions—With two fingers press firmly up/side/down/side eight times massaging each vaginal wall direction. Keep it slow.

The Goddess Spot (the G-Spot)—Massage her urethral sponge area thoroughly with one or two fingers.

The Doorbell—Press very firmly on her G-spot, as if you were ringing a doorbell. Press/release/press/release . . . repeat.

Rock and Roll—Using two hands, alternate between G-spot stimulation and clitoral stimulation, about ten seconds on each.

Twist and Shout!—You twist, she shouts. Using however few or as many fingers she chooses, penetrate her in and out while twisting at the wrist.

The Pit Stop—Hold completely still while your fingers are inside her. Don't move; just be there, even if she begs you to move. And she probably will.

Be here now—Whenever you take your fingers out, remove them ever so slowly, and then simply rest your hands on her body, to give her time to integrate all the good feelings and give her a rest.

Vibrator Massage

Good, Good, Good Vibrations—Using a vibrator, vibrate the bottoms of her feet, between her breasts, her belly, lips, temples, nipples, and all manner of other erogenous zones. Vibrate the areas around her inner thighs and labia to get her accustomed to the intensity of the vibrator, and then move toward more sensitive areas of her vulva. If it's too intense for her, use your hand as a buffer between her and the vibrator. Tease around her vaginal opening with the vibrator, with a very slight touch.

Necking— Place one vibrator on the back of her neck while you massage her clitoris with the other vibrator. This draws the energy from her genitals up her body.

Pubic Relations—Press/release/press/release the vibrator on her clitoral area.

Vibrate, Penetrate, Levitate—Hold the vibrator with one hand on her clitoris and penetrate her vagina with the other. Watch her levitate.

Rosebud Massage

Spend some time massaging the outside of her anus, with your thumbs and fingertips. If she likes it, massage inside her anus. Don't then go back to her vagina without washing your hands, as it can spread bacteria to her vagina. You can also tease her anus with the vibrator. You can have several condoms on the vibrator before you start the massage, then just strip them off when you go back and forth to avoid spreading bacteria.

As She Likes It

Now you've likely got her fully tumesced (turned-on), so give her more of whatever it is she desires for a while, be it more clitoral massage, intervaginal massage, vibrator massage, intercourse, or whatever. Perhaps add some tongue massage if desired. A massage table is the perfect height for oral sex if you pull up a chair as she scoots down to the end of the table. She can rest her legs on your shoulders. Or better yet use a chair with arms so she can put her feet on the arms of the chair while you dine. Delicious.

The Grand Finale

By now she will likely be extremely blissed out. How you end the massage is really crucial. Skip down past the men's strokes to the section below for further instructions.

FOR MEN

(Continue here after you've completed the Basic Body Worship section described before.)

Waking Up the Neighborhood

Belly Circles—Rub his whole belly and groin in circles with your flat palms and fingers. Vary the speed and pressure. Massaging counterclockwise stirs up powerful male erotic energy. Build up a rhythm.

Nipple Circles—Men's nipples can be awakened to generate exquisite pleasure. Massage them lightly with your fingertips, pinch and pull with your fingernails, and massage with palms circling the tips.

Buddha Belly Press—Press your fingertips into the area just above his pubic bone. Pressing on the bladder area can feel really sexy.

Massaging the (Other) Magic Wand (Penis)

Good Vibrations—Gently rest one hand on your lover's heart area (between his nipples) and the other on the genital area. Take some big breaths and vibrate your hands on both areas.

Anointing with Oil—Now is the time to oil up. The tissues of the magic wand are very sensitive, so use gobs of oil. Be sure to oil the testicles and the perineum (under the testicles), too.

Penis Shiatsu—*Shiatsu* is a Japanese word meaning "finger pressure." With your thumb and forefinger squeeze up and down the magic wand, front and back and sides. This rhythmic stroke begins to wake up the inner tissues of the penis.

Rock Around the Cock Clock—Imagine the magic wand pointing toward the belly button is twelve o'clock. Alternate your hands sensuously and slowly rubbing the magic wand like the hand of a clock to point to his right (3:00), down toward his feet (6:00), and to his left (9:00). Circle his penis all around, so it gets a good stretch at the base.

The King's Delight—Give some special attention to the place just below the head on the underside of his penis. It's called the frenum. This area contains a concentration of nerve endings. With one thumb on each side of the underside of the head, press and rub with thumb circles. Then do cross-country skiing with your thumbs to make alternating strokes up and down.

Healing—With the magic wand resting on his belly, glide the heel of your hand up and down the underside of his penis with your fingers toward the feet. This massages the spine of the cock, and when rubbed it generates a tremendous amount of erotic energy. Don't forget to use the other hand to massage other parts of the body simultaneously whenever you can.

Twist and Shout—You twist, he shouts . . . with ecstasy. Pull the skin taut toward the base with one hand. With the other hand corkscrew up and down the shaft.

Heart Circles—One hand does the Healing stroke while the other massages the heart area. Watch him become putty in your hands.

Juicer—Pull the skin of the penis down toward the base and juice as you would an orange. This stroke is done mostly with the fingers and fingertips. Don't put too much pressure on the head, just the shaft. But don't juice too much—you don't want him to ejaculate.

Fire—With the magic wand pointed straight up, rub with different speeds between your palms. This is a high-friction stroke, so be sure to use enough oil. Feel the heat!

Head Massage—Hold his magic wand pointing up toward the ceiling with one hand. Using the other (well-oiled) palm, slowly circle the middle of your palm over the head of his wand. Do it slowly and with great sensitivity.

Sunrise—Start each stroke at the base of the penis, wrapping your hand around the magic wand and gliding up and off at the tip. Alternate, using both hands, stroking the energy up toward the sky. This can be done relatively firmly.

Superstretch—Stroke the magic wand toward the heart, and at the same time tug the balls toward the feet. Give it a good stretch several times. Watch your partner's face during this stroke, to make sure you've got the right amount of pressure.

Testicle Massage

Ring the Balls—Twist the testicle sac as if you were wringing out a washcloth with two hands, but more gently.

Nuts and Jolts—Scratch the testicles lightly with your fingernails.

Scrotum Massage—Massage, stretch, and stroke the skin that covers the testicles with your fingertips and thumb. But be careful; the testicles can be very sensitive. This area is often ignored and needs a little loving attention.

Vibrator Massage

Good, Good, Good Vibrations—Using a vibrator, vibrate the bottoms of his feet, around his heart area, nipples, belly, lips, temples, and all other erogenous zones. Vibrate the areas around his inner thighs to get him accustomed to the intensity of the vibrator, and then move toward his penis. Vibrate the base of his penis, and go up and down the shaft. Tickle his pickle.

Necking—Put the vibrator on the back of his neck while you massage his magic wand. This draws energy from his genitals up his spine, to blow his mind.

Perineum and Rosebud Massage

Core Vibrations—Vibrate his perineum (under the testicles) with the heel of your palm, or your fist, or with the vibrator. Or all of these.

Rosebud Massage—Using lots of lube, massage the outside of his anus with your thumb and fingertips. Be creative. If he likes it (and believe me, many men do), gently massage around the inside of his anus. Stimulate his prostate.

As He Likes It

Whatever it is he seems to like best and desire, do it freestyle with gusto. You can include a massage with your mouth and tongue, and add intercourse if desired.

ENDING THE SPECTACULAR SEX MASSAGE FOR BOTH MEN AND WOMEN

If you ended up having oral sex or intercourse, you will likely want to end the massage in your own delicious way. But if you didn't, here's a beautiful ending.

A Happy Ending

Rock-a-Bye Baby—With your palms, rock her/his body from side to side.

The Brush Rush—Gently brush her/his whole body with your fingertips.

Sensorium—Do some sensual things such as kiss some wine or juice into your lover's mouth, feed a grape, ring a bell in his/her ear, tease him/her with a feather or silk scarf, or feed him/her a chocolate.

The Cocoon—Wrap her/him in a sheet or blanket. Let her/him be still for a few minutes. Don't touch or fluff her/him. Just stay present with her/him. After this massage, many people feel very blissed out and are in an erotic trace. Let them enjoy it.

The Baby Wipe—After you slowly open up the cocoon/sheet, take a towel and towel off your lover's skin. Remove powder or oil, lovingly and tenderly, as if he/she had just been reborn.

Love Sweet Love—Whisper compliments and sweet words into her/his ears. Kiss the forehead. Give her/him plenty of time to bask in the afterglow.

And in the End . . .

After the massage, you may want to give your partner time with himself/herself or you may want to snuggle together for a while. Notice how transformed you feel in comparison with when you started? You'll likely say, "I needed that." Feel the new energy you have created in your immediate environment. Let it move through you and you through it. Enjoy your intimate connection and the good feelings it has generated in your bodies. That connection is a little bit of heaven. You may want to say thank you.

Dr. Sprinkle's Orgasm 101

The orgasm is no longer a mere biological function, nor the side effect of casual pleasure . . . It is the very center of human experience and ultimately determines the happiness of the human race.

WILHELM REICH

*G*rab yourself some of our delicious buttery organic popcorn and follow me into the center's screening room for a power-point presentation of orgasm's greatest hits. Storing this information in your memory bank will help ensure that you won't be shortchanged when it comes to your orgasm opportunities. Taking this class is a good investment in your erotic future.

First I will tell you a bit about the history of orgasm research. Then I will share with you a way to become much more orgasmic by expanding your concept and definition of orgasm. In the next Step, 13, I'll discuss a whole bunch of possibilities for different types of orgasms and ways to have them.

While there is plenty of information here about both the male and the female orgasm experience, I will focus more on the female orgasm, partly because I am a female and I want to share from personal experience, but also because many men tell me they want to learn more about female orgasm as well. So if you are a man who loves women, I hope this will be helpful for you in pleasuring your partner.

You Can Do It— You Probably Already Have

If I had a dollar for every woman who's told me she can have great orgasms when masturbating alone but has trouble coming when with a lover, I'd be rich. Some women tell me they have never, ever had an orgasm. When they tell me about their difficulties with orgasm, they are desperate, often on the verge of tears. I feel their pain and frustration. This is no joke. They consider themselves "nonorgasmic." First I usually suggest that they probably *have* had orgasms but weren't yet conscious of them, just as we all dream every night but aren't always aware of our dreams. (I'll explain more later.) Then I assure them that they can learn to be (more) orgasmic.

Diversified Portfolio

I also meet women who tell me they're very orgasmic, but they've heard about various super-duper orgasms. They want to know how they can have an orgasm that lasts an hour or an orgasm that requires no physical contact; an orgasm that includes female ejaculation or the mysterious full-body orgasm. Women want to learn how to experience all these— and they can.

Are you one of the many women who feel that they could have better orgasms, or more varied orgasms, or more frequent orgasms? Or perhaps you have yet to experience your first orgasm. If you are "preorgasmic," it simply means you think you have not had an orgasm . . . yet. Do not despair. You very likely will.

Almost everyone has had difficulty reaching orgasm at some time in his or her life. If you have, too, it's likely there isn't a thing wrong with you. In fact, you belong to a big sorority— 10 to 15 percent of adult women claim they've never had an orgasm. Far more say they have difficulty having orgasms; some studies estimate the number to be as high as 50 percent.

The reasons we don't have orgasms can be emotional, hormonal, or psychological; a side effect of medication; or the result of communication problems with our partners. Or lack of a (helpful) partner. Far less frequently, the problem is physical. Negative thinking, anxiety, expectations, boredom, past trauma, and low levels of desire and passion can be factors. The good news is that, as we age and become more at home in our own lovely bodies, most of us do become more orgasmic. If you are not yet deep into your thirties, you should understand that you are very likely still just learning, and have a lot to look forward to. How to experience a wide variety of orgasms can be learned and developed— and is a skill worth learning. We are going to make you much more orgasmic in a variety of ways, primarily by making over your mind about how you think about orgasm.

Early Withdrawal

Research has shown that human infants and preadolescents can actually have a simple kind of energy release that could be called "orgasm" and that looks something like a sneeze or a yawn. This was reported in Alfred Kinsey's famous study *Sexual Behavior in the Human Female* (1953). What he documented was that ". . . there is a buildup of neuromuscular tensions which may culminate at a peak—from which there may be a sudden discharge of tensions, followed by a return to a normal physiologic state." But even if we once knew, we can forget how to have orgasms for a while or become socially conditioned into not having them. Orgasm is a natural bodily function. We have to get our minds out of the way and let our bodies do what comes naturally.

If you've been beating yourself up for not being orgasmic enough (or for the common male concerns—being nonorgasmic or prematurely orgasmic), the first thing to do is to stop. Right now, just stop! There's no sense in making yourself more miserable, and it doesn't help change things at all. Rather than putting terrible pressure on yourself, use love—self-love—to get yourself where you want to go.

Trust Fund

Begin by developing positive thoughts and feelings around orgasm. Whenever you can, practice the following:

Cheer Yourself On—Tell yourself silently or, better yet, out loud, "I am at the right place at the right time in learning about my orgasms. I love myself unconditionally, and day by day I'm learning more."

Trust Your Process—Pat yourself on the back, caress your forehead, put your hand on your heart, or perform some gesture that expresses love and support for yourself, as you are quite perfect as you are. If someone doesn't speak French, would we think less of him or her? If you don't yet speak the language of orgasm, that's perfectly okay. In time and with practice, you will become fluent.

Be Compassionate with Yourself—Develop acceptance of wherever you are now. Try to let go of all expectations and self-imposed pressures. Don't buy into any pressure tactic, whether it's coming from a partner or from the media or from your own self. Instead, put your energy into creating the right conditions for you to enjoy orgasms on your own terms. You will get there on your own timetable, in your own way. Don't you feel better already?

Listen to the Wisdom of Your Body—Your body is a great coach, and it's trying to tell you things. Listen.

PROSPERITY CONSCIOUSNESS

If you are already an orgasmic woman, or even a glutton for 'gasms, I guarantee there is more you (we all) can learn. If you've had any experience with yoga, you know that it's a process where you learn more and get better at it the more you practice. You won't be assuming the advanced postures during your first classes. While it doesn't take very long to learn the basic concepts, postures, and activities, it is only through months and even years of practice that the experience of yoga deepens and transforms us. Exploring orgasm is a lot like yoga. The basic concepts can come easily, but it takes some practice and commitment to get really good at it. Yet anyone can do it.

The Fun and Functions of the Orgasm or Why Cum?

Why have orgasms? Allow Dr. Sprinkle, certified sexologist and orgasm Olympian, to start with some basics: First, there's pleasure—pure and simple. For most of us, orgasms feel extraordinarily good. During orgasm, wonderful sensations wave and pulse through our genitals and, on a good day, can spread throughout our bodies.

Orgasm can lead us toward our more relaxed selves. They can make us happier as they change our body chemistry, releasing endorphins, serotonin, oxytocin, and who-knows-what other biological happy dust the scientific researchers have yet to discover.

Sometimes the benefits of orgasm are simply practical. For example, orgasms can help us sleep better by releasing pent-up sexual tension. Orgasms can help repair damaged relationships. Some women who've felt frustration and bitterness in their relationships report that they become much less angry, and more contented and loving, when they regularly experience good orgasms. Orgasms can make us feel closer to our partners, open our hearts, and reboot the romance in a relationship.

Then there's the energy-lifting aspect of orgasm. Orgasms can put a bounce in your step, and make you feel more confident and optimistic. If you're feeling drowsy, I prescribe a quick orgasm. Orgasm has been known to work as excellent intervention against writer's block, so my Hitachi Magic Wand is never far from my computer.

For many people, orgasm is the climax to a lovely evening. It signals the end of a sexual encounter, the way a period marks the end of a sentence. Treating orgasm as the end of a sexual encounter can be handy at times. But beware: Orgasm certainly isn't the be-all and end-all of every sexual encounter. We are not socially programmed to have non-goal-oriented, playful, euphoric sex without worrying about a crescendo tying everything in a bow. We are taught that sex is incomplete or unsatisfactory without an orgasm and that when we "achieve" orgasm we achieve success. So when we don't, we "fail." However, as sex therapists say, "Sex is not a competitive sport," not at its heart. Making love is a dance with its own dips and twirls and turns. If orgasm is the only goal, we miss most of the tango by focusing only on the back-bending finale.

Off the Charts

For some of us, orgasm can be a highly spiritual experience. Human beings have a longing to go beyond everyday reality to a kind of mystical state. Nothing makes a girl feel more like a real live goddess than a full-body orgasm. We can let go of our ego and everyday reality for some moments and feel as beautiful as one hundred sunsets. (See below for how to do this, if you don't already know.)

How to Make Your Orgasms More Spiritual and Your Spirit More Sex-Ful

If you have not experienced sex or orgasm as a spiritual event, I suggest you consider this:

Imagine that you are sitting on top of a hill watching a sunrise. There are two ways to watch.

1. The Unconscious Way—You are not really paying much attention to the sunrise at all. You're sitting there, thinking about the things you have to do later that day. You feel uncomfortable sitting on the ground. Your mind wanders all over the place. You think you don't really care much about sunrises in the first place. You don't feel much or see much. The sunrise is pretty, but it doesn't mean much to you.

2. The Conscious Way—You are sitting on a hill watching a sunrise. You give it all your attention and go deeply into its beauty and mystery. You imagine the sunlight filling you until you positively glow. You ponder the miracle of the sun rising every morning. You feel the sun's rays on your skin and soak up their warmth. You focus your thoughts on the sunrise, letting other thoughts go by, without giving them attention. Suddenly you become overwhelmed

with the perfection of the moment and you are moved to cry. You breathe into the feelings, until you have what you could call a spiritual experience.

Now try it with a sexual situation.

1. There's the unconscious way.
2. There's the conscious way.

Whether your orgasm is a spiritual and enlightening experience or not is pretty much up to you. Your orgasm can take over, or expand, or enlighten your whole being simply because you have focused your entire attention on it and looked for the magnificence of it.

Mourning Glory

Orgasm can be excellent therapy. Very recently a friend of mine died. I was very busy, unable to get in touch with any grief, and I felt rather numb, until about a week later when I had an orgasm with my lover. The intensity of feeling and the relaxation from the orgasm allowed me to release the pent-up feelings of grief I had not acknowledged, and I fell weeping into my lover's supportive arms. That's what I call a "crygasm," and it's one of my favorite kinds of orgasms. Many women tell me they sometimes cry when they come, not because they feel sad but because they feel deeply happy and moved. Sometimes our sex partners think it's weird, or they may worry that they're hurting us. But if we just explain to them how good it feels to come and cry at the same time, they usually get it. On the other hand—and I believe this requires less explanation for most women—orgasms can also trigger hearty laughter. I call those "laughgasms."

Double Digits

Orgasm is a handy painkiller. Once I volunteered to be a laboratory guinea pig for sex researchers Gina Ogden and Beverly Whipple, who did a scientific study of the power of orgasm to change a woman's experience of the pain threshold. They wired me up to machines that measured physiological responses, then put my finger in a little mechanized vise that could squeeze my finger—a little, a lot, and fairly hard. Then they asked me to masturbate to orgasm. They discovered they could squeeze my finger (and many other women's fingers) much harder after an orgasm! Why was I not surprised?

Ya Can't Foil Me

Another time, I used orgasm as a pain reliever after gum surgery, when pain pills weren't enough. I had tinfoil on all my teeth, a swollen face, and I didn't look or feel the least bit sexy, but my lover compassionately applied oral sex, just to make me feel better and to ease the pain. It worked like a charm.

Lust in the Dust

Author of *Sacred Orgasms,* Ray Stubbs, believes that orgasm generates "primordial healing energy." I'm not totally sure about the primordial part, but I couldn't agree more about the healing part, as illustrated by an experience I had with my former lover Willem De Ridder. He had very bad asthma, and when we visited Pompeii and spent a day in the dust, he had a serious attack in the middle of the night. It was one of those moments that every asthmatic fears: medical help was far away, and the attack was one of those terrifying ones that could have become fatal. I tried everything I could think of to help Willem breathe more easily, but nothing calmed him enough to lessen the attack. Finally, in a panic, though sex was the last thing on our minds, I administered oral sex. He had an orgasm, which relaxed him enough to take some deep breaths. To this day he swears that that blow job saved his life.

Orgasm (and sex) also works wonders to ease menstrual cramps and migraine headaches. Studies show that some people with arthritis can achieve significant pain relief for several hours after orgasm. It also boosts the immune system, strengthens the heart, and decreases blood pressure.

Exit This Way

Joseph Kramer believes that orgasms can help prepare us for our death, because they teach us how to surrender and let go. Kramer isn't the first to make this connection between orgasm and final, existential surrender. The French even refer to orgasm as *le petit mort*, the little death. My friend Norma Wilcox, a nurse, told me about her husband's dying moments. He had suffered a long time from cancer. He actually died having a great big orgasm while she was changing the catheter in his penis. "It's exactly how he would have wanted to go," she said with a smile.

Mini-exercise: Think of three ways you have used, could use, or would like to use orgasm in positive ways in your life.

1. _____

2. _____

3. _____

Misappropriation of Fun

A note of caution: Anything this good is bound to be misused. Sometimes orgasms are used to express anger, control, and power. Sometimes orgasm can actually take away intimacy, or become a chore, or be used as an agent of control. My friend Sharon had a mean boyfriend who consistently withheld his orgasm to make her feel she was a lousy lover. Another woman I once knew consistently put down her lover for not being an orgasmic woman. Sometimes women really berate their man if he comes before she'd like him to. That kind of misuse of orgasm really hurts, and no one should have to put up with it. And let's not forget the antisex fanatics and extremists who threaten us, saying that orgasm for pleasure's sake is sinful and dooms us to hell. Well, at least we'll all have plenty of company!

Sit down and ask yourself if there are any negative associations with orgasm you might be harboring. Does a part of you think orgasm is disgusting, gross, dirty? Do you find it embarrassing, humiliating, unattractive, shameful? Do you feel that it makes you a weak person? Or that you don't deserve that pleasure? Do you associate orgasm with a negative experience from your past? Does the pressure to have them or not have them create a lot of anxiety and disappointment? If you answered yes to any of these, ask yourself more about why. These are not uncommon thoughts and feelings.

Would you like to reprogram yourself so you can enjoy more of the benefits and beauties of orgasm? Here's how. Before, during, and after orgasm, aim to think only wonderful, positive, loving thoughts. Rewrite your own internal script by using helpful fantasies. When you come, simply accentuate the positive. You've got nothing to lose and a lot to gain.

ORGASMS AREN'T EVERYTHING

There are so many wonderful reasons to have orgasms; however, I don't mean to say that you can't have a fulfilling sex life without orgasms. You certainly can live a wonderful, fruitful, glorious, satisfying life without ever having a single orgasm. Truly.

Anthropologists have noted that some entire societies virtually ignore female orgasm. But happily I don't belong to that society. I highly recommend the experience.

If this last exercise was hard for you, you are not alone. Most other people can't do it, either. The truth is, there is no one definitive answer to the question; there are many. When I set out to study more about orgasm, I was amazed to discover how little was actually known about the topic even by scientists and academics; it was just like knowing the top of an iceberg or the principle of a big long-term loan. Since orgasm is such a common experience, and the experience is among the most pleasurable most human beings will ever know in their lifetimes, one would think that this would be worthy of investing enormous study. The scientific community is not immune to sex-phobic thinking and politics, though, and many professionals are not willing to risk the shame and stigma of doing orgasm research; even if they are, they can't get the funding.

Fortunately, there have been a few brave souls who have overcome the obstacles and devoted themselves to at least a bit of the study of orgasm. They have come up with a variety of theories about orgasm and how it occurs. These theories are also known as "models of orgasm."

Freudian Slipup

Naturally orgasm has been studied and written about for many centuries. But let's start with Freud's thoughts on the subject, which still really affect us today. He believed there were two types of female orgasm—vaginal and clitoral. (To me, that's like saying there are two kinds of fruit—bananas and blueberries.) Brilliant as he was, Freud believed that vaginal orgasms were the true, "mature" orgasms. Meaning that clitoral orgasms were "immature"? Since he saw the clitoris as a stunted penis, a clitoral orgasm would be both "masculine" and "immature." Some feminists conjecture that Freud said this in part because as a man deep down he hoped the ultimate orgasm was from penetration. In any case, Freud's belief informed much of twentieth-century thinking about female orgasm and went far to screw things up for women (and for men, too, for that matter) for a long time. It got to the point where it was not all that uncommon for doctors a century ago (shortly after Freud's time) to remove a young girl's clitoris if they were afraid she was masturbating her clitoris too much, or just might try. *Oy vey!*

Who's Counting?

From the mid-1950s, through the '80s, Dr. William Masters and his assistant-turned-wife, Virginia Johnson, researched human sexuality. They studied hundreds of women (and men) having orgasms in the laboratory. (Doesn't that sound like a fascinating job?) Moving away from the Freudian distinction between mature and immature orgasm, they basically proved that Freud's theory was erroneous. They defined the "sexual response cycle" in four phases: excitement, plateau, orgasm, and resolution. In so doing, Masters and Johnson made a huge contribution to the research about orgasm. However, they focused almost exclusively on the physiological aspects and mechanics of orgasm, which is a bit like saying that life is about heartbeats, blood flow, and sweat glands.

Market Research

Among the next generation of orgasm researchers was Helen Singer Kaplan, who was a sex therapist. In 1979, she defined three arousal states: desire, excitement, and orgasm. What made her theory special is that she included "desire" as an important part of the cycle. This seems obvious to us now, but back then it was a new concept. Certainly levels of desire can indeed affect our orgasms and our potential for them.

Descriptions of the varieties of female orgasm have been offered by some other folks. Researchers Josephine and Irving Singer suggested that there are three different types of female orgasm—vulval, uterine, and blended (vulval plus uterine). Dr. Michael Perry, a friend of mine in Los Angeles who produces sex-education films, managed to videotape the inside of several vaginas before, during, and after various kinds of orgasms. He said he found four different types of female orgasm, which he coined "plateau," "tonic," "clonic," and "fusion." The variables of each of these and their descriptions are too lengthy and complex to go into here. But the point is that different people have defined various different kinds of orgasms, categorized them, and given them a variety of names.

Women Invested in More Orgasm Research

Today some wonderful women are challenging the old models of orgasm. Sexologist Leonore Tiefer (who was mentioned in Step 3) criticizes Masters and Johnson's four-phase model on which so many sexologists and sex therapists today still rely. She argues that their theory is limited by an exclusive focus on the physical, that the psychological and social aspects of human experience are ignored. Tiefer suggests that when it comes to orgasm, it is really important to "combine psychophysiological sophistication with respect for individual and couple diversity."

Mikaya Hart, who wrote a book about female orgasm called *When the Earth Moves*, similarly writes that "we need to stop defining sex as merely physical function, and begin to acknowledge its emotional and spiritual depth." Some aspects of orgasm may be impossible to ever define. But clearly we need more research.

Talk to Me, Baby

Then there's Bob Schwartz, a successful author who teaches a class about "extended sexual orgasm," also known as E.S.O. Naturally, I took his class. Schwartz suggests that sex partners use a system of telling each other their exact degree of arousal, which he breaks down into five basic levels. They are flat, a little turned-on, turned-on, highly passionate, and feeling out of control (too high). Schwartz says that the idea is to get to, and stay in, an extended orgasmic state through constant verbal communication between partners. I find it really difficult to talk continually when I am most excited, but, hey, it seems to work for some folks.

Triple Yield

In a nutshell, contemporary Western sexologists generally define the orgasm cycle as a buildup of muscular tension in the genitals, called "myotonia," with an engorgement of blood, called "tumescence" or "vasocongestion." With increasingly intensifying sensation this leads to a grand release of the muscular tension, called "orgasm." Multiple orgasms are a repeat of this pattern.

There is only an armful of good books specifically about orgasm, and my favorite one is *The Essential Tantra,* by Ray Stubbs, Ph.D. His definition is: "Orgasm is an event where two or more vibratory patterns change so that they resonate with each other, and a new vibratory pattern occurs which consists of the initial vibratory patterns, plus the vibratory pattern of primordial incarnated energy." Pretty heady, eh? He has named four types of orgasms: "sexual orgasm, light body orgasm, spirit body orgasm and soul body orgasm." Did you get all that? To translate and simplify, Ray takes an energy-oriented approach to orgasm, as opposed to a physical-muscular/tension-release approach. He believes that we are more than our physical body and that orgasms can also occur in our "light body," "spiritual body," and our "soul system," or several of these at a time. Furthermore, he says that *sexual* orgasms are just one kind of orgasm, that orgasm can occur while sky-diving, climbing a rope, listening to *Tristan and Isolde,* during a religious service, etc. I totally agree with Ray, that orgasm is largely an energy-oriented experience besides the physiological aspects, that it is a fuller, more helpful way to view and define this amazing phenomenon.

Clitoral Analysis

Betty Dodson, Ph.D., whom I have mentioned before, is the sex educator widely known for writing the first feminist book on masturbation. Since 1970, she's been teaching mas-turbation skills. In her amazing women's Bodysex Workshops, she has taught many women about orgasm. She has been my beloved mentor and role model since the mid-1970s. We are of like mind on most issues, except when it comes to defining orgasm, a mat-ter on which we differ and have heated disagreements. Betty basically believes the exact opposite of Freud. She feels that the clitoris is a woman's primary sex organ and that cli-toral orgasms are the real, worthwhile, true orgasms. She feels that women must learn to master their clitoral orgasms. Although she teaches women to combine vaginal penetra-tion along with their clitoral stimulation for a "combination orgasm," you could say Betty is clit-centric. If anyone can kick Freud's butt, it's Betty.

Given how Freud and his anticlitoral-orgasm followers have influenced so many people's thinking about women's sexual pleasure, I do see Betty's point. But I know a lot of women who just wouldn't put their bets on Clits Rule.

Some feminists believe that the clitoris is relatively a much larger body part than previ-ously thought, that it has "legs"—I call them "roots"—that branch down into the vaginal area. So it could be said that vaginal orgasms could in fact be clitoral orgasms, too. Redefining the clitoris as a huge area is somewhat controversial, and some folks think this adds to the confusion as to what kind of orgasm is what. But one thing I know is that orgasms from clitoral stimulation feel really different than those from vaginal stimulation. Certainly clitoral orgasms are terrific. But my experience tells me that we can have many different kinds of orgasms that actually don't involve the clitoris at all.

My Way

My own definition of orgasm is this:

> *Orgasm is the pleasurable release, explosion, or streaming of built-up erotic or sexual energy in its broadest sense. And it can occur in many different areas of the body, in many different ways.*

In my book (and this is my book), if you feel that you might be having some kind of orgasm, then you likely are. By claiming more of our pleasurable energy releases as kinds of orgasmic experience, we become more and more orgasmic, live more orgasmic lives, and develop our full orgasmic potential—which can be phenomenal. Although there are some fine lines as to what I'd consider or not consider an orgasm, no one is going to give you a pass/fail grade. So stake your claim.

The same goes for men, of course. Orgasm doesn't necessarily mean ejaculation. Men are capable of all kinds of orgasms, too, that don't even have anything to do with their penises. Although from what I hear, penile orgasms with ejaculation are wonderful. Just not the only game in town.

Orgasm Disclaimer

There are as many different theories of orgasm as there are orgasm experts. Some theories are contradictory. Others have similarities. We may have come a long way when it comes to orgasm research, but there's still a heck of a long way to go.

Please know that the following information is based on my own view, study, and experience, which can vary from those of other people, and from yours.

Granted my ideas about orgasm, although shared by many other orgasm experts I know, are outside the usual paradigm of orgasm used by the general public and the sexology community. That makes it somewhat revolutionary, all the more interesting, and, I believe, the wave of the future.

Expand Your Idea of What Orgasm Is

One of the first things we need to do in order to expand our orgasm opportunities is to expand our idea of what an orgasm is. Let's begin with a true story:

LEFT FOR BROKE

A young man suffered a radical spinal-cord break in an accident when he was eleven years old; his entire body was paralyzed, and he was left without a sense of touch anywhere below his neck. There was no hope that one day he might actually enjoy sex in any conventional sense of the word. He never had a girlfriend, or any kind of sexual experience, and there was little chance he ever would.

When he was twenty-five, he told his parents he wanted to know about and perhaps experience something sexual. Fortunately, he had compassionate and loving parents who hired a sex surrogate (a trained professional who is part therapist, part educator, and part boudoir companion).

The surrogate worked with him weekly over the course of several months, making him feel safe and winning his trust. Then she began to explore his body, inch by inch, to see if there were any places where his skin would respond to pleasurable stimulation, some place where he might have some feeling. Sure enough, they discovered an area on the inside of his upper left arm, about two square inches of skin, where his injury had apparently left him with a modest level of sensory response. Over time and with much patience and encouragement, the surrogate brought him to feel an increasingly intense sensual pleasure in response to her kisses and licks of that one small place.

COMING TO MATURITY

On the day of his twenty-sixth birthday, the surrogate went all out, teasing and playing with that spot, sucking and nibbling, to the point where the young man cried out in pleasure in a way she had not witnessed from him before. The concentrated sensual stimulation led to an extremely pleasurable energy burst, which in turn, compelled him to cry out in joy. What he experienced that day could only be called an orgasm. With tears welling up in his eyes and laughter in his voice, he told the surrogate that it had been the best birthday present he had ever received.

Perhaps you are not prepared to describe what this man experienced as orgasm, because it lacked the physical evidence we usually associate with male orgasm—the blood-engorged penis, the ejaculation, and so forth. But to him, as well as to the sex surrogate—who had helped her share of men reach orgasm under difficult circumstances—it was a bona fide orgasm.

EXTENDING CREDIT

The point is that in my view there are all kinds of orgasms, and virtually anyone can learn to experience them. Like the young man in the above story, some quadriplegics and paraplegics who have lost or never had genital sensation have reported experiences that are undeniably orgasmic. If they can have a variety of orgasmic experiences, so can you.

Then again, perhaps you share the same view and definition of orgasm as I do and you've had experiences similar to mine. Terrific. Isn't it nice to know that you aren't alone?

I have experienced many types of orgasms myself, have observed them in other women and in men, and have received reports of others. But before I share them with you, I would like you to please take this oath:

Orgasm Oath

I solemnly swear that to the best of my ability I will not use any of this information to make myself feel inadequate in any way. I intend to use this information to learn and grow. I am willing to open my mind to new ideas about orgasm and to perhaps try an orgasm makeover on for size.

Step Thirteen

Seize Your Orgasm Opportunities

*It may be discovered someday that an orgasm actually
lasts for hours and only seems like a few seconds.*
DOLLY PARTON

Come, I've prepared a beautiful room for you that makes you feel positively royal. The room is lit by the large crystal chandelier that seems to hold a whole world in each droplet. Listen to the music: It matches the rhythm of your heartbeat and entices your body to follow its call. There are delicious treats for you, an ambrosia of exotic fruits and sweet nectars. A very comfortable bed to luxuriate in. Your immediate needs are fulfilled. There is nothing to do but to lie back and enjoy. The time has come for you to cum. Let me offer you a selection.

Dr. Sprinkle's Orgasm Sampler

Here is a sprinkling of different kinds of orgasms that I've come, literally, to believe you are capable of experiencing:

1. *Genital Orgasms.* These are orgasms that occur in the genital area. They require some level of physical stimulation (analogous to BodySex).
2. *Energy Orgasms.* These orgasms occur without genital physical stimulation (analogous to EnergySex).
3. *Hybrid Orgasms.* These are the neoclassics—designer orgasms, if you will. They occur through physical stimulation but with an awareness of energy release or energy flow (analogous to Body+EnergySex).

1. BELOW THE GARTER BELT—GENITAL ORGASMS

Clitoral Orgasms

Clitoral orgasms are the most common and popular kind of female orgasm today. (Fifty years from now that could possibly change. Who knows?) These are generally the kind of orgasms most gals long to have, or to have more of. The clitoris is stimulated, energy builds in the form of muscular tension, and orgasm occurs when this explodes or releases. A clitoral orgasm can be small, hiccuplike, and just in the pelvic area, or it can radiate out of the pelvis into an overwhelming, full-bodied rush. My friend Kembra describes her clitoral orgasms beautifully, as being like a glass of cool water that fills up slowly and, when it's full, overflows down the sides of the glass.

Physically, some of the following things may happen: Your clitoris becomes engorged and throbs, your heart rate speeds up, your toes curl, your vagina lubricates, your pelvic floor contracts, your nipples turn to pebbles, your breathing changes, your back arches, you claw your lover's back . . . and you yell, "*Eeee, yes, yes, oh, God! Don't stop!*"

If you have never had a clitoral orgasm, or you want to have more of them, what can you do? The only correct answer to this question, or any other questions about female sexuality, for that matter, is "It depends." You simply have to find what combination of things work for *you* and realize that whatever worked before can change at any time. Begin by practicing alone masturbating. Here are some ideas that could help:

PLEASURE PRIMER

- First and foremost, *think positively,* by replacing any negative thoughts with positive thoughts.
- *Stimulate your clitoris* in whatever way feels best. Some women like indirect stimulation, some direct, some to the right side or left side, top or bottom. Although you don't necessarily need to start with clitoral stimulation to have a clitoral orgasm. Sometimes it's best to start vaginally or labially and work toward the clitoris, teasing slowly.
- I strongly recommend that you *practice regularly.* Once a month, or even once a week isn't enough. The more you practice, the quicker you will learn.
- *Use a vibrator.* Most women learn to come or learn to have multiple orgasms by using a good sturdy vibrator, as it provides constant and steady stimulation. Start by vibrating the back of your neck, forehead, hands, feet, thighs, and belly to warm up.
- *Masturbate* with something (safe) inside your vagina: a dildo, a candlestick, or a nice cool cucumber, etc. (Put a condom over objects which might have chemicals or pesticides on them.)
- *Relax.* Don't worry; be horny.
- *Use music* and do the orgasm dance. Just let go and have fun doing a horizontal erotic dance. Let the music turn you on.
- *Don't analyze; fantasize.* Let your analytical thoughts just pass right through your pretty head. Fantasize unabashedly.
- *Focus totally on the physical sensations* you're having. This "sensate focus" can work even better than fantasizing for some women.
- *Experiment with your breath.* Hold it, breathe deeply, then try very fast and shallow breaths. Not necessarily in that order. Breathing helps you focus on and intensify the physical sensations.
- *Read erotica, look at sexy pictures, or watch a good porn movie.*
- *Undulate your hips.* Try lifts and circles and bucking your hips as if into a lover.
- *Use variety.* Try face up, down, side, standing, sitting, etc. Alternate between ex-

tending your legs and bending your knees, flexing your feet and pointing your toes. Try masturbating in a shoulder stand, on your tummy, in front of a mirror, in the bathtub, *however you can!* Experimentation is the name of the game.

- *Add Kegel kisses* (as described in Step 6).
- *Lie with pillows under your buttocks,* so your pelvis is raised higher than your head. This can be a real turn-on.
- *Pinch, pull, and tickle your nipples.* Hold your breasts in your hands, squeeze and roll them around the way a lover would. This can be a delightful distraction from trying too hard to orgasm.
- *Make sexy sounds!* Moan, whisper, say "dirty" words to yourself or to an imaginary lover.
- *Go with the flow.* Follow your body's natural urges. If you feel an impulse to roll over and hump the covers, do it. If you really listen to your body, it will let you know what it needs and wants.
- *Let yourself be wild, free, and outrageous.*
- Some women learn to have clitoral orgasms by *working with a sex therapist.* The sex therapist will usually give you homework, exercises to practice at home alone. You can contact the American Association of Sex Educators, Counselors and Therapists for referrals. Also, now there are actually "orgasm coaches" who can sit with you and watch how you masturbate and give you pointers. (See the Resources.) This can be highly successful, fun, and a unique experience, although it's not every woman's cup of tea.
- *Don't give up too quickly.* It's likely that a few minutes are not long enough for you. Hang in there for an hour if need be, or even longer. So, when practicing having orgasms, take all the time you need. And take heart—the longer it takes to get there, the better it can be!
- *Try self-pleasuring with your vulva facing into a mirror.* This can look really hot and send you right over the edge.

TIPS FOR THE DYNAMIC DUO

If you find it very difficult to have a clitoral orgasm when you are having sex with a lover, what can you do?

- First, *think hard about why* it might be difficult for you. Visualize your lover and pay attention to the thoughts and feelings that arise. Do you have any fears or concerns about coming with any lover, or just with that particular person? Are you embarrassed about what turns you on? Afraid of too much intimacy or looking like a crazy woman? Worried that you'll mess up your eyeliner, wet the bed, or wake the neighbors? Fear a heart attack or spontaneous combustion? You probably can intuit the answer. Unrealistic fears aren't serving you, so try to use positive thinking to rise above them.

- *Think about whether there are mechanical reasons to explain why* you aren't getting over the hump. Are the ways in which your partner stimulates you optimal? Are you in the position that feels best for you?

- *Is your partner really taking enough time* to stimulate you to orgasm? If not, explain to your partner that it takes more time for you to reach orgasm. Do not be afraid of alienating or turning off your lover; most people really want to please their lovers.

- *Tell your partner exactly what you like and want.* You can do it! If you've discovered, through solo research, what helps you to come, you must show your lover the way. Once you begin sharing sexual information with your partner, it will get easier and easier, until it feels as natural and necessary as talking about what to make for dinner, but much more interesting and fun.

- *Let go of always needing to give.* Kick back and *totally* receive, guilt-free. Most women have been taught that it's "better to give than to receive." In some instances I'd agree, but when we take it as far as to feel we don't deserve sexual satisfaction, it's time to throw out guilt-inducing ideas and receive, baby, receive!

- *If you are having a relationship issue, clear it up* before you get in the sack.

- If you are on *antidepressants or medications that make it hard to orgasm,* talk to your doctor about changing the kind you take. If you can't reach orgasm for a long time because of a drug's side effects, you might get even more depressed and anxious than you'd be without the darned pills!

- *Lend your lover a hand!* Massage your clitoris with your fingers or with a vibrator during intercourse or even oral sex. I've never had a lover (and I've had many) who didn't like it when I massaged my own clit during sex, particularly when he/she saw how good it made me feel.

- *Add Kegels.* Remember: These can help stimulate you from the inside and pump up more volts of sexual energy.
- *Think erotic thoughts.* Besides being a turn-on, thinking erotic thoughts keeps your mind off any worries, insecurities, mind chatter, or negative thinking.
- One thing you can do to help yourself orgasm with a partner is to *simulate partner sex* a bit more when you masturbate. Often women have a specific, very efficient pattern of masturbation to orgasm that works for them. But partner sex is a different dance. So during your solo practice, move the way you'd move with your lover and act as if your partner is there.
- *Do anything you can* to get more turned-on—within reason.
- If nothing else seems to work, you might want to *consider the possibility that the barrier between you and orgasm is biological.* If you have pain when you orgasm, you must discuss this with your gynecologist. If you are an older woman, perhaps you need to consider hormone adjustments. Judy, the most orgasmic woman I've ever met, was suddenly unable to have any kind of orgasm when she hit menopause. She was devastated because she loved her orgasms. Her doctor suggested that she try taking some natural hormone replacement, and she did. Almost immediately she was back in the saddle again. Although certainly many postmenopausal women have plenty of orgasms without any hormone replacement.

If you've tried all the above and you still are not having orgasms with your partner, please remember that not having an orgasm can also be very exciting and energizing. Simply enjoy not having orgasm. It's perfectly fine and normal and even sometimes desirable not to come. Think of it as building up the charge for the next time you make love, or use the energy for cleaning the house or winning a boxing competition.

GO FORTH AND MULTIPLY YOUR ORGASMS

The term "multiple orgasms" is nebulous, as it describes a variety of experiences. It could mean having a clitoral orgasm and a few minutes later having another one. Or it could mean having several orgasms right in a row. It could mean having many small orgasm waves with a big clitoral climaxing orgasm at the end.

Here's something for you more experienced gals: Can you distinguish between a clitoral orgasm wave and a clitoral climaxing orgasm? If not, then here's how to learn. Observe your body closely. Stimulate yourself to the verge of orgasm. Then let yourself have some little, short clitoral orgasms. Hold back the urge to have a big one. See how many tiny orgasms you can have without letting yourself go all the way over the "cliff." Then, after you've had several tiny orgasms, let yourself go for as big a climax as you can. After you try this, you will very likely understand the difference between an orgasm wave and a climaxing orgasm. A clitoral orgasm wave is like standing in the ocean, bobbing up and down in about four feet of water with small waves passing gently through you. A clitoral climaxing orgasm is more like riding a huge wave all the way to the shoreline, until you come to a complete stop.

Vaginal Orgasms

I believe that most sexually active women who are enjoying penetration are having what are popularly called "vaginal orgasms," but they often don't acknowledge them as such because they expect them to feel like clitoral orgasms, and they simply don't. I was having G-spot and vaginal orgasms for years before I became conscious that they were, in fact, orgasms. Once I realized that those feelings were orgasms, I nurtured and developed them and let go of my confusion about them, and they grew stronger and more distinct. Eventually I became quite clear as to what was an orgasm and what wasn't. A simple pleasurable body rush wasn't an orgasm, but a very pleasurable energy release or explosion that swept over me at the end of an arousal peak was. For me it was a learning process—and a very pleasurable one at that. I hope you will get the same rewards from your learning process.

In this category are orgasms that occur with vaginal penetration, be it with penises, fingers, dildos, or a fresh green cucumber. These would include vaginal, G-spot, and cervical orgasms. The borders between these different kinds of orgasms are blurry, but each kind has a slightly different feel. For me, a G-spot orgasm feels electric and tingly. A cervical orgasm (which can occur when there's repeated pressure on the cervix, which is deeper in than the G-spot) feels like a bass drum being hit and reverberating. A vaginal orgasm (it encompasses the whole vaginal area, including G-spot and cervix) feels like a big stone landing in a calm lake making ripples. *Ker-plop!* However, these might feel different for you.

TIPS FOR DEEP INSIDE

If you want to learn how to have, or have more, vaginal orgasms, try some of these tips:

- *Realize* that a vaginal orgasm is pretty easy to have. Don't make it difficult. Call whatever you think might be a vaginal orgasm a vaginal orgasm. It very likely is.
- *Pay attention* to those very first moments of penetration. If you are highly aroused and ready and your lover inserts a penis, finger, dildo, or whatever inside you, those first moments of penetration can trigger a vaginal orgasm—especially if you haven't had any sex in a while. Check it out.
- *Try to learn to distinguish* between energy building up and energy releasing or exploding, simply by paying close attention.
- *Ask your lover* to start with slow penetration, then build it up to go as fast and as hard as you can take it. Then stop suddenly. If you feel a nice energy release or burst, that is probably a vaginal orgasm.
- *Notice your sex sounds.* If you suddenly scream at the top of your lungs or make a very deep loud groan, that could very likely be a vaginal orgasm of some kind.
- To trigger a G-spot orgasm, *ask your lover to stimulate your G-spot area* for a good amount of time. Some women find firm pressure uncomfortable, but some women report that they need a lot of very firm pressure on their G-spots to orgasm from there. Some gals get triggered from being penetrated with a twisting motion from fingers or a dildo—like a washing-machine motion. Some gals come from a feeling of being stretched open.

BLENDED ORGASMS

These are when a woman has orgasm with stimulation of her clitoris while being stimulated vaginally and/or anally at the same time. Where this kind of orgasm starts and ends is difficult to tell. One thing is certain; it's a winner.

What a man, or woman, needs to remember to bring a woman to this kind of orgasm is to build arousal levels, keep focused, then keep a steady rhythm with only minor adjustments, and just don't stop!

2. Energy Orgasms—Look, Ma, No Hands!

Nocturnal Orgasms: Snoregasms and Dreamgasms

Did you ever wake up from a deep sleep and find that you were having an orgasm and you weren't even touching yourself or anything? *The Kinsey Report* found that 37 percent of American females had this experience at least once by the age of forty-five. Kinsey called them "nocturnal orgasms." I jokingly call them "snoregasms." Sometimes they are very mild, sometimes really strong. They sometimes occur with strong vaginal contractions, or they might not. Sometimes we dream we are having an orgasm and wake up and we are. As there is no genital stimulation, a nocturnal orgasm is a great example of an "energy orgasm."

A Group Energy Orgasm Story

At a certain point in my orgasm experiments, I and some of my peers discovered that it was possible simply to lie down, with our clothes on, and just will ourselves into a very yummy orgasmic state.

Once I experimented with this type of energy orgasm with a group of forty-five women and men at the end of a weeklong erotic massage seminar I was teaching called "Cosmic Orgasm Awareness Week," at a northern California resort. By the final hour of the seminar everyone was highly energized, excited, and wound up. I wanted people to leave fully satisfied and sensed they still needed some release. So I invited them to "lie down, keeping clothes on, just relax, and without any touching, let erotic feelings and energy rise to the surface." Imagine, if you will, a group of folks, lying on the floor, doing seemingly nothing, and then suddenly all together they quiver into a simultaneous energy orgasm, starting slowly, peaking, and then coming back down into an afterglow phase lasting several minutes. Everyone's orgasm sounds mixed with giggles were the sweetest music I think I've ever heard. By the time the workshop came to the very end (pun intended), everyone was fully satisfied, and quite amazed. It was so easy and natural, yet most of the participants would have thought it impossible before actually doing it.

Thinking Off

If all this sounds hard to believe, there is scientific proof that this kind of thing can happen. Sex researchers Beverly Whipple and Gina Ogden did a laboratory study where they looked into the possibility of what they called "thinking off." They studied several dozen female volunteers who claimed they could have orgasms without any genital stimulation. I was one of their volunteers. Hey, anything for science.

In their laboratory at Rutgers University, they wired me up to several machines that would measure my physiological responses, such as my heart rate and vaginal contractions. First I was instructed to have an orgasm in the "usual way," by self-stimulating my clitoris. So I did. After a few minutes' break, they asked me to try to have an orgasm without any physical stimulation. So I relaxed, fantasized sexual energy building, and mentally opened my body and mind up to let orgasmic energy build and then pulse through me. After a few minutes I had a release, an energy orgasm. According to their machines, my body had some of the same physiological responses as it did to the clitoral orgasm. Most of the other women they studied had similar results. They showed, scientifically, that some women can in fact "think off."

I Think, Therefore I Orgasm

Here are some tips to learn how to "think off" and have energy orgasms:

- *Realize* that energy orgasms feel very different from clitoral orgasms.
- *Believe* that it is possible; otherwise it's virtually impossible.
- *Pay attention.* Energy orgasms can be very subtle as well as very intense. You'll know that energy is being released when you feel little quivers and quakes and maybe some chills. These sensations are there just for the asking, residing just below the surface. All you need to do is let them bubble up, and pop! Dr. Ray Stubbs calls these "light-body orgasm" and notes that "they can be easily missed if we are not looking for them."
- *Expand your definition.* You can have various kinds of little microgasms, small energy orgasms, while doing nonsexual activities that you find highly pleasurable. Like riding fast on a motorcycle ("windgasms"), lying in the sun ("sungasms"), and listening to Anita Baker sing ("eargasms").

- *Take some classes* in tai chi, chi kung, yoga, karate, or any other discipline that works with energy. Although usually there is no mention of energy orgasms in these classes, they can help teach you about subtle energy.
- *Fake it 'til you feel it.* Acting as if you are having an energy orgasm can lead you into the actual experience.
- *Use your mind and erotic thoughts* to coax your body to respond orgasmically. Call on your memories of how orgasm feels.
- *Will your body* to erotically shake like a leaf on a tree in the wind.
- *Imagine that your heart area is opening up.* I find that if I imagine that my heart is opening up, creating a feeling of spaciousness, it can help open me up to the orgasmic energy.
- *Watch someone who knows how to do it.* The very best way to learn about energy orgasms is to watch someone have them. There are several videos where energy orgasms are demonstrated. In my documentary film, *Annie Sprinkle's Amazing World of Orgasm,* my friend Jwala demonstrates a doozie. The wonderful DVD *Ancient Secrets of Sexual Ecstasy* has some excellent examples (as well as other great information on how men can have long multiple orgasms without ejaculating).

Breath Orgasms

If you look into the history of various ancient, sexually wise cultures (such as the Tantrics, Taoists, and some Native American cultures), you will find that people have been having breath orgasms for thousands of years. Knowledge of them got suppressed and went underground because of the tyrannical oppression by antisex fanatics. But everything old is new again, and today "breathgasms" are all the rage. Quite a few sexuality teachers are teaching breath-orgasm techniques. Besides feeling really good, they're totally safe sex!

The first time I had a breath orgasm, it came as a surprise—you could say it was an electric shock! I was in a class learning a breathing technique called "rebirthing." Our group had been rhythmically breathing together for a couple of hours straight. It felt good, and everyone was highly energized. Suddenly I felt electricity shoot through my whole body, as if it had been plugged into an electrical outlet and had become a conduit for orgasmic energy. Intensely pleasurable feelings came in through my toes and shot out my fingers and the top of my head. It was the best physical feeling I had ever had. It was far more intense than any clitoral orgasm I'd had, and it kept going and going. Fortunately, the workshop leader, Joseph Kramer, had a sense of what was happening to me and was supportive, letting me go with the experience. I felt so much aliveness in my body, and all around me, and felt totally psychically cleansed and revitalized for days. After that I was hooked and started practicing how to have breath orgasms. It took me about a year to really get the hang of it, but sometimes people do learn how it works on their first try.

Only an Ecstasy Breath Away

Remember the Ecstasy Breathing technique you did in Step 6? Where you breathed energy up your body? Well guess what? If you do the ecstasy breathing for long enough you can experience a full-body energy orgasm, when the energy shoots out the top of your head. There are many different kinds of breath orgasms you can have; each one is quite unique. It can take some practice, but I've seen literally hundreds of people learn to do it.

3. Hybrid Orgasms—The Neoclassics

These orgasms occur with physical stimulation combined with an awareness of energy orgasms.

Body-Part-Gasms

Years ago I had a delightful lover who just loved to suck my nipples. He'd suck them for a long time, and suck them in a way that would turn me on incredibly. Then, *wow*, suddenly it felt as if my nipple were shooting electricity, and I screamed in ecstasy. If you know what I'm talking about, then you've probably had "nipplegasms," too. If you enjoy anal sex, you might at some point have had an "analgasm," where you felt like your anus happily exploded with the most beautiful fireworks. (Some women, and men, swear by them.) Some people orgasm in their lips just from extended passionate kissing. Under the right conditions, you can in fact experience orgasm in any erogenous part of your body, as you learned in the story about the man with the spinal-cord injury.

Here's how to have a body-part-gasm:

a. *Have your partner make love very intensely to one particular erogenous zone* for at least ten minutes, caressing, licking, sucking, biting, or whatever feels good.

b. With all your attention, *imagine erotic energy building* in that spot.

c. *Watch* for the moment when pleasurable energy releases from that spot or feelings of electricity shoot out. Those are body-part-gasms.

We are equipped with starter buttons all over our bodies. It's simply about getting the right kind of stimulation and inspiration, then building to that energy-release phase, letting it happen, and surrendering to the good feelings.

Body-to-Body-Gasms

Like rubbing two sticks together to make fire, the rubbing, humping, grinding of bodies together with genitals against thighs or bellies can eventually ignite incredible full-body energy orgasms. Sometimes this action is called "frottage" (French for *rubbing*), "tribadism" (usually used to describe lesbians rubbing their clits together), or "dry humping" (when a man and woman make like they're having intercourse, but with the penis outside the vagina—hence "dry"—but this can actually make you very wet).

Imagine your body is a big balloon. It inflates with energy when you passionately and enthusiastically rub your body against your lover's body. The deeper the breaths you take, the more your body fills with the energy. Do this for a while. When you feel really full of energy, tense your body tightly and hold your breath. Then let yourself "pop" as you exhale. You may feel the energy release into an orgasm.

The Megagasm

Now it's time I told you about what I call the "megagasm," the tsunami of orgasms.

As women, too often we spend time restraining our sexuality. We are conditioned to make no disturbance. Moisture on the sheets or otherworldly sounds emanating from our bodies are considered unladylike. Well, get ready all you unladylike ladies because the megagasm is for the woman who is ready to make a ruckus. It is an intense, full-body, and beyond-the-body experience. An enormous tension release occurs, to the point that you're virtually unable to stand up or think for a while after you've had one. I've had fewer than a dozen of these in my lifetime. One was when we were filming my experimental sex film, *Sluts and Goddesses*. We captured my megagasm on tape, so we were able to time it. It was five minutes long, very intense, and not at all ladylike! My face looked as if I were having

Basic Masters and Johnson
model of Female Sexual Response Cycle

ORGASM

Plateau

Resolution

excitement

Draw your own Orgasm here

Here is how I would chart some of my orgasm experiences. How would you chart yours?

a baby. Several women who saw the movie told me that they'd also had similar kinds of megagasms. So I'm definitely not the only one who has had them.

RIDE THE MEGAGASM WAVE

During a megagasm it can feel as if there were a lifetime of pent-up emotion bursting free—and it is. You might feel a sensation of being "breathed by the universe," your body open with electricity streaming through. You may experience lots of tingling in your hands and lips, your jaw may chatter, and your lover may end up having some kind of contact orgasm, too. Just hold on tight, and ride, ride, ride that humongous wild tidal wave of bliss.

Some people get scared of, or are uncomfortable with, the force of a woman's megagasm—or, for that matter, her other orgasms. Women tell me they feel they have to hold back the full force of their orgasms because their lovers can't handle it. That's a crying shame. To begin resolving this issue, I suggest that, when you're not in bed, you talk with your lover(s) about their fears and concerns. Explain to them how you feel and that you want the freedom to really be the powerful volcano that you are. (Of course, *you* have to give yourself that freedom as well.)

MEGAGASM MEMO

It's rather difficult to describe exactly how to have a megagasm, because women and their lovers are all so different. But here are some notes about megagasms:

Megagasms happen at times in your life when you need to release *a lot* of energy. You have to be in the mood to have such an intense release. From what I have gathered, megagasms don't happen all that often. In my experience, megagasms are brought about through very intense physical, sexual stimulation: very hard and fast vaginal penetration combined with really strong and steady clitoral stimulation. Sometimes they can be triggered by "erotic pain," such as from biting or stretching the vagina wider.

Some women I know have had their megagasms from "fisting." Fisting is when someone gets penetrated not just with fingers but with a whole hand. Then there's "semi-fisting," where several fingers and part of the thumb are inside, but not going past the knuckles. The stretching feeling can be really exciting for some folks, and some need that intense stimulation to trigger their biggest orgasms.

Give yourself permission to delve as deeply as possible into your biggest and strongest orgasm. Keep going beyond your threshold, beyond what you thought you were capable of.

To have more powerful orgasms, get in touch with your physical power in places other than the bedroom. Practice karate, do Tai Bo, kickboxing, dance wildly, etc. Just a few lessons can have a big impact. Be willing to express your power. Let the lion inside you roar!

Remember: Don't let any of this information make you feel inadequate if you have not yet experienced any of these orgasms. You are at the right place at the right time in learning about your orgasms. Or perhaps you've had various kinds of orgasms that I haven't even touched upon.

In Cum-clusion

Okay, let me guess what you might be thinking. You've read through this orgasm sampler, but you still feel resistant to some of these ideas about orgasm. You just don't buy this new expanded view, or that you can orgasm without genital stimulation. How do you really *know* that some of the things I've described aren't possible, just because maybe you haven't experienced them? Does an orgasm have to be limited to a certain sensation? Why *can't* an orgasm be very subtle, seem to start from somewhere other than the genitals, or make us feel a wide variety of ways?

Over the years I have taught women about the wide variety of orgasms in dozens of workshops and private sessions. Some of them were resistant at first, too, but eventually they "came" to understand. We start by planting little seeds, first learning that new things are possible. Eventually the ideas grow and turn into realities. I encourage you to keep an open mind, actually try some of the things I've suggested, and see for yourself what happens. If not much happens, then consider that perhaps maybe it will at some future time.

A big part of making over your sex life involves making over your thinking. The power of the mind is awesome; once we change our thinking, our bodies will follow.

Your Orgasm Homework

For the next month, as an experiment, try calling more of your detectable pleasurable sexual energy releases, explosions, and electrical streaming sensations "orgasm." You can do this yourself privately, or share this experiment with your lover. See if, by the end of the month you are feeling and being more orgasmic, and experiencing some interesting new sensations. If so, then you are seizing more of your orgasm opportunities and you've undergone an orgasm makeover!

Step Fourteen

Bask in Your Afterglow

The sex was so good that even the neighbors had a cigarette.

UNKNOWN

Are You Experiencing Premature Afterglow?

Your lovemaking or masturbation session has come to a grand finale, and now you are ready to bask in the afterglow. Wait, wait! Don't be too quick! Sometimes the point when you think you are finished having sex is exactly the point for you to push further. You're at your most relaxed, you're in a highly aroused state, and you've reached a certain level of bliss. Why not go for the big beyond?

But you say, "I can't take it anymore."

You can't take what? The pleasure?

"My clit is too sensitive," you say.

After clitoral orgasm(s), there are often some moments when your clitoris seems way too sensitive to keep going. If you wait just a minute or two, this passes. Also, if you, or your lover, provide indirect stimulation—not on the clitoris but around it—you'll find you can "take" more.

Testimonials

When I lead groups of people in sexual massage workshops, over and over I hear women say, "That was the most intense sexual experience I ever had," or "That was the most ecstasy I've ever experienced," or "That was the most orgasmic I've ever felt." Sure, I lead a great group massage, but to be honest, I know that the main reason they had such a good experience was because they got continually sexually stimulated for about an hour and a half, and generally women don't get continually stimulated for that long. Researchers have shown that most sex sessions last just for a few minutes.

In my own personal research, it's often the times when I have pushed beyond the point I or my lover has felt done that I've had the most transcendental, deeply satisfying, spectacular sexual experiences. Perhaps you've had that experience, too, but need to be reminded. Really spectacular sex sometimes takes time. Once you experience the great results of going beyond what you thought you were capable of a few times, you'll be raising your pleasure bar higher and higher. Going for more and more intensive stimulation can get you to deeper and deeper levels of satisfaction. As my shero Mae West once said, "Too much of a good thing is wonderful."

How to Keep the Glow Glowing

Okay. So, now you are definitely done. Your lovemaking has come to a crescendo, and you are entering the afterglow phase.

I love the word *afterglow*; it's such a lovely, poetic term and describes the experience so beautifully. In the afterglow we can feel we are glowing with love, with satisfaction, with a lightness of being, with pleasure. In the afterglow we can experience a heightened sense of peace, beauty, and connection—connection with our self, our body, our lover, and, on a really good day, the whole universe!

Interestingly, in movies and in pornography, they rarely ever show the afterglow phase. An exception was an episode of *Sex and the City* that shows Miranda jumping up after sex with her lover. He pulls her back, insisting on cuddle time. Eventually he teaches her the joys of staying in afterglow. But as I said, this is not a common topic in movies, probably because not much happens on the outside; there isn't much movement or action. But a lot is actually happening; your heart and blood are pumping, your energy is flowing, your body is tingling. It's just mostly internal rather than external.

Savor the Flavor

In general, unfortunately, there isn't much public awareness of how special afterglow is. All too often, after the grand finale climax, lovers jump up and go to the bathroom, light up a cigarette, or pull away emotionally. Men are notorious for this, but women certainly do it, too. The afterglow can be the most precious part of lovemaking, yet many people throw it away and don't take advantage of it.

Your afterglow can easily be nurtured and extended. My feeling is that at least a quarter of the time spent making love can be dedicated to a wonderful afterglow phase. So if you have sex for one hour, fifteen minutes after climax (energetic or orgasmic) is the minimum. More is even better.

Make It Last

How to extend your afterglows:

- *Acknowledge to yourself and your lover that the afterglow is an important and wonderful part of lovemaking.* Just being aware of this is a great start.

- *Stay physically connected.* Refrain from getting up or pulling away.
- *Pay attention.* Use your intention to keep all the good feelings going.
- *Don't talk for a while.* Communicate with touch, with eyes, with stillness—but avoid words for a while. Talking can break the mood and bring you out of your body and heart, and back into your head. Pillow talk can come later.
- *Take big, slow, natural breaths.*
- *Add some Kegels if desired* to help keep sexual energy pumping through you.
- *Gaze into your lover's eyes.* It keeps the connection going.
- *Do extended kissing.* Try making a kiss last for several minutes. Some of the best, most delicious kisses of all take place in the glow.
- *Keep focused on the bliss.* Avoid thinking about things outside of lovemaking, like bills, the mess in the other room, or work.

Gratitude Adjustment

The afterglow phase is the time I most love to express my gratitude. If I'm with a lover I might say something like "Thank you, sweetheart. I'm so grateful you are in my life. I feel so lucky that I can feel these wonderful sensations. I'm grateful for your love, your touch, your breath, your scent . . . Thank you for *schtupping* me so beautifully!" If I'm alone and I've just masturbated and I'm in the afterglow, I might put my hand on my heart and say (silently or out loud), "I'm so grateful for my healthy body. I'm grateful for my life, for my beautiful home, friends, and family. I'm grateful for my electric vibrator . . ."

Expressing gratitude is another wonderful way to make love. Accentuate and appreciate the positive, and watch how good you and your lover feel. Say "Thank you" every which way you can, as often as you can. Say thank you outside the bedroom, too. In love notes, write it with a stick in the sand on the beach, or on a big homemade cake with hot-pink frosting, and of course—say it with Hallmark.

Sometimes I also like to take a moment to thank those people who made all the pleasure I experience in my life today possible. I might say something like "I'm so grateful to all the people who have taught me something about sex, and love, and relationships. I'm grateful to my former lovers. I'm grateful to all the heroic people who fought for my sexual freedoms. It's because of them that I can be who I want to be and do what I want to do today. I'm enormously grateful for the abundance of choices that I have today in my life . . ."

Glow Forth

Once you've learned to give the afterglow phase as much time and attention as it deserves, it will feel so natural that you'll never again be tempted to have that cigarette or shower prematurely. No more "Wham, bam, thank you ma'am"s, unless of course it's one of those special occasions when that is part of the fun.

When you think of the afterglow as an integral and very special part of lovemaking rather than as something that happens occasionally, you'll add another beautiful dimension to your sex life. In other words, the afterglow can be a very special part of your spectacular sex.

Your Big Reveal

A sexually satisfied person is a happy person.

You did it! You've completed the Sex Life Makeover Program. Let's take a moment to assess what you got out of it. Which kind of makeover do you feel you've undergone?

- **The Mini Makeover.** You chose to go through the program purely on an intellectual level. You checked out what was being offered here and chose not utilize the tips, do the exercises, try the experiments, or practice the techniques. You simply read through this book. Maybe you didn't feel ready, or you felt you knew a lot of what was offered. Perhaps you came to realize that you are actually content with the current state of your affairs. Coming to that realization is progress in itself. If any of these is the case, don't think that nothing has changed. Some changes might actually have occurred without your conscious awareness. If you made even the slightest shift in attitude or picked up just one little key piece of information, then it's likely some seeds have been planted that are yet to blossom.

- **The Medium Makeover.** You made some positive changes, internally, externally, or both. You tried some of the sex tips and experiments, and they worked well for you. Perhaps you shared them with a lover, and you can hardly wait to do them again. You worked through some of your issues and feel better able to communicate your desires. The path of your sex life seems clear. You now have a more expanded idea of what sex is, and you are enjoying a wider variety of kinds of things. Terrific!

- **The X-treme Makeover.** You took advantage of everything this program has to offer. You tried the suggested steps, made some wonderful changes; you eroticized your environment, had some fun with your new alter egos, and are asking for more of what you want sexually. You improved your sexual relationship, both with your lover(s) and with yourself. You feel your sexual energy flowing freely, and you put it to good use. You continue to rebalance your sex life, got some sexy new things to wear, and appreciate and love your body more. You kicked out a party pooper or two. You're more orgasmic than you were. You feel like a new woman or man, with a new sex life, and a fantastically sexy future ahead of you.

- **The XXX-treme Makeover.** You did all the steps, with unbridled enthusiasm. You've quit your day job and now you wear a vibrator around your neck. You've set up a Web cam in your home and have started your own Sex Life Make Over Center to teach people how to have the kind of spectacular sex that you do. Good luck, and welcome to the club!

Whatever kind of makeover you chose and whatever changes you made or didn't make were just right for you.

So What's Next?

It's almost time for you to leave the safety and comfort of the Sex Life Makeover Center and to go on and resume your daily life. I hope you're feeling terrific, optimistic, and excited about taking what you learned here and applying more of it in the future.

After you leave here, you may have to go through some growing pains and face some challenges. Your lovers may have to adjust to the new you. But you are more prepared than ever, for whatever and whoever may come. When you change your sex life, you might find you want to change other things in your life as well. Go with the "flow."

Don't be surprised if someday in the future you find yourself feeling that you want or need another sex-life makeover. Things invariably change and shift over time, and your sex life may need additional attention—some more "psychic surgery," stimulus, and nurturance—in the future. You are always welcome to come back and reenter the program. No doubt, each time will be different. Just know that I and other support systems are always here for you.

Your Graduation Ceremony

Now follow me into the famed Sprinkle Salon, where I have prepared a graduation ceremony just for you. Sit on this plush red velvet throne with the ornate gold trim—it's the "hot woman seat" or the "hot man seat." Take a few deep breaths and some moments to feel how far you have come in your life, in your own personal sexual evolution. Feel your magnificence, take a deep breath, and appreciate *all* your accomplishments over the years. Give yourself a pat on the back and a coupla Kegel kisses just for being YOU.

My Commencement Speech

Remember my credo? "Let there be pleasure on earth and let it begin with me." Never forget that when you receive pleasure, you will be contributing to the pleasure in the world. So have a lot.

Make no mistake about it; human sexuality is as complex and full of contradictions as life itself. Just when you think you know a lot and understand it, another door opens and there is much more to learn. Go forth and learn more about sexuality with a sense of wonder and curiosity. Studying more about sex will help you build confidence and make you more knowledgeable. How fortunate we are that nowadays there are numerous safe, highly regarded, fun classes and workshops all over the country, and so many wonderful books and films to teach us. There are panels, forums, lectures, and some even some great television shows about sex. But always remember that the best way to learn about love and sex is not by reading about it but by practicing it, by trial and error. Be brave in love. Be brave in sex. Be brave in your ecstasy. Be brave in your orgasms. Be brave in being who you truly are.

As a sexually awakened person, you have enormous power. Own that power. Don't let anyone take it from you.

Do the best you can, and that's fantastic. Stay open. Be compassionate. Expect miracles. Do it *your* way.

Remember, you are an important part of the future. You can change the world either in a small way—in your marriage, relationship, or in your circle of friends—or in a broader way—in your community or even globally.

Envision your sex-life makeover going beyond yourself. You may want to become a "pleasure activist." There are many ways to do this. Think of ways you can make the world just a little bit sexier every day. Share your sexual knowledge with others. Help a friend with her/his sexual issue, rejoice in others' successes. Support sex education and sex research. Make a donation or volunteer to help a cause that is near and dear to your heart, such as fighting censorship, rape crisis and prevention, helping children heal from sexual abuse, AIDS prevention, sexual health, and . . . There are so many worthy causes. In fact much of the world could benefit from a giant sex-life makeover.

Let's imagine a beautiful future for people of the next generations. Let us hope that the world becomes a safer place in which to live, love, and be sexy. Let's make a wish that everyone gets the love, affection, and sexual satisfaction they desire.

Now I'd like to make a toast "to the wonderful, sexy human being that YOU are. May you have many years of sexy fun, abundant love, exquisite pleasures, and many glorious orgasms. I wish you lots of spectacular sex."

Your Big Reveal

Go and celebrate the new you however you'd like. Do something really special. Do it alone, with friends, or with your lover. Here are some things other graduates have done: took a trip, got a tattoo, got married, got unmarried, performed a ritual, threw a party, put on a show, spent a weekend in a fancy hotel room with a lover, took a special workshop or went on a retreat with a lover, went for a weekend to a hot spring, etc.

If you'd like to, please do send me the story of your personal sex-life makeover and your "big reveal." I'd love to hear all about them. I'll keep your story absolutely private and confidential. Or if you prefer, I'll post it on my Web site at www.anniesprinkle.org for you to share with others.

My Venus Vow

I, _____ , vow to honor the gift of my sexuality. I utilize my sexuality to express my creativity, my passion, and the love I have inside me. Everything that happens in my sex life happens in the perfect right order. I learn and grow from every sexual experience. I follow my muse. I take good care of myself. I honor and adore my body and see it as beautiful and sexy exactly as it is. All the love and pleasure I give comes back to me in the most delightful ways.

Your Venus Award

Congratulations! You have earned the Venus Award for making the world a sexier and more pleasure-filled place. Copy and enlarge the following page, or simply cut it out of the book. Then fill in your name (either your born name or the name of an alter ego). Frame it, and hang it proudly in your boudoir.

THE DR. ANNIE M. SPRINKLE

✕ *Venus Award* ✕

has been conferred upon

_____

For Making the World a Sexier, More Pleasure-Filled Place

Annie M. Sprinkle, Ph. D.

Farewell

It's been my honor and pleasure to guide you through these steps and to be of service to you. You've been a perfectly lovely, charming, and sexy guest.

Be sure to visit our spa boutique for your own goody bag filled with Dr. Sprinkle's Sparkle Bath, sexy soaps, delicious lubes, condoms, and essential oils. Here is the stretch limousine, complete with hot tub and Hitachi Magic Wand vibrators to keep you humming while it whisks you home. You'll find the driver most attractive and accommodating.

Stay sex-sea. Ya'll come! And come back any time. Bye bye.

How to Get in Touch with Me

Please do contact me with your suggestions, feedback, and comments. While I can't promise to respond to your letter, I will if I can. If you want to produce a Dr. Sprinkle event or workshop, do invite me to come to your town, city, state, and country. I'll come if I can. You can email me at *drsprinkle@anniesprinkle.org*. Or write to me at:

Annie Sprinkle
P.O. Box 720044
San Francisco, CA 94172

Resources

● ● ○

The Sex Life Makeover Center Library
of Recommended Reading

PERSONAL TRANSFORMATION AND EMPOWERMENT

Big Big Love: A Sourcebook on Sex for People of Size and Those Who Love Them by Hanne Blank (Greenery Press, 2000)

Exhibitionism for the Shy by Carol Queen (Down There Press, 1995)

It's Not About Food by Carol Emery Normandi and Laurelee Roark (Grosset/Putnam, 1998)

Life Makeovers: 52 Practical and Inspiring Ways to Improve Your Life One Week at a Time by Cheryl Richardson (Broadway, 2002)

The Queen of My Self: Stepping into Sovereignty in Midlife by Donna Henes (Monarch Press, 2004)

You Can Heal Your Life by Louise Hay (Hay House, 1985)

RELATIONSHIPS AND INTIMACY

Codependent No More by Melody Beattie (Hazelden, 15th Edition, 2001)

The Ethical Slut by Dossie Easton and Catherine A. Liszt (Greenery Press, 1998)

For Each Other: Sharing Sexual Intimacy by Lonnie Barbach, Ph.D. (Signet Books, Revised Edition, 2001)

Getting the Love You Want: A Guide for Couples and *Keeping the Love You Find: A Personal Guide* by Harville Hendrix (Owl Books, 2001 and Pocket Books, 1992)

Passionate Marriage by David Schnarch, Ph.D. (Owl Books, 1997)

SEX EDUCATION

Anal Pleasure & Health by Jack Morin, Ph.D. (Down There Press, 3rd Edition, 1998)

Becoming Orgasmic: A Sexual and Personal Growth Program for Women by Julia Heiman, Ph.D., and Joseph LoPiccolo, Ph.D. (Fireside, 1987)

The Clitoral Truth by Rebecca Chalker (Seven Stories Press, 2000)

The Erotic Mind by Jack Morin, Ph.D. (HarperPerennial, Reprint Edition, 1996)

ESO: How You and Your Lover Can Give Each Other Hours of Extended Sexual Orgasm by Donna and Alan Brauer (Warner Books, Revised Edition, 2001)

Female Ejaculation and the G-Spot by Deborah Sundahl (Hunter House, 2003)

Femalia (photographs of vulva) edited by Joani Blank (Down There Press, 1993)

The Good Vibrations Guide to Sex by Cathy Winks and Anne Semans (Cleis Press, 3rd Edition, 2002)

Guide to Getting It On! by Paul Joannides and Daerick Gross (Goofy Foot Press, 3rd Edition, 2000)

How to Tell a Naked Man What to Do: Sex Advice from a Woman Who Knows by Candida Royalle (Fireside, 2004)

The Many Joys of Sex Toys by Anne Semans (Broadway, 2004)

The New Male Sexuality by Bernie Zilbergeld, Ph.D. (Bantam, Revised Edition, 1999)

A New View of a Woman's Body by the Federation of Feminist Women's Health Center (Feminist Press, 2nd Edition, 1991)

A New View of Women's Sexual Problems edited by Ellyn Kaschak and Leonore Tiefer (Haworth Press, 2002)

9 Secrets to Bedroom Bliss: Exploring Sexual Archetypes to Reveal Your Lover's Passions and Discover What Turns You On by James Herriot, Ph.D., and Oona Mourier, Ph.D. (Fair Winds Press, 2003)

Orgasms for Two and *Sex for One* by Betty Dodson, Ph.D. (Harmony Books, 2002, 1987)

Real Live Nude Girl: Chronicles of Sex-Positive Culture by Carol Queen (Cleis Press, 2nd Edition, 2002)

Safer Sex: The Complete Guide to Safer Sex (Barricade Books, Updated 2004 Edition)

Sex, Love and Health: A Self-Help Health Guide to Love and Sex by Brigitte Mars (Basic Health Publications, 2002)

The Survivor's Guide to Sex by Staci Haines (Cleis Press, 1999)

The Ultimate Guide to Adult Videos: How to Watch Adult Videos and Make Your Sex Life Sizzle by Violet Blue (Cleis Press, 2003)

The Ultimate Guide to Anal Sex for Women by Tristan Taormino (Cleis Press, 1997)

The Ultimate Guide to Sex and Disability: For All of Us Who Live with Disabilities, Chronic Pain and Illness by Miriam Kaufman, M.D., Cory Silverberg, and Fran Odette (Cleis Press, 2003)

The Ultimate Guide to Sexual Fantasy: How to Turn Your Fantasies into Reality by Violet Blue (Cleis Press, 2004)

The Whole Lesbian Sex Book by Felice Newman (Cleis Press, 2004)

The Woman's Guide to Sex on the Web by Anne Semans and Cathy Winks (Harper San Francisco, 1999)

GENDER AND IDENTITY

Miss Vera's Cross-Dress for Success: A Resource Guide for Boys Who Want to Be Girls by Veronica Vera (Villard, 2003)

Miss Vera's Finishing School for Boys Who Want to Be Girls by Veronica Vera (Main Street Books, 1997)

My Gender Workbook by Kate Bornstein (Routledge, 1998)

BDSM INFORMATION

Deviant Desires: Incredibly Strange Sex by Katharine Gates (Juno Books, 2000)

Different Loving by William Brame, Gloria Brame, and Jon Jacobs (Villard, 1996)

The New Bottoming Book by Dossie Easton and Janet Hardy (Greenery Press, 2001)

The New Topping Book by Dossie Easton and Janet Hardy (Greenery Press, 2003)

The Seductive Art of Japanese Bondage by Midori with Craig Morey (Greenery Press, 2003)

SM 101: A Realistic Introduction by Jay Wiseman (Greenery Press, 1998)

Tied Up with Love; The Making of Mistress Antoinette autobiography by Jeanette Luther "Mistress Antoinette" (Versatile Fashions, 2nd Printing, 2003)

SACRED SEXUALITY

The Essential Tantra by Kenneth Ray Stubbs, Ph.D. (Tarcher, 2000)

The Kama Sutra of Erotic Massage and *The Kama Sutra of Sensual Bathing* by Kenneth Ray Stubbs, Ph.D. (Secret Garden Publishing, 2004)

Radical Ecstasy by Janet W. Hardy and Dossie Easton (Greenery Press, 2004)

Sacred Sex: Ecstatic Techniques for Empowering Relationships by Jwala with Robb Smith (Mandala, 1994)

Sexual Energy Ecstasy by David and Ellen Ramsdale (Bantam, 1993)

Urban Tantra by Barbara Carrellas (Cleis Press, 2005). I highly recommend this unique book.

OTHER MISCELLANEOUS GREAT BOOKS AND EROTICA

Erotic by Nature by David Steinberg (Down There Press, 1988)

The Erotic Comedies by Marco Vassi (Permanent Press, 1996)

Nothing But the Girl: The Blatant Lesbian Image edited by Susie Bright and Jill Posener (Freedom Editions, 1996)

Photo Sex: Fine Art Sexual Photography Comes of Age edited by David Steinberg (Down There Press, 2003)

Susie Bright Presents: Three Kinds of Asking for It—Erotic Novellas by Eric Albert, Greta Christina, and Jill Soloway (Simon & Schuster, 2005)

Unrepentant Whore by Scarlot Harlot (Last Gasp, 2004)

BOOKS BY AND ABOUT ANNIE SPRINKLE

Annie Sprinkle: A Cartoon History. From Carnal Comics' Legends of Porn series (Re-Visionary Press)

Hardcore from the Heart: The Pleasures, Profits and Politics of Sex in Performance (Continuum International Publishing Group, 2001)

Post-Porn Modernist: My 25 Years as a Multimedia Whore by Annie Sprinkle (Cleis Press, 1998)

Videos and DVDs for Your Viewing Pleasure— Homeschooling Has Never Been So Much Fun!

(Most of these films are available from the wonderful sexuality boutiques and their Web sites listed later.)

Ageless Desire by Juliet Carr

Explicit lovemaking by experienced couples over sixty years old. Very inspiring!

Anal Massage for Relaxation and Pleasure by Joseph Kramer and Chrys Curtis-Fawley

Learn tender loving touch for one of the most sensitive parts of the body.

Ancient Secrets of Sexual Ecstasy, produced by the folks at Tantra.com

Wonderful information about Tantra and the spiritual side of sexuality illustrated by experienced couples. Includes an excellent demonstration of ecstasy breathing into a full-body energy orgasm.

Annie Sprinkle's Amazing World of Orgasm by Annie Sprinkle and Sheila Malone

A sexually explicit documentary about the big O, including interviews with twenty-four orgasm experts. Features a wonderful example of ecstasy breathing into full-body energy orgasm.

Bend Over Boyfriend (Fatale video) and *Bend Over Boyfriend 2: More Rockin', Less Talkin'* (SIR Video)

Hot and smart education for couples who like strap-on sex!

The Best of Vulva Massage: An Anthology of Erotic Touch by Joseph Kramer

A terrific collection of footage from the sex films of over a dozen erotic pioneers.

Deep Inside Annie Sprinkle, directed by Annie Sprinkle (Distripix)

If you want to see a classic 1980s porn flick, this is a good one.

Fire in the Valley: Female Genital Massage by Joseph Kramer with Annie Sprinkle

Learn the amazing female genital massage from the experts.

Fire on the Mountain: Male Genital Massage by Joseph Kramer

Learn the amazing male erotic massage from the experts.

The Full Load: Scenes from ssspread.com directed by Barbara DeGenevieve (Fatale Media)

Lesbian lovers of all types—butch, femme, and trans. Extremely hot and well made.

Healing Sex (SIR Video)

An amazing resource for anyone affected by sexual abuse. Based on Staci Haine's book, *The Survivor's Guide to Sex.*

Masturbation Memoirs by Dorrie Lane with the House O'Chicks
> Women share their personal masturbation styles.

The Pain Game by Cleo Dubois
> Probably the best "real S/M" video out there.

Self Loving: Portrait of a Women's Sexuality Seminar and Celebrating Orgasm: Women's Private Self Loving Sessions by Betty Dodson
> Betty Dodson shows women how to improve their self-loving sessions in these classic videos.

The Sluts and Goddesses Video Workshop: Or How to Be a Sex Goddess in 101 Easy Steps by Annie Sprinkle
> This alternative, arty sex film features my five-minute-long megagasm.

Sugar High Glitter City and *Hard Love and How to Fuck in High Heels* (Sir Video)
> Genuine lesbian porn from San Francisco.

A Tantric Journey to Female Orgasm and Female Ejaculation for Couples by Deborah Sundahl
> *Journey* is Deborah's labor-of-love film featuring several couples. Includes a fantastic sexual healing scene with Jwala using G-spot stimulation.

Tristan Taormino's Ultimate Guide to Anal Sex for Women by John Stagliano and Evil Angel Productions

Urban Friction: A Tale of Love and Sex in the Big City and *Ecstatic Moments* (Libido Films)
> Intelligent "couples erotica" porn that's well done and heated.

Voluptuous Vixens, Slide Bi Me, Please Don't Stop and *Carol Queen's G Mark the Spot* (Sex Positive Productions)
> Four alternative-style sex films featuring a diverse casts of folks of all shapes, sizes, and colors.

Internet Resources

GOOD SEX/SAFER SEX INFORMATION SITES

www.sexuality.org
A huge Web site devoted to the acceptance and understanding of all sexual orientations and all consensual and safe sexual practices. Includes resources, local guides, essays, reviews, and FAQs.

www.safersex.org
Safer sex in all of its yummy forms: latex, toys, erotica, and politics.

www.thebody.com
A comprehensive HIV/AIDS resource.

www.itsyoursexlife.com
A guide to safe and responsible sexual pleasure from the Kaiser Family Foundation

INTERNET MAGAZINES AND EROTICA SITES

CLEAN SHEETS
www.cleansheets.com
An online magazine of erotic fiction and poetry.

LIBIDO
www.libidomag.com
The Journal of Sex and Sensibility

MIKEY AND MANDY'S PORN EMPORIUM
www.mikeyandmandy.com
View this unique collection of two discriminating porn connoisseurs.

NERVE MAGAZINE
www.nerve.com
A smart, sexy site with great personal ads and fabulous photo galleries.

TANTRA.COM
www.tantra.com
This site is a central hub of the online Tantra community, offering articles and resources as well as listings of teachers and workshops.

THE CELIBATE FAQ
http://www.glandscape.com/celibate.html

LOVING MORE
www.lovemore.com
Explores and shares information about new models for
adult relationships.

Erotic Education: Workshops, Weekends, and Homeschooling

BODY ELECTRIC SCHOOL OF MASSAGE
www.bodyelectric.org
Body Electric presents fantastic erotic massage and sacred
sexuality workshops all over the country for men, women,
singles, and couples.

DARK ODYSSEY
www.darkodyssey.com
Weekend conventions that bring together sexuality, spirituality, education, and play in a fun, supportive, nonjudgmental, diverse environment.

DRAG KING FOR A DAY
www.dianetorr.com
Explore your masculine side in a workshop led by Diane
Torr. It's a blast.

THE DEER TRIBE METIS MEDICINE SOCIETY
www.dtmms.org
Among the many transformational teachings of the Deer
tribe and Harley Swiftdeer are the classes in Quodoushka,
based on sacred shamanic traditions that integrate spirituality and sexuality into your life.

ESALEN INSTITUTE
www.esalen.org
A famous retreat center in Big Sur, California, that offers
massage, Tantra, and other transformational workshops
and seminars.

HUMAN AWARENESS INSTITUTE
www.hai.org
Helps couples improve relationships through embodied
erotic learning weekends and communication skills.

INSTITUTE FOR ADVANCED STUDY
OF HUMAN SEXUALITY
www.iashs.edu
A graduate school offering certificate programs, master's
degrees, and doctorates in human sexuality.

KAHUA HAWAIIAN INSTITUTE
www.kahuainstitute.com
My friends Kutira and Raphael will enrich your life with
their unforgettable Oceanic Tantra workshops. They also
create music and workshops on CD made especially for
lovers. Rent their bamboo lovers' temple in Maui. It's divine.

LIFESTYLES
www.lifestyles.org
This is a for-profit company that specializes in vacations,
conventions, and parties for the swinging lifestyle.

THE NEW SCHOOL OF EROTIC TOUCH
www.eroticmassage.com
Homeschooling for the erotically gifted and adventurous.

MISS VERA'S FINISHING SCHOOL
FOR BOYS WHO WANT TO BE GIRLS
www.missvera.com
A unique cross-dressing academy run by my dear and very
talented friend Veronica Vera.

UNIVERSAL TAO CENTER
www.universal-tao.com
Features the wisdom and work of Taoist master Mantak
Chia. They offer workshops and retreats all over the world,
as well as many educational books and videos.

VULVA UNIVERSITY
www.houseochicks.com/vulvauniversity
They offer sex wisdom online classes. You can also purchase your own custom-made vulva hand puppet here.

THE WOMEN'S SEXUALITY CENTER
www.womensexualitycenter.com
Pamela Madison and her staff are devoted to the sexual
empowerment and fulfillment of all women through education, healing, and support.

Shopping

SEX TOYS, CONDOMS, LUBRICANTS, DVDs, AND OTHER FUN STUFF

(An asterisk* means they also offer classes and workshops.)

BLOWFISH
www.blowfish.com
A great feminist sex store, with a slant toward the kinky side.

DR. G
www.doctorg.com
An internet site that offers "movies, tools, and education
for a better sex life," from Dr. Gary Schubach.

GOOD VIBRATIONS*
www.goodvibes.com
The original worker-owned sex-positive store: a fantastic
place to buy all your toys, books, and videos.

GRAND OPENING!*
www.grandopening.com
A woman-owned and -run sex-positive store with locations
in Boston, West Hollywood, and on the Web.

MEDICAL TOYS
www.medicaltoys.com
You can buy speculums in all shapes, materials, and sizes
here for your own cervix exam.

TOYS IN BABELAND*
www.babeland.com
Feminist sex-toy store "selling toys for a passionate world."

A WOMAN S TOUCH*
www.a-womanstouch.com
A Madison, Wisconsin, woman-owned store and site "celebrating romance and sensuality."

SEXY CLOTHING, HOT LINGERIE, AND EXTRA TOUCHES

ANGELIC AROMAS
www.angelicaromas.com
These massage oils, lubes, and yummy sprays will evoke
romance and sensuality on any occasion.

BODY CIRCLE DESIGNS
www.bodycircle.com
The best body-piercing jewelry.

GINA'S INTIMATES
www.g-intimates.com
Very sensuous nippleless bras.

GLAMA-RAMA
www.glamarama.com
My favorite hair salon ever, featuring the most sexy hair extensions ever and wig styling. Based in San Francisco.

PIEDMONT BOUTIQUE
www.piedmontsf.com
My favorite clothing store where most of my outfits are
bought or made. For all genders.

SECRETS IN LACE
www.secretsinlace.com
Sexy lingerie for all body shapes and sizes.

TWIRLY GIRL PASTIES
www.twirlygirl.net
Fabulous, superbly made pasties for all occasions.

VERSATILE FASHIONS
www.versatile-fashions.com
Mistress Antoinette's fetish fashion creations for all genders. They make my favorite corsets and PVC attire.

Sex-Positive Organizations

BEYOND HUNGER
www.beyondhunger.org
Beyond Hunger is a nonprofit organization dedicated to helping individuals overcome the obsession with food and weight and find a natural, loving, and peaceful relationship with their food, weight, and selves.

THE BODY POSITIVE
www.thebodypositive.org
A nonprofit organization whose mission is to reduce the suffering caused by preoccupation with, and pursuit of, our culture's unrealistic beauty ideals.

CENTER FOR SEX AND CULTURE
www.centerforsexandculture.com
Sexologists Carol Queen and Robert Lawrence have created a sex-positive community learning center, archives, and library.

THE FREE SPEECH COALITION
www.freespeechcoalition.com
Defending sexual freedom through legislative advocacy for civil and sexual rights.

MUSEUM OF SEX——"MOSEX"
http://www.museumofsex.org
An excellent and unique museum in Manhattan.

NATIONAL COALITION FOR SEXUAL FREEDOM
www.ncsfreedom.org
A grass roots organization dedicated to defending the sexual rights of all people.

PLANNED PARENTHOOD
www.plannedparenthood.org
A national federation of clinics and educational centers offering all women and men sexual health services.

Professional Assistance for Personal Transformation and Sex Information

THE AMERICAN ASSOCIATON OF SEX EDUCATORS, COUNSELORS, AND THERAPISTS
www.aasect.org
(804) 644-3288
AASECT is a nonprofit, interdisciplinary professional organization of sex educators, therapists, and coaches.

INGERSOLL GENDER CENTER
www.ingersollcenter.org
A nonprofit agency that gives information about gender, transvestism, and transsexualism.

KINK AWARE PROFESSIONALS
www.bannon.com/kap
A resource for people seeking psychotherapeutic, medical, complementary healing, legal, financial, and computer professionals who are informed about the diversity of consensual adult sexuality.

THE NATIONAL DOMESTIC VIOLENCE/ABUSE HOTLINES
1-800-799-SAFE
If you or someone you know needs assistance, please call and ask for it.

SAN FRANCISCO SEX INFORMATION (SFSI)
www.sfsi.org
(877) 472-SFSI
SFSI is a free information and referral switchboard providing anonymous, accurate, nonjudgmental information about sex. Call them from anywhere in the world.

SEXOLOGICAL BODYWORK
www.sexologicalbodywork.com
Sexological body workers are erotic educators certified by the state of California to assist individuals, couples, and groups to deepen their experience of embodiment.

Fabulous Sex Educators

KIM AIRS
http://www.grandopening.com/
Kim teaches many different workshops ranging from striptease to safer-sex techniques, to bisexuality and everything in between.

ANNIE BODY
www.anniebody.com
Adult entertainer, nude model, party girl, stripper.

DAVID JAY BROWN
www.sexanddrugs.info
David's site explores the relationship between sex and drugs, from caffeine to herbal aphrodisiacs to entheogens.

BARBARA CARRELLAS AND KATE BORNSTEIN
www.tootallblondes.com
Innovative sex educators, performance artists, gender pioneers, and authors.

FRANCESCA DE GRANDIS
www.well.com/user/zthirdrd/WiccanMiscellany.html
Francesca is an author and traditional spiritual healer, focusing her work on helping others celebrate life, create their own destiny, and make a difference in the world.

BETTY DODSON
www.bettydodson.com
Though she no longer offers group classes, Betty Dodson continues to hold private sex-coaching sessions.

DUCKY DOOLITTLE
www.duckydoolittle.com
Smart, sexy, and fun sex educator, artist, and performer.

CLEO DUBOIS' ACADEMY OF SM ARTS
www.sm-arts.com
Cleo offers fantastic erotic dominance intensives and guided play sessions for those looking to explore consensual BDSM and power play.

NINA HARTLEY
www.nina.com
Nina is the world's most beloved porn star, erotic educator, and sexual entrepreneur. Check out her porn movies and her sex education videos and DVDs.

LORAINE HUTCHENS, PH.D.
www.lorainehutchins.com
Author, sex coach, teacher, and very brilliant gal. An expert on bisexuality.

JWALA
www.jwalaji.com
Jwala is an ecstatic Tantra teacher who has her own line of sexy clothes for you and your bedroom!

JOSEPH KRAMER, PH.D.
www.eroticmassage.com
www.sexologicalbodywork.com
My mentor and a fantastic sex educator. Teaches advanced sexological bodywork courses among others.

ISA MAGDALENA
www.xtasia.info
One of the most spirited and wise teachers of erotic possibility, Isa Magdalena offers a wider variety of services to awaken your potential, including sex coaching.

MIDORI
www.fhp-inc.com
Fetish diva Midori is an incredible teacher of sexuality and seduction. She is one of the world's masters of Japanese rope bondage. Thoughtful erotic education for adventurous adults.

FRANK MOORE
www.eroplay.com
This is the inspiring performance artist whom I wrote about.

CAROL QUEEN
www.carolqueen.com
Carol Queen, her partner Robert Lawrence, and her organization, the Center for Sex and Culture, are on the cutting edge of sexual politics and sex education.

CANDIDA ROYALLE
www.royalle.com
One of the leading female directors in the adult-movie industry, Candida is also an inspirational author and guide for directing your own fabulous sex life!

K. RUBY
www.sexologicalbodywork.com/html/ruby.html
A wonderful sexual healer and teacher. Sexological body-work, workshops, private sessions.

RAY STUBBS, PH.D.
www.secretgardenpublishing.com
Ray is a wise sex visionary, with many wonderful books and videos.

DEBORAH SUNDAHL
www.isismedia.org
Deborah's specialty is teaching women about the G-spot and female ejaculation.

LEILA SWAN
Leila@leilaswan.com
Adult entertainer, nude model, and sex coach who teaches stripping.

TANTRIKAS, DAKINIS AND DAKAS
www.goddesstemple.com
An experienced Tantra teacher can help you explore your sexuality and teach you and your lover technique. This Web site lists many male and female teachers, erotic masseurs, sex coaches, and sexual healers from all over the world.

TRISTAN TAORMINO
www.puckerup.com
Author, teacher, and all-around sex goddess. Coproduces the annual Dark Odyssey retreats that offer dozens of workshops.

SUSUN WEED
www.susunweed.com
Susun Weed is the creator of the Wise Woman Center in Upstate New York, where she teaches about herbal medicine and spiritual healing. She and her fellow teachers host many wonderful workshops.

Photographers for Boudoir, Erotic, or Sexual Portraits

VIVIENNE MARICEVIC
www.sheshootsmen.com
Vivienne specializes in shooting naked men as well as women, and is available for private shoots. (East Coast)

RANDAL ALAN SMITH
www.furtographer.com/
Randal shot most of the photos of me in this book. He's a terrific guy, and a makeup artist. He will do great sexy shots of women, men, and couples. (West Coast)

Acknowledgments

My deeply heartfelt gratitude to . . .

Veronica Vera for twenty-three years of a golden friendship and for being an inspiration in ways too numerous to count. She flew cross-country and spent ten days with me to generously add the delicious frosting and decorations on top of this book-cake. Such a gift! I love you, V.V.!

Scott Mendel, my very charming and wonderful literary agent/angel, who encouraged me to do this project. He has not only done a great job representing me; he's gone above and beyond to guide and help me.

To the wonderful Penguin/Tarcher family for cocreating this book and sprinkling it generously around the world. Sara Carder, my editor, who made the magic happen by choosing me, gracing me with her experience and editing talents, and making nothing but positive changes. Joel Fotinos, publisher of Jeremy P. Tarcher/Penguin, for taking this project, giving it his all, and giving me freedom. A big thank-you to cover designer Laurin Lucaire, interior designer Meighan Cavanaugh, and the head of the interior design department, Claire Vaccaro, for doing such wonderful work. Also, special thanks to assistant editor Ashley Shelby, to copy editor Barbara Grenquist, to my publicist Kat Kimball, and marketing goddess Kristen Giorgio.

Marcy Sheiner, Bayla Travis, Andrew Ramer, Chrys Curtis Fawley, and Margaret Wade for helping me with production of this book in various important ways. You're all so talented and sweet. Sexologist Loraine Hutchens, Ph.D., for being a reader and helping with accuracy. Anne Harless and Howie Gordon for giving me honest feedback in the early stages. Erica Rand, in the later stages. My colleague Kenneth Ray Stubbs, Ph.D., for his enlightening comments on what I had written about orgasm.

Randal Alan Smith and Julian Cash, who did the photographs for this book. Thanks, Randal, for doing my excellent makeup (and everyone else's) and the preliminary page mock-ups on the computer. Jackie Jack, who created the sweet drawings and charts. You were all so much fun to collaborate with, and I'm so glad we worked together. Let's do it again sometime.

The brave women and men who allowed me to photograph them for this book, each based on real clients who had sex-life makeovers: Gwen Perry, Shelly Compton, Carol Leigh, Annie Body, Leila Swan, Juliet Carr, Sarah Kiron-Moore, Rick "Mud" Abruzzo, Roxane Williams, Elliot Pisor, Judiann Simon, Thomas Stevenson, Jane Sumner, Megan Tennity.

Dr. Joseph Kramer, Ph.D., for being my sounding board, mentor, loving friend, business partner, confidant extraordinaire, and for teaching me about ecstatic breathing and sexual massage.

My sex teachers: especially Jwala, Betty Dodson, Frank Moore, Kutira Decosterd, Dieter Jarzombec, Kenneth Ray Stubbs, Xaviera Hollander, Linda Lovelace, Alan Lowen, Harley Swiftedeer, and Gypsy Rose Lee. All sex researchers before me.

My life, art, and spiritual teachers: especially Linda M. Montano, Martha Wilson, Wendy Raw, Susun Weed, Louise Hay, Keith Hennessy, Seth Eisen, Spider Webb, and Willem De Ridder.

Every former lover, workshop participant, costar, and client. I certainly couldn't have created a Spectacular Sex program without you.

To the ladies of Club 90, my fabulous porn star support group of twenty years: Veronica Hart, Candida Royalle, Gloria Leonard, and Veronica Vera. Special thanks to Barbara Carrellas, who gave me extra support on this project, who has been my workshop cofacilitator, theater director, and former manager extraordinaire. Throughout the years you have all been my wise and loyal friends.

To my wonderful blood family, especially my mom, Lucille Malvani, dad, Raymond Malvani, my brothers, David Steinberg and Adam Malvani, and my sister, Lora Malvani.

Those who made a contribution to this book in various miscellaneous ways: Carol Queen; Robert Lawrence; Katharine Gates; Gina Ogden; my computer doctor, Julia Page; Susie Hara; David Steinberg; Francesca De Grandes; Sheila Malone; my massage therapist, Melusina; my wonderful Web master, Daniel Wasko; Ross Thomas; Jeff Suttor; my black lab, Bob; Neon Weiss; Imad of Deli Pub (S.F.); Kate Bornstein; Dr. Sharon Mitchell; Linda Hirsch; Idexa of Black and Blue Tattoo; my brilliant fabulous hair artist for the heart photos, Deena Davenport of Glama-rama! hair salon (S.F.); my hair stylist for the photos of me in the white lab coat, Tom Walls of Tom's on Cortland. To my favorite clothing designers, Uti at Piedmont Boutique (S.F.) and Ms. Antoinette at Versatile Fashions (L.A.). Thanks to the Common Grounds coffee shop folks, especially Jamel, who chased the thieves when my laptop was stolen (S.F.). My art dealers, Adriaan Van Der Have of Torch Gallery (Amsterdam), Jerome Jacobs of Aeroplastics Gallery (Brussels), Pet and Tammey Stubbs of *Art@Large* Gallery (New York), Peter Huttinger of Volatile (Cincinnati). Thanks, Sharon and Hy Mariampolski, Lynn Barrett, and Suzanne Geneste de Besme.

Last, and certainly not least, my delightful mate, E. Marshall Stephens, for cheering me on all the way.

Special thanks to anyone I accidentally forgot to thank.

I'm eternally grateful to you all. May all that you have given me come back to you tenfold, and may you have lots of spectacular sex.

Annie M. Sprinkle

Permissions for Photos

Randal Alan Smith photographed Annie Sprinkle for the cover, title page, and pages 15, 37, 104, 109, 136, 141, 160, 216, and 272. He also shot all the photographs and did the models' makeup in the color insert. His Web site is furtographer.com.

Julian Cash photographed Annie Sprinkle for pages 67, 87, 126, 129, 145, 164, 180, 193, 200, 231, 250, and 267. His Web site is juliancash.com.

Jackie Jack did the drawings on pages 87, 99, 145, 156, 206, 263, and 277.
Her Web site is jackiejack.com.

Center photograph of Annie on page 7: Bobby Hanson. Other photos of Annie on page 7 (*clockwise*): Charles Gatewood (charlesgatewood.com), Fakir Musafar (fakir.org), Jean Marie Guyaux, Julian Cash, Fakir Musafar, and Joegh Bullock (anonsalon.com).

Index

About the Author

Annie Sprinkle is a sex-life coach, sex educator, artist, and performer. For over three decades, she has been passionately researching and exploring sexuality and sharing the knowledge she has gained in her own unique style and through a wide variety of media.

Annie began her career in adult entertainment (she has been inducted into all four sex film halls of fame). From this, she bridged into a successful performance art career, traveling the world doing theater about her life in sex. Sprinkle earned a Ph.D. in Human Sexuality from the Institute for Advanced Study of Human Sexuality in 2002. Now a faculty member at the Institute, she lectures widely around the world at museums, universities, and colleges. She also facilitates workshops at such esteemed wellness centers as the Open Center, the Wise Woman Center, and the Omega Institute.

Annie has been the subject of four HBO Real Sex segments as well as several documentaries, including *Female Misbehavior,* a film about how she transformed herself from a shy, insecure gal to a vibrant, sexy star. Her film *Sluts and Goddesses* has been shown around the world at such venerable institutions as the Museum of Modern Art in New York City. *Annie Sprinkle's Herstory of Porn* won the Erotic Oscar for Film of the Year. Her book *Hardcore from the Heart* won the Firecracker Alternative Book Award.

Currently, Sprinkle lives and loves in San Francisco. She's a member of the American College of Sexologists, the Free Speech Coalition, and Feminists for Free Expression; she is also on the board of the St. James Infirmary, a free health care clinic.

Sprinkle has been called the "Mother Teresa of sex" for her compassion, the "Yoko Ono of sex" for her creative arty flair, and the "renaissance woman of sex" for her wide array of talents. She has dedicated her life to helping people utilize their sexuality to bring more love into their lives and into the world.